ITALIANS FIRST!

December 1901, Poldhu, Cornwall, England. Marconi seated at the apparatus by means of which the first trans-Atlantic signal — the letter 'S' — was received at St Johns, Newfoundland, Canada
Published by kind permission of the Marquis Lorenzo Solari.

ITALIANS
FIRST!
FROM A TO Z

Arturo Barone

Paul Norbury Publications
Sandgate, Folkestone, Kent

ITALIANS FIRST!
From A-Z

First published 1989 by
PAUL NORBURY PUBLICATIONS
Knoll House, 35 The Crescent
Sandgate, Folkestone, Kent, England CT20 3EE

ISBN 0-904404-69-2

British Library Cataloguing in Publication Data
Barone, Arturo, *1933-*
  Italians first!: from A to Z.
  1. Italy, history
  I. Title
  945

  ISBN 0-904404-69-2

Keywork by Ann Tiltman; photoset in Rockwell by Visual
Typesetting of Harrow, Middlesex. Printed in England by BPCC
Wheatons Ltd, Exeter.

This book was written for my family and is
dedicated to Lord Forte

GALILEO, 1564-1642

Acknowledgements

To list all the people who have been of help to me in compiling this work would take too long. They range from my schoolteachers, to whom I am indebted for a broad classical education, to Elio Nissim for his unfailing encouragement, to Pietro del Giudice for details of his brother's career, to Keith Moore, Archivist to The Royal Society for his helpful suggestions, to the staff of Dacorum Public Library for their unfailing courtesy, and to my elder son Franco for checking the various references.

Of the writers who have gone before me, I should mention Luigi Barzini because, essentially, he put the Italians so to say on the literary map of the general reader in a particular manner and in inimitable style. His analysis of them is quite perceptive, although not always faultless.

I am almost equally indebted to Stendhal but for a completely different reason. He loved Italy and its inhabitants so much that his love has served to reassure me that we can't be all that bad, because if a Frenchman loves an Italian, then there must be more to the Italians than meets the eye. I have always subscribed to the view that on the whole the French don't really like the Italians; but then, neither do we like the French too much either. The greater affinity amongst the Mediterranean people as far as Italians are concerned lies with the Greeks and not with either the French or the Spanish. The common language bond with these last two peoples does not make up for many fundamental differences in temperament and outlook.

I owe a great deal to John Addington Symonds. His hymn of glory to the Italian Renaissance was a great boost for my ego; his occasional analyses of the Italian temperament are perfectly accurate. My debt to him is indeed notable.

Furthermore, I must acknowledge an even greater debt to all my friends, particularly my English friends who have enabled me to put matters in a better perspective.

Lastly, I am grateful to my family because they actually provoked me into putting pen to paper. But the views expressed by me are not necessarily shared by them . . .

A.B.

7

Acknowledgements

LEONARDO DA VINCI, 1452-1519

Contents

Section 10: Sport and Travel

Section 11: The Sciences

PART 2: THE DEBATE

Foreword

Every Italian and most Englishmen should read this book. It is a comprehensive and witty account of many Italian achievements. Arturo Barone allows no sense of false modesty to dim his admiration for the achievements of his 'native' land. In this he is surely right, for do they not say that those who are born in Italy are blessed by God.

My claims to introduce his work are limited to the fact that I was fortunate enough to marry an Italian wife and to pass some time each year in the Italian countryside, and importantly in that unique city of Venice.

Arturo Barone's book is an A to Z examination of some of the remarkable Italian discoveries and achievements of the last 1000 years. True, we all learn from one another and Italy learnt much from Greece and from Byzantium and even from China, as we ourselves in England learnt much from Italy.

I was disturbed by the author's doubts on English painting and would remind him that the English watercolorists led the rest of Europe in the practice of this very special art. Nevertheless, he is right to put Italy first in many things — for her cities, her sculpture, her paintings and her glorious countryside, concealing as they lie bathed in sunshine, a wealth of achievement which spans from the Renaissance to the development of modern banking. It is to me rather a relief to remember that Arturo Barone, despite all this and his love of Italy, has made his life in England.

THORNEYCROFT
House of Lords
May 1989

GIOVANNI MOSCA

The Author and Publisher are most grateful to the heirs of Giovanni Mosca for permission to publish a selection of his witty and entertaining cartoons which first appeared in Italy in 1975 under the title *La Storia D'Italia in 200 Vignette*, published by Rizzoli of Milan. Those selected for *Italians First!* are based entirely on a subjective choice without any particular regard for the original historical sequence.

Introduction

Some General Observations

It is my intention to project a totally different picture of the Italians from that which normally springs to mind. The popular stereotype projects an exceptionally pleasant and easy image of Italy and the Italians but inevitably it is rather superficial. I hasten to say that it is not entirely the fault of other nationalities that such an image prevails; in my view, the Italians themselves have to carry a great deal of responsibility for it. Yet the image is almost an inevitable one, as it emerges from concepts, attitudes and patterns of behaviour and of living which in themselves are very easy. After all, who would expect the Italians to be complicated people, capable of anything exceptional, when they have with so much ease and success provided the world with 'spaghetti,' 'pizza,' 'vino,' 'la dolce vita,' Ferrari motor cars, etc. All these things are so pleasant and so universally acceptable that the Italians themselves must by definition be pleasant and likeable people; but they cannot be capable of anything very great. So runs the generally accepted view.

I mean to surprise you. I intend to show you that the Italians are in fact great.

Furthermore, I intend to show you that the contribution made by Italians to world knowledge and well-being is very substantial indeed, if not unique. I am reluctant myself to qualify it by saying that it is the greatest in the world, or the second best, or whatever; I shall leave that judgement to you.

But I must warn you that in the course of this exercise you will come across a number of unexpected features. You will also have to reconsider your attitude as regards what you believe to be the common traits of the Italians.

It is of course true that we all have a mental picture of the various nationalities: we associate diverse people with different results and outlooks. Most of the time this process of association is inevitable because we all, to some extent, live by generalisations. But it is not always meaningful.

Let me give you an example. It is a commonly held view that we associate the English with reserve, democracy and an empire. In my experience, however, English reserve evaporates under the influence of alcohol, our democracy is at the moment under a certain amount of pressure and the empire, as everybody knows, has gone. Incidentally, I should make the point straight away that, for the sake of simplicity, I refer throughout to 'England' and the 'English,' meaning 'Britain' and the 'British.' This is imprecise, but convenient, since many foreigners also use the word 'England' indiscriminately. Any remark I make about England and its inhabitants, therefore, should be understood as including also the Scots, the Welsh and, to a lesser degree, the inhabitants of Northern Ireland.

Most people tend to associate the French with high fashion and first-class cuisine. It seems to me that very few people nowadays can afford the former and indeed, when it comes to it, Italian fashions at the moment, at least for the man in the street, are a great deal more popular than French fashions; and when it comes to the latter, you will find that the French learnt it from us. Indeed, anyone who frequents restaurants as a matter of course, knows only too well that, at least as far as London is concerned, Italian or even Chinese or other restaurants provide better food than the French.

I believe the man in the street will associate Germans with militarism and efficiency. A cynic would remark that, despite both these traits, they managed to lose two great wars and it is conceivable that today the Japanese are proving themselves more efficient.

One could go on generalising and the exercise would not be too productive, for there are absurdities in the patterns of behaviour of most people. But as regards the Italians, I think it is fair to say that they are the most misunderstood people in Europe, because of generalisations about them.

The view, for example, that the average Englishman has of the Italian (and probably, for that matter, the average American, Australian, German etc) goes from one extreme of great liking and sometimes even love, to the other, of utter disregard and sometimes contempt. It is an interesting situation which I shall return to later and it has developed out of a love/hate relationship which has some historical justification.

Nevertheless, it is a fact that for an Englishman the typical Italian is a short, black-haired, romantic with a more or less lovely voice, who is either a gigolo, a waiter, an ice-cream vendor or a footballer, and goes around pinching girls' bottoms (more about bottoms later).

The Italian woman is a large, pasta-eating person, with many 'bambinos,' who slaves away in the kitchen.

Both pictures are a travesty of reality and lead to much misunderstanding. For example, contrary to popular belief, Italian men are anything but romantic (more about this, too, later on); they do not pinch girls' bottoms, although they may caress them; present-day Italian families are anything but large; Italian women may or may not be fat, etc, etc.; the commonplaces are legion, as are the misunderstandings.

It is a pity, of course, that the Italians should be so misunderstood for, as I have said, their contribution to life has been very great indeed. The most modern authority in this regard is Luigi Barzini whose book *The Italians* published in 1964 is, to me at any rate, the most perceptive study of his fellow countrymen I have encountered so far. Let me quote from its introduction:

'One of the sources of confusion was the absurd discrepancy between the quantity and dazzling array of the inhabitants' achievements through many centuries and the mediocre quality of their national history. Italians have impressively filled Europe and most of the world with the fame of their larger-than-life-size famous men. Italian architects and masons built part of the Kremlin in Moscow and the Winter Palace in Leningrad; Italian artists have embellished the Capitol in Washington. They have strewn churches, princely palaces, and stately villas all over Catholic Europe, especially in Vienna, Madrid, Prague, and Warsaw; their influence on architecture was felt almost everywhere else, exterior architecture, to be sure, designed to impress and please the on-looker more than to serve strictly practical purposes. They have filled South America with ornate and rhetorical monuments to the local heroes.

'Italy's smaller contributions to everyday life are so numerous as to go unnoticed. There would be no pistols but for the city of Pistoia; no savon in France but for the city of Savona; no faience anywhere but for the city of Faenza; no millinery but for the city of Milan; no blue jeans but for Genes, the city of Genoa, where the blue cotton cloth was first produced, and no Genoa jibs; no Neapolitan ice-cream, no Roman candles, no Venetian blinds, no Bologna sausages, no Parmesan cheese, no Leghorn hens. Italians have discovered America for the Americans; taught poetry, statesmanship, and the ruses of trade to the English; military art to the Germans; cuisine to the French; acting and ballet dancing to the Russians; and music to everybody. If some day this world of ours should be turned into a cloud of radioactive dust in space, it will be by nuclear contrivances developed with the decisive aid of Italian scientists.'

And I add:

There would be no America but for Amerigo Vespucci who gave his name to it. No Ancona hens but for the town of Ancona where they originated. No ballet but for the Italian verb 'ballare'. No bankrupt or bankruptcy but for the Italian 'banca rotta.' No burlesque but for the Italian 'burla.' No carbines but for the carabin soldiers from Calabria. No Dantesque but for Dante, the great Italian poet. No Diocletian windows but for Palladio who revived their use in the sixteenth-century. No Fallopian tubes but for Fallopio who discovered them. No florins but for Florence where they were first minted in 1252. No galvanometer but for Galvani who invented it. No garibaldi biscuits but for Garibaldi, the Italian national hero. No gazettes but for the Gazetta, in Italy a small coin and later a newspaper. No Justerini and Brooks ('JB Whisky') but for Giacomo Justerini of Bologna who founded the well-known firm of wine merchants in the early eighteenth-century. No Lippizaner horses but for the town of Lippiza near Trieste. No machiavellian thoughts but for Machiavelli, the founder of political science. No madrigals but for the Latin/Italian 'matricale'. No maiolica but for the style that the Italians gave to a particular kind of ceramic decoration which they got from the Arabs through Mallorca (Majorca or Majolica). No mantuas but for the town of Mantova (Mantua) famous for its silks in the seventeenth and eighteenth centuries. No Pall Mall but for the Italian game of 'palla maglia,' (ball and mallet). No marconigram but for Marconi who discovered radio. No pants or pantaloons but for the 'commedia dell'arte' character Pantalone. No Punch but for Punchinello which was the Italian 'commedia dell'arte' mask. No sardines but for Sardinia (or is it the other way round?). No sequins but for the Italian 'zecchino,' another small coin. No spaghetti but for the Italian noun 'spago,' meaning string. No sybaritic behaviour but for the town of Sybaris in Calabria where it is said they really enjoyed themselves. No volts but for Volta who discovered electricity. And no White's Club in St James's but for Francesco Bianchi who founded it, (originally as 'White's Chocolate House') in 1693.

Incidentally, it is interesting to note that the Italian language has contributed a large number of words to the English vocabulary. As will become more apparent later on, Italian literature was read and cultivated in England since the time of Chaucer (fourteenth century) and the arts and artists of Italy exerted a great influence in England. Apart from those words which relate either to poetry, music, architecture, sculpture or painting, there are many others for which England is indebted to Italy. The following random selection ignores English words with more direct derivation from Latin as well as the substantial contributions made by the Italian language to musical and art terms, from *allegro* and *forte* to *intaglio* and *chiaroscuro*.

Alarm, Alert, Alto, Arcade, Argosy, Arsenal, Balcony, Balustrade, Bandit, Bankrupt, Bordello, Bravo, Brigade, Brigand, Broccoli, Burlesque, Bust, Cabriolet, Calepin, Cameo, Canteen, Canto, Cappuccino, Caprice, Caricature, Carnival, Cartoon, Cascade, Casemate, Cavalcade, Charlatan, Citadel, Colonnade, Confetti, Concert, Contralto, Conversazione, Cornice, Corporal, Corridor, Courtesan, Credenza, Cupola, Curvet, Dilettante, Ditto, Doge, Domino, Espresso, Extravaganza, Fata morgana, Fiasco, Flask, Florin, Folio, Fresco(al), Gazette, Gondola, Granite, Grotto, Guitar, Impresario, Inferno, Influenza, Lagoon, Lava, Lazaretto, Macaroni, Machiavellian, Madonna, Madrigal, Mafia-mafioso, Magazine, Malaria, Manifesto, Mask (masque), Motto, Moustache, Niche, Opera, Oratorio, Padre, Palette, Paparazzo, Pantaloon, Parapet, Patch, Pedant, Pedestal, Pergola, Pianoforte, Piazza, Pistol, Pizza, Policy, Porcelain, Portico, Quarantine, Proviso, Quarto, Regatta, Ridotto, Ruffian, Scenario, Sentry, Sequin, Seraglio, Serenade, Soffione, Soffit, Sonnet, Soprano, Spaghetti, Stanza, Stiletto, Stucco, Studio, Tenor, Terra-cotta, Terra-firma, Tirade, Torso, Trombone, Trump, Umbrella, Vendetta, Vermilion, Vertu, Virtuoso, Vista, Vogue, Volcano, Zany.

[Furthermore, it has been suggested that the expressions 'Dear me' and 'Fiddle de dee' are taken from the Italian (respectively, from *Diomi (salvi)* — God save me — and *Fe di Dio* (by the faith of God).]

But let's go back to Barzini.

'The list of the famous Italians is awe-inspiring. It is as well to record them here, as they will scarcely be mentioned in the rest of the book, written with the presumption that the reader is well acquainted with them. Here are some of the main ones: the saints: Saint Francis, Santa Caterina da Siena, San Bernardino da Siena, San Luigi Gonzaga, Saint Thomas of Aquino. The sinners: The Borgia family (Spanish but acclimatized), Cellini, Caravaggio, Cagliostro, Casanova. The political thinkers: Dante Alighieri, King Frederick of Hohenstaufen of the two Sicilies (born in Italy, the inventor of the "balance of power,") Machiavelli, Guicciardini, Mazzini, Cavour. The military leaders: Giovanni della Bande Nere, Raimondo Montecucoli (who led Austrian armies), Napoleon, Garibaldi. The admirals: Andrea Doria, Mocenigo, Morosini, Bragadin, Caracciolo. The scientists: Galileo Galilei, Leonardo da Vinci, Volta, Marconi, Fermi. The navigators: Columbus, Vespucci, the Cabots. The thinkers: Saint Thomas of Aquino, Campanella, Croce, Vico. The poets: Dante Alighieri, Boccaccio, Petrarch, Leopardi, Manzoni. The sculptors: Verrocchio, Donatello, Ghiberti, della Robbia, Cellini, Michelangelo, Bernini. The painters: Giotto, Botticelli, Fra Angelico, Leonardo da Vinci, Piero della Francesca, Perugino, Michelangelo, Raphael, Titian, Tintoretto, Tiepolo, Modigliani. The musicians: Palestrina, Pergolesi, Monteverdi, Vivaldi, Rossini, Verdi, Bellini, Donizetti, Puccini, Toscanini. These are, of course, the names of first magnitude. The second and third could easily fill a small city's telephone book.'

Having read Barzini's magnificent commentary, you may well have been left wondering whether what he says is true. Admittedly, some of the names he mentions you will surely have heard of before; but is it all possible? Can he be trusted? Or is he just being Machiavellian as are all Italians? Is he displaying our well known so-called duplicity?

I must admit that after I had myself read what I have just transcribed it occurred to me that I should go and check out everything he said; and I did. I discovered that Barzini had actually understated the position and it struck me that his grandiloquence ought to be supported by facts.

It was at that point that I decided that I should put pen to paper. I did so for a combination of reasons, some selfish, some disinterested.

The first reason was that I reacted against Barzini's unsubstantiated generalisations much as I react against politicians who also indulge in generalisations (mainly false) without citing any authority to support their view.

There was a second reason. My three children were all born in England and despite the fact that their mother is also Italian, they are hardly aware of the real traditions of their parents' country. Do not misunderstand me; it is not that they are not aware, say, that Italian food is the best in the world. They know that only too well, because of their mother's cooking. Nor do they have any doubt that, when it comes to things of beauty, it is difficult to beat what comes out of Italy. In due course, as they grow older, they will realise that there is more to being Italian than just good food and taste.

But apart from these concepts, and the fact that Italian opera is more enjoyable than any other, the cultural tradition of Italy is almost non-existent as far as they are concerned. And it occurred to me that this must be the position with a number of children of Italians, either born in England or America or wherever, expatriates, who, apart from their name, have little left of what is Italian.

This is not their fault, of course, because England and the New World have the great ability to absorb, to permeate and, inevitably, to corrupt national characteristics. There are a number of reasons why England in particular has so far succeeded in this process. The principal reason is that the English damp weather has a softening and sobering effect in all areas of life. But there is a second and much more important reason and it is that England offers what for example Italy lacks, namely a political tradition, a tradition of freedom and respectability and of obvious patriotism. All this is kept alive by public ceremony and impeccably executed parades, the sensible, elegant display of pomp and the superb orchestration of displays of national history, the National Anthem and an efficient and dutiful monarchy.

It therefore provides something which people can cling to and, as far as the Italians are concerned, it offers an excellent substitute. Whatever traditions Italians may have, they are of a cultural and certainly not of a political nature.

For all these reasons the Italians have blended in with the English community quite well. I remember that in the early fifties the brick industry in Bedfordshire needed cheap labour. Thousands of Italian workers were imported from southern Italy. There was a great outcry locally. It was said that the morals of the community would be corrupted, that these Italians would turn into criminals, that they could not be trusted and so on. Strangely, the same remarks were made then (and I recall them well) which have been made over the past twenty years about other 'importations' into this country.

Fears for the well-being of the local women were very prominent. Fears for their virtue, and for their physical safety.

I also remember, almost with nostalgia, the names of the brick companies involved (The London Brick Company, The Marston Valley Brick Company; the latter no longer in existence). A lot of fuss about nothing. The workers blended in perfectly, and as far as I know, they now represent a substantial, law-abiding section of the Bedford community; I am not aware of any problems. They even have their own Radio Bedford. Just imagine!

The point I am trying to make is that by blending in so well with the environment of their 'adopted' country, very many of the new generation of Italians (who have gone into management, politics, medicine, the law, etc.) have forgotten the contributions that their mother country has made to man's technical and cultural progress - at least in the western world. I thought some of them might welcome the opportunity to get hold of the facts. Having done so, they may well come to the conclusion that Italians are a lot better at some things than they are normally given credit for. Of course, some might comment that it is a pity Italy did not produce a Beethoven or a Shakespeare (more about that later, though). Putting that line of argument to one side, it has to be said that, in general, Italy's sum total of creativity is fantastic and, happily, continues to be so.

But there was a third reason for writing this book. On 17 January 1986 *The Times* published a letter from one of its readers where, in congratulating the Italian government on the manner in which they had dealt with the outbreak of violence at Rome Airport earlier on, the author indirectly expressed the view that it was probably the first time that the Italians had ever got anything right. That letter made me angry. My pride was hurt, my dignity offended, my self-respect slighted. I asked myself: How dare he? Who does he think he is? What were his ancestors doing when mine were civilising the then known world? Are his traditions, cultural or otherwise, such as to entitle him to proffer public criticism of a whole nation?

My anger subsided because it struck me that the fault was not his, but it was ours, the Italians', and that his reaction was totally understandable. It was the reaction of the ordinary Englishman for whom the Italians are not too important. As has been said, thank God for the Spaniards for, without them, the Italians would be the last people in Europe.

It is of little use to remind the man in the street of what Dr Johnson said about Italy and the Mediterranean. The man in the street in England does not read Boswell. The passage I have in mind occurs in Boswell's Life of Johnson (Thursday, 11 April 1776): 'A man who has not been in Italy is always conscious of an inferiority from his not having seen what it is expected a man should see ... all our religion, almost all our law, almost all our arts, almost all that sets us above savages, has come to us from the shores of the Mediterranean.'

The normal reaction to Italians cannot be helped, because we have encouraged it. We Italians deserve the way in which others, especially the English, think of us. We seem to enjoy projecting and encouraging the projection of a wrong image. We make everything easy, we behave in a clownish fashion, we never take anything seriously, we have no sense of duty, we are corrupt.

Our language itself is misleading. I remember that when I was a student here, I had to support myself by teaching Italian, amongst other things, at evening classes. And one of my greatest difficulties lay in disabusing my students of the notion that Italian was an easy language. After all, how deceptively easy it sounds: '*Grazie*', '*prego*', '*buon giorno*', '*buonasera*'. Anybody can learn that, it is so easy; but it is hardly the truth.

Indeed, it is so especially easy that when people, particularly English-speaking people, make an attempt to utter it, they do not bother to get the pronunciation or the spelling right. They seem to be incapable of finding out how they should pronounce or write Italian. The very same people who would go to the trouble of looking up a French or German word in the dictionary blissfully embark upon Italian without consulting anyone. This attitude can be traced to the Victorian era, when Italian was considered as a light and frivolous language, the language of lovers and minor poets, and as such fit to be taught only to wealthy young girls so that they might, perhaps, gain more appreciation of music and opera.

Leaving aside the absurdity of pronouncing the name of a well-known, but not terribly good, Italian actress as Ghinay Laulaubreegheeday, it is fascinating for an Italian to note the absurdities that flow when Englishmen (Americans, Australians?) speak Italian. And I am not considering the uneducated or the ignorant.

I was listening to a programme on BBC Radio 3 recently where someone was discussing the relationship between Verdi and his librettist Boito. He kept referring to Bóito as Boìto. It was really painful for me; it was painful because apart from the grammatical unlikelihood of having a diphthong with the accent on the second vowel, the only word I could at the time think of in Italian with a comparable sound was 'guaîto', which is the representation of the sound that an animal makes when it is kicked or hurt. It was an interesting association of ideas, for me at any rate, as I felt like kicking back myself.

But there was an even more delightful nonsense shortly after, this time on television, when in the course of an interesting programme on crime in Italy, the presenter referred to the code of solidarity amongst criminals in Italy as 'Omêrta'. The combination of the soft English-style pronunciation of the dental consonant and the accent on the 'e' will no doubt strike Italian readers as entertaining. For those who do not know Italian, may I add that, as a result, instead of pronouncing the word 'Omertá' with an accent on the last syllable, which Italians all understand as representing a noun of strength, meaning and passion, whatever view one forms of the criminal aspects of it, one heard the pronunciation of a word which closely approximates to the Italian word for excrement. A suitable connotation for those who do not have sufficient respect for other people to bother to pronounce their language correctly.

So what? you may well remark. Well, it is important. I do not like that any more than I like people who purport to sing Italian opera in Italian with a foreign accent. After all, would you like it if a very primitive, ignorant Italian with a horrible accent stood on stage declaiming 'Friends, Romans, countrymen, lend me your ears' in tones and an accent that were totally alien to you? Would you not consider him presumptuous?

Furthermore, if I cannot trust you to get such a simple thing as the pronunciation or spelling of a word correct, how can I trust you to get the all important facts correct? Carelessness in one is an inevitable concomitant of sloppiness in the other.

At this point you may well be wondering, what gives Arturo Barone the right to don the mantle of criticism and censure. Well, other than my legal training which helps in factual analysis, I have no particular right, of course, any more than anyone else does; but I think my background and experience provide some justification. I have been living in England for over 30 years.

My three children were born in England and I have inevitably made a very long study, in comparative terms, of the English (but not forgetting our New World cousins either) and the Italians. Lest you should be misled by some of my critical terms into believing that I do not like England, let me make my position perfectly clear straight away: I love England. I love it despite all its shortcomings. I love it despite the present mood of materialism, self-aggrandisement and aggression; I love it even despite the break-up of the middle class centre ground and of the erosion and sometimes disappearance of traditional values. I should add at this point that in all honesty I have to say that my 'long study' has been of the English - as opposed to the Welsh, Scots or the Irish. I therefore refer mostly to England throughout.

I love the English countryside. I can think of nothing more beautiful, and now sadly missed, than the hedgerows of England stretching over undulating landscapes, with the English elm vibrating in the wind. I had always compared that lovely tree to the Greek statue of the victory (Nike) of Samothrace which adorns one of the landings in the Louvre. I think the description of that statue - 'Clothed in Wind' - given by Gabriele D'Annunzio, one of the most successful of modern Italian poets, could happily be applied to the English elm. But I digress.

The reader should also know that I consider myself to be Italian by tradition and English (British) by custom. I see no contradiction whatsoever in this, any more than a Welshman or a Scot might. Most of us have two parents anyhow; why not two cultures?

This duality of feeling, which I am certain is common to all those like myself who, originating from one country, live in another, is not even, and seldom has an equilibrium. I live in England and not in Italy; since I am not sufficiently wealthy to have my private jet and to go for medical or cosmetic treatment to Switzerland, I prefer to fly British Airways, and if I had to enter hospital, I would by choice go in England. If I had to be arrested and tried for any offence, I would prefer that it happened here. Whilst I am in England, I complain about a number of things; when I am in Italy, I will not hear a word said against England.

This patriotic ambiguity, if one could term it that, may appear almost schizophrenic: but it is not so. It is probably a good thing, because it enables one to broaden one's mind through close contact with two societies and two cultures. To that extent, it is a source of spiritual and, sometimes, material satisfaction.

At this stage, therefore, I have to make two apologies and two points. One apology follows from what I have just said, namely, that in the course of setting out what I consider to be the achievements of the Italian people I shall lapse from time to time into some form of comment or comparison; I shall digress. I know that, according to Byron, ('Beppo' stanza L) 'digression is a sin that by degrees becomes exceeding tedious ... and therefore may the reader too displease', but I should not be criticised too much for doing so because I hope at least that, by using this approach, I may be able to break up the monotony and the repetitiveness of those achievements.

The second thing for which I 'apologise' in advance is a certain pride and relish in what I have to say about Italian 'firsts'. But why apologise? The fact is I am proud of my Italian origins; I do not subscribe to the view that pride is a cardinal sin. Indeed, I firmly believe that it is one of the qualities that is missing in today's world and its absence causes very many of the problems with which we have to live. But that is another story. By the way, in a book of this kind, there is a tendency to repetition because in attempting to examine so many traits and characteristics from different aspects and points in time, my thoughts inevitably meet the same milestones or 'tributaries' of fact and information. I apologise in advance if this becomes tiresome to the reader

One final observation. In researching my subject I found a considerable scarcity of material, especially contemporary references, published in English. There are, of course, innumerable books on Italy, whether travel books or books on food and wine or art and architecture. The country itself has been dealt with quite extensively. But to my way of thinking, it has always been dealt with somewhat superficially and the Italians themselves have been avoided. It is difficult to say whether this was done because the writers felt, possibly with some degree of justification, that they preferred the country without the Italians, or whether because they took the view that we were not worthy of detailed analysis, or, as I surmise, because they reached the conclusion that we defy classification.

The more I pursue the topic the more I am convinced that the challenge of classification is the reason why so little has been published about the Italians as a people, as distinct from Italy as a nation. There is an elusiveness about us that can be troublesome. The moment you think you have understood what it is all about, something happens which causes you to ponder; you have developed a certain theory and immediately something crops up to destroy it.

As a result, there is really no *detailed* analysis of the Italians in the English language that I could find. There are two modern works, however - one by Luigi Barzini (from which I have already quoted) and the other by David Willey. They are totally different and indeed cannot be compared in any way.

Barzini, a writer of considerable experience, knows and understands the subject matter quite well, since presumably he knew and understood himself quite well. (He has since died). His analysis of Italian temperament and character is excellent. For that, he has only himself to thank. But some of his conclusions are wrong. For example, he says that divorce would never be introduced into Italy; he was, regrettably, wholly mistaken about this.

For his historical analysis and perception I think he owes a great debt to John Addington Symonds, as he himself acknowledges. But even with him, the reasons why we are as we are seem to elude him. I think this is probably because he was essentially a journalist and he was not prepared to delve too deeply into the subject matter, although the historical background which he provides is extensive.

At the opposite end of the spectrum, David Willey is basically a reporter. He is content to tell us what features the Italians of today display. His book really is almost a television documentary; all the more so because the text is copiously interspersed with photographs. His is a reasonably accurate portrait, but it does not purport to represent an in-depth study.

I'm not ignoring the late Peter Nichols's *Italia, Italia*. But he is more concerned with modern Italy - its politics, its economics, what makes it tick - than with the reasons why Italians are as they are in the historical sense. As a lover of Italy, he is worthy of my respect.

The only other modern contributor in this field is David Scott Fox whose book *Mediterranean Heritage*, first published in 1978, betrays his approach in its title. Although it is dedicated 'To Italy and Greece' - and I suggest that the order in which he puts the two countries, which is neither alphabetical nor historical, shows where his heart really is - most of what he says applies to Italy much more than to Greece. This is really inevitable, because the later Italian developments were more extensive and had a much more immediate and greater impact than those of Greece. And indeed, if one indulged in an analysis of his book page by page, one would find that the number of times Italy or the adjective 'Italian' is used is infinitely greater than that when Greece or 'Greek' are referred to.

Even so, if, as the cover records, his book is based on a lifetime's observation and enjoyment, then he must be reckoned amongst the many inspired Englishmen who despite all our faults have learnt to appreciate us.

The Scott Fox book was written long before two very recent contributions appeared on the scene. They are *Democracy Italian-Style* by Jack La Palombara (Yale University Press 1988) and *Agnelli and the Network of Italian Power* by Alan Friedman (Harrap 1988).

The former considers the Italians purely as political creatures and is, overall, a flattering exercise as far as Italy is concerned; the latter is effectively a biography of the Chairman of Fiat and is on the whole less flattering of him, if not of the Italians.

But enough of the preliminaries. As regards the task ahead, I should advise the reader that I had to draw the line somewhere in deciding at which point to start. I took the view that the achievements of ancient Rome are so well documented they could be taken for granted. Thus, I have ignored Roman civilisation completely even though Italians claim to be the successors of the Romans. By the way, it is interesting that the English themselves have claimed to be successors of the Romans at least in the sense that they applied the same political criteria when founding an empire and, as the Romans used to extend their nationality to all those whom they conquered, so did the British. Whether the Italians are the true successors of the Romans is a matter I shall return to later on.

So, for this reason, and because it seemed like a sensible departure point, I have started at the year 1000 AD. Furthermore, some of the most reliable records commence roundabout the beginning of the second millennium. I should also advise the reader not to be surprised by the absence of many of the 'great' Italian names, such as Verdi and Michelangelo. The reason is simple: they were great, but they were not the first at what they did. Opera had existed before Verdi and, obviously, so had sculpture, painting and architecture, let alone poetry, before Michelangelo.

In this book (at least in Part I which provides the Facts) I am only interested in the things that Italians did first. Indeed, the title is *Italians First!* but it could just as easily have been 'Italian Firsts'. I am concerned only with discoveries and first events and with those concepts which some authors might call seminal. To date, I have recorded over 400 'firsts'. The list does not purport to be exhaustive and I am quite certain that many others will be found by more zealous researchers than I. But it is nevertheless an impressive list; and a start. (I have to confess, however, that I did allow myself to meander amongst some less important, though equally interesting, achievements; and for this I call on the reader's indulgence.)

I can almost hear some of you thinking 'So, what is all the fuss about? The only good things that Italians have discovered are pasta and America.' If you are thinking that, you are totally mistaken. The discoveries made by Italians are of enormous importance. If I took you now through a whole day, as I will in my Conclusion at the end, you would find that if you wake up with an alarm and you go to bed listening to the radio, not only will you have started and ended the day with an Italian invention but throughout the day you will not have been able to live or move or even eat, yes, even eat, decently, but for the Italians!

You do not believe me? Then let me assure you that every statement of fact (not my digressions, of course) is backed up by an authoritative source. Wherever possible, for example, I have referred to the *Encyclopaedia Britannica*. All references to the *Encyclopaedia Britannica* are drawn from the 15th Edition. But there are other authorities and other encyclopaedias that are also referred to.

I have divided the factual entries into eleven sections for ease of reference, set out alphabetically according to subject matter. Thus, if you are interested in finding out what discoveries Italians have made in, say, physics, look under the section 'Sciences' sub-heading 'Physics'. In this way, you do not have to read through the whole of any one section to check a possible entry.

Are you still in some doubt? Let us try one out. As I have already mentioned, French cooking stems from Italian cooking, although most people, it appears, believe that it was the other way round. Well, it was Italian cooking that was the turning point in the development of gastronomic excellence and Italy influenced France extensively. If you want to check this statement, look it up in the *Encyclopaedia Britannica* under the heading

'Gastronomy', Volume 7, page 940. (If necessary, go to the library and look it up!) I should like you to do so because I wish my readers to be convinced at the outset that whenever a statement of fact is made in the pages that follow (indicated by a solid dot at the head of each entry) then, unless I have myself qualified that fact, it is incontrovertible.

You may think that is a tall order. But as the saying goes, the proof of the pudding is in the eating. Go and check the heading 'Gastronomy'. And whilst we are on the subject of food, did you know that it was the Italians who invented the fork for use at table? Yes, I know, Italian eating habits are dreadful, all that spaghetti being twirled around, splashing one's clothes and dropping on to one's lap. Nevertheless the dining fork was invented in Italy in the sixteenth century, It did not come into use in England until 100 years later. I do not say this, the *Encyclopaedia Britannica* does and the reference is Volume IV page 230. Go on, look that up too!

Am I provoking you? I am not surprised. It is exactly what I intended to do. You will find in what follows a number of provocative statements based on provocative, established, but usually unacknowledged facts.

Let's make a start.

LEONARDO

LEONARDO

No, signori, ogni insistenza è inutile.
Mi rifiuto fermamente
d'inventare la televisione.

"No, gentlemen, it is useless pressing me any
further. I refuse to invent television — and that's
the end of the matter!"

PART 1:
THE FACTS

Section 1:
Architecture
& Buildings

Architecture

● In 1432 Filippo BRUNELLESCHI (born in Florence) developed the concept of the negative side thrust and designed and built the dome on the Florence Duomo.

● In 1485 Leon Battista ALBERTI (born in Florence) wrote the first textbook ever on architecture. It was written in Latin and it was called *De Re Aedificatoria*.

Alberti was responsible for the Tempio Malatestiano at Rimini and the façade of Santa Maria Novella in Florence. He was a man of many parts: one of the earlier Italian humanists, a lawyer, a mathematician, a cartographer and an educator. (In this last capacity he is referred to later on.) He was also one of the first developers of ciphers, (see 'Cryptography').

● In 1437 Alberti gave the first pinhole demonstration of the perspective view. He systematized the plan and layout of houses.

He also pioneered the designing of houses in particular locations, with special reference to the physical features of the surrounding landscape, particularly gardens.

● In 1570, ANDREA PALLADIO (born in Padua) published his four books 'On Architecture' which were translated into all modern languages. His style was easily assimilated in England and influenced all subsequent English architects including Sir Christopher Wren. There is still extant a copy of Palladio's work signed by Lord Burlington and dated by him 1728.

His *Quattro libri dell'architettura* were also read and annotated by Inigo Jones when he accompanied the second Earl of Arundel on a tour of Italy.

The effects can be seen in everything Inigo Jones did, from the Palladian bridge at Wilton to the house layout at Burghley.

Indeed, it can be said that the English country house would not exist but for Palladio and the influence of Italian architecture throughout the world, stemming from Palladio's style, is too well known to need detailed re-statement here. Suffice it to say, however, that the earliest example of Palladian influence is to be found at Houghton House, built between 1712 and 1726 as a residence for Robert Walpole. The influence of Italy there is all pervasive; in the outline, in the stucco ceilings, in William Kent's work. It was Lord Burlington who had spotted Kent's potential and had taken him on a tour of Italy; when Kent came back, he profitably and stylishly applied to the English environment all he had learnt in Italy.

One more example: Dashwood House at West Wycombe, the home of Sir Francis Dashwood, the founder of the Dilettanti Society, continued the Palladian and Italianate tradition particularly in its double loggia, a rarity in England.

Sir Francis Dashwood was himself somewhat of an exception because he was a merchant and not a nobleman by birth. But he appreciated fine things: Dashwood House is Italian both in thought and effectuation. Nor should this be surprising to accept in any event, because since Elizabeth I the English had had a love affair with Roman architecture generally: to superimpose on it, or to blend it with, Palladian influences, came very naturally. Just as the English ruling class could be compared to that of Rome, so its taste and appreciation of things Italian was a mark of refinement; just as Rome had defeated the Gauls, so had England subdued the French. This is apparent if one visits Syon House in Isleworth, Middx, where Robert Adam gave the Dukes of Northumberland what one could describe, if one may be forgiven the pun, as a home from Rome.

From England the Palladian style was exported to the Empire. It lent itself, imposing as it is and easy to assimilate, to the embassies, residences of High Commissioners, palaces, mansions, etc. which were erected wherever British rule extended. It is a solid, reliable style: it pleased the rulers, enhanced their status in the eyes of the local population and added to their power and majesty.

The Victorians were particularly enamoured of it as it suited the great power of England at that time with territories throughout the world. Furthermore, Queen Victoria's personal style in architecture was somewhat italianate, as witness her Isle of Wight residence, Osborne House.

It is built in the manner of an Italian seaside villa, with a 'campanile'-type tower. Indeed, if one just saw a photo of it, one would probably want to place it somewhere along the shores of the Riviera.

Skyscrapers

• It is San Gimignano in Tuscany, not New York, which boasts the first skyscrapers in the world.

Known as 'tower houses,' they were built in about 1200 when San Gimignano came under the dominance of the Etruscan town Volterra. San Gimignano itself is of Etruscan origin.

According to extant records, about 76 of these towers were built, but only 13 are left standing today. They were quite a feature at the time as each of the owners vied with the other to build a taller and more impressive residence. They were so famous that the town itself became known as San Gimignano 'of the beautiful towers'.

Indeed, there were complaints of overcrowding of buildings right up to the

fourteenth century when the town passed within the sphere of influence of Florence.

The towers (some of which are over 175 feet high) rise well above the rooftops, and they stand out against the sky as sentinels, almost as though they were endeavouring to protect the architecture of the place and its historical heritage.

Pedestrianisation

SIENA The central square (the Piazza del Campo) and adjacent streets were closed to traffic in July 1965. The local authority order to that effect came into force after the Palio of that year was run.

ROME As far as Rome is concerned what are known as the Seven Sectors of its 'historical centre' were all closed to motor traffic in 1973 and 1974.

Section 2:
The Arts

Ballet

It is the Italian verb *ballare* from which the word 'ballet' is taken. During my investigations I was surprised to find that the Italian contribution to ballet is quite substantial.

I had always looked upon the ballet as a Russian development, but I was wrong. As Barzini said, it was the Italians who taught dancing to the Russians.

In case you think this statement rash, look at the facts.

• In 1400 Domenico da PIACENZA wrote the first book on the dances of Europe. It was written, as was then customary, in the Latin language and it was called *De Arte Saltandi Et Choreas Ducendi*.

• The first ballet was produced by Baltazarini Di BELGIOIOSO. It is not clear whether he did so in Tortona in Italy in 1489, or in France in 1581.

Let's not however worry too much about the dates; according to the *Encyclopaedia Britannica*, he did so.

• It was Salvatore VIGANÓ (born in Naples) who really established dramatic ballet in Milan in 1809.

It was of him that Stendhal ('Rome Naples and Florence') wrote: 'the finest tragedy that Shakespeare ever wrote can scarcely move me half as much as a ballet by Viganó ... he is a genius whose art will die with him.' [see page 90 of the 1959 John Calder edition, translated by Richard Coe].

• At about the same time, Gasparo ANGIOLINI (born in Naples) was the first to integrate dance music and plot.

• In 1591 the term 'balletto' was used for the first time by Giovanni GASTOLDI.

• In 1747 Gaetano VESTRIS (born in Florence) established himself as the first male ballet dancer. In his day, he was referred to as the god of the dance.

• In 1820, Carlo BLASIS (born in Naples) codified the techniques of classical ballet.

• In 1887 Enrico CECCHETTI (born in Rome) developed his method of training for dancers which is still widely used throughout the world and is known as Cecchetti's Method.

But even before Cecchetti established his method of training, the great dancing tradition had found its best nineteenth-century exponent of the Romantic style in Marie Taglioni, whose debut in Vienna in

1822 was as notable as that of our next character. Taglioni was among the first to dance on tiptoes. Ten years later, in *La Sylphide*, she displayed leaps, arabesques and, above all, a dress of a style which has continued almost to this day.

• In 1893 Pierina LEGNANI established her virtuoso ballet technique which formed the basis for the Russian School of Ballet.

She did so in a rather flamboyant fashion when she made her debut in Saint Petersburg. She executed a series of 32 fouettés, a technical feat never before seen on stage.

The Russian audience was ecstatic. Her positioning was so true to the vertical that she is said not to have moved one inch from the spot on which such brilliant execution occurred. It was left to her and to the Italian ballet corps to salvage Tchaikovsky's *Swan Lake*, which had not received a good press the first time it was performed by Russian dancers.

Caricatures

• According to the *Encyclopaedia Britannica*, the first caricaturist was Pier Leone GHEZZI (born in Rome).

Britannica seems to wander a little when it comes to caricature. For example, if you turn to page 37 (in this book) you will find that *Britannica* also attributes caricature to Bernini, whereas Scott Fox in his book *Mediterranean Heritage* attributes it to Annibale Carracci, who was born at least 200 years before Ghezzi.

I shall opt for Leonardo da Vinci as the true Italian originator of caricature, as some of the drawings in the Louvre (and there are many) clearly show. However, according to the Harwin chronology of Inventions, Innovations and Discoveries, there is an even earlier attribution: this publication ascribes it to Buffalmacco Buonamico De Cristofaro in 1330, a 'painter of the earlier Florentine School, with a great reputation as a practical joker. He drew comic figures and put labels to their mouths with sentences.'

Whichever way you look at it, it does not really matter, because Ghezzi, Bernini, Carracci, Leonardo and Buffalmacco were all Italians.

It is a matter of choice as to who deserves the accolade but it is an historical fact that caricature portraits became exceptionally popular with English visitors who went to Italy on their grand tour. As a result, the English developed the Italian caricature into a satirical and political weapon (see Hogarth); and that tradition is maintained to this day (see the television programme 'Spitting Image').

Literary Criticism

- In 1498 Lorenzo VALLA (born in Rome) proved the forgery of the donation of Constantine. He also happens to have translated Aristotle's poetics into Latin.

- 1570 saw the establishment of the first literary critic in the person of Lodovico CASTELVETRO (born in Modena).

Our criticism, however, is not confined to literature. The Italians are constantly criticizing. They criticize their neighbours, their friends, their nation, other peoples, but never themselves.

We have a very highly developed critical sense that knows no social, political or religious barrier; but we seem quite incapable of turning it inwards. To this extent, we are continuing the Roman tradition. We hardly need reminding of Horace's satire, which in laughter reproaches customs (*Castigat ridendo mores*).

We are also in this sense continuing the other Roman tradition of the Fescennine Verses that, roundabout the middle of the first century B.C., became so offensive that they had to be banned. I still remember from my school days how Horace puts it: *Donec iam saevus apertam in rabiem coepit verti et per honestas ire domos impune minax*, which roughly translated means that the jocular dialogues which were already offensive became vicious and more open and affected even reputable homes. An early version of *Private Eye!*

But as I have said, I am not sure how good we are at self-criticism. If we were better at it, we might be more willing to make allowances for others. We would then find it somewhat easier to remedy one of our major faults namely, our utter inability to pull together as a nation.

Music and Musical Instruments

In the list that follows there will be names you know and names you think are 'missing'; there will also be names, no doubt, that you have never heard before. As I said earlier, this should not be considered unusual. For example, Puccini may have been the initiator of a particular type of melodic line, but he discovered nothing. Opera and music pre-existed him.

The names that follow are the names of people who were, each in their own way, the first in their fields; alternatively, the events that are recorded occurred in Italy for the first time ever.

• In 1028 Guido D'AREZZO established the western system of notation based on eight notes in an octave which is still used extensively throughout the western world despite attempts by Schoenberg and others to upstage it with a 12-note system. D'Arezzo is said to have produced his system while in the Benedictine Abbey at Pomposa, on the Adriatic.

• In 1634 Francesco LANDINI established the cadence that bears his name.

• In 1490 the 'frottola' came into existence as the predecessor of the madrigal.

• In 1492, whilst Christopher Columbus was travelling to the Indies, Franchino GRIFFORI first described tuned glasses.

• Around the year 1500 the first thin-cased harpsicord construction was achieved in Italy.

• AFRANIO (of Pavia) was a Canon at the cathedral in Ferrara and is said to have invented the bassoon. He is certainly given as the inventor of the bassoon in the year 1500 in the Harwin Chronology of Inventions, Innovations and Discoveries. But according to Treccani, whatever he did invent it was not the same instrument as the modern bassoon.

• During the Renaissance, the violin evolved in Italy.

• In the sixteenth and seventeenth centuries the first virginals and spinets were built in Italy.

• In 1520 Andrea GABRIELI (born in Venice) established the procedures that were later to result in the sonata and started the western system of orchestration.

• In 1597 Ottavio RINUCCINI (born in Florence) wrote his Dafne, thus becoming the first musician to use a libretto.

• In 1600 Agostino AGAZZARI (born in Siena) wrote the earliest known musical instruction book.

• The oratorio originated in Italy.

The oratorio was originally a musical entertainment mixed with religious education and evolved around the middle of the sixteenth century. Saint Filippo Neri instituted it in the oratory of the Roman Church which takes its name from him and which is still in existence. The earliest surviving oratorio was written by Emilio del Cavaliere in 1600.

• In 1607 Girolamo FRESCOBALDI (born in Ferrara) established himself as the first master of organ composition.

• In 1607 Claudio MONTEVERDI (born in Cremona) had his opera Orfeo first performed in Mantova. He had started his musical career some twenty years earlier and from about the year 1587, he can to all intents and purposes be considered the founder of modern music.

• In 1617 Biagio MARINI (born in Brescia) wrote the first sonata for solo violin.

• In 1622 Salomone ROSSI wrote the first specification of instruments for dance sets.

• In 1698 Bartolomeo CRISTOFORI (born in Padova) constructed the first pianoforte.

What Cristofori did was to combine the qualities of the clavichord and the harpsichord into a single instrument. The clavichord would produce numerous shades of sound, but it was not a powerful instrument; the harpsichord had a bigger sound, but did not lend itself to crescendos or diminuendos. Hence his brilliant synthesis.

• Around the year 1700 the modern violin was first manufactured in Italy. Its principal makers were Gasparo Da SALO', Andrea AMATI and Giovanni Paolo MAGGINI. A few years later they were joined by the maker of the Rolls Royce of violins, namely Antonio STRADIVARIO (born in Cremona).

Stradivario's violins are world famous for their tone, power and beauty. For over 200 years violin makers have been trying to reproduce the same features that make a Stradivarius unique, but so far without success.

Indeed, despite all the technical resources at our disposal, we do not even know whether such features are due to the varnish used, to the especially high mineral content of the wood, to a combination of both, to a special film of 'pozzolana' ash, or just to a special knack he had. Even so, he was unique as were his instruments.

Stradivario also manufactured cellos, violas, lutes, mandolins, guitars and bows. His output was enormous: it is claimed that he manufactured between 700 and 1500 instruments.

When he died in 1737, aged 93, he was universally acclaimed as the successor of Amati; he was also the richest man in Cremona. He certainly lived life to the full, in a city full of life. He had two wives each of whom had five children.

Stradivario had started his apprenticeship quite early, so that by the time he was 18 he was already in the workshop of his master, Nicolo Amati. Even in his lifetime, people were conscious of his greatness. The world's most famous scientist, Galileo, himself the son of a musician, called Stradivario's instruments 'incomparable'. Most interesting of all, perhaps, is the fact that he made his greatest and most successful instruments during his seventies.

Stradivario also devised the violin bridge in modern form and the proportions of the violins which he manufactured set the standard which has prevailed to this day: his patterns have been followed by all subsequent manufacturers of stringed instruments, particularly cellos.

I have already remarked on our inability to explain away the success, in tonal terms, of what he produced. But apart from tone, the instruments that he made were unique because they were exceptionally strong, and yet light, resonant, without being harsh, and of an outstanding patination. The Stradivari sound has been variously described as warm, glowing, rich, deep; it

is not so strong as that of a Guarneri, and yet it is more vital: it is almost as though his instruments are living things and they gain from the association with the human being who plays them.

To all intents and purposes his instruments are his heirs, and, as far as one can tell, all those that have survived are in excellent condition. Most of them are dated and many of them have names; for example, the Rawlins guitar, the Cristiani, Tuscan and Davidoff cellos, the Hellier, Tuscan and Archinto violas, the Emiliani, Tuscan, Cathedrale, Amatise, Soil, Reyner, Francescatti, Kreutzer, Marie Hall, Gibson and Parke violins, each with its own history and personality, style and sound, all members of a unique family of exceptional vitality and continuity. For over 300 years Stradivario's techniques have given the world the joy of the sounds of his instruments. Cristofori produced the piano, Stradivario developed the violin: how much delight and pleasure have these two names provided for future generations. Pleasure for the performers as well as for the audiences.

It is no small claim to lay, that one has been able to give pleasure; others may have fared better in different fields but when it comes to style and pleasure (whether of the table, of the arts or particularly of music) the Italians' claim is paramount: it would appear that the Almighty has endowed Italy with the ability to make people happy.

One final consideration: with such a plethora of first-class instruments available, it must have been comparatively easy for Stradivario's esteemed contemporary, Antonio Vivaldi, to write his music, especially *The Four Seasons*. (Incidentally, Vivaldi was the son of a barber.)

● In 1712 Francesco Antonio BONPORTI (born in Trento) wrote his *Invenzioni* for the harpsicord. You may well wonder what the significance of this fact is. Let me tell you. Bach (JS) got his ideas from Bonporti.

● In 1721 Pietro LOCATELLI (born in

Bergamo) anticipated Paganini by being the first virtuoso violinist and bravura performer.

• Not a particularly exciting first, but nevertheless worth recording for the sake of completeness: Carlo BROSCHI, otherwise known as Farinelli, established himself as the most celebrated castrato singer ever in 1721. He was Neapolitan, like Caruso, and was at least as famous as the latter. He was the best known 'soprano' of his generation and sang in most places in Europe. He spent a long time at the Spanish Court and had an outstanding success in London. Being to all intents and purposes a 'primadonna', it is recorded that he behaved exactly like one. He was jealous of his reputation as a singer and whenever he was on stage with anyone whose voice might compete with his, to ensure that in the high notes they did not out-perform him, he would either tread on the toes of the other singers or actually pinch their thighs in order to upset their vocal balance. He had been preceded by another 'castrato', Niccoló Grimaldi, otherwise known as 'Nicolini', who however did not quite achieve the same notoriety as Farinelli. Other 'male' singers taking female roles in the eighteenth century were Giovanni Carestini and Giacinto Conti Gizziello.

• In 1740 Francesco GEMINIANI (born at Lucca) wrote the first published violin method.

• In 1750 Giuseppe TARTINI (born in Padova) discovered the so-called 'difference tone' or 'resultant tone'. This has the effect that a note emitted a third sound. (Tartini was famous for the short violin piece known as the 'Devil's Trill', the result, so it is said, of his having made a pact with the devil that he would be the greatest violinist ever. Curiously enough, the foremost virtuoso of the following century, Nicolo PAGANINI, took it up as one of his own show pieces.)

• In 1758 Tommaso TRAETTA (born at Bitonto) started operatic reform. His works

were accompanied by the orchestra, the chorus as well as ballet sequences and were all brought more closely into the action and integrated, thus anticipating Gluck and future operatic developments.

• The first mechanical piano was invented towards the end of the eighteenth century by Nicolo FRABRIS. Around the same time, Muzio CLEMENTI invented a self-performing piano.

• The first song specifically written for recording was, according to its label, 'Mattinata' by Ruggero LEONCAVALLO. It was published in 1904.

• In 1913 Luigi RUSSOLO experimented with electronic music, thereby anticipating synthesized music.

• In 1981 Giuseppe DI GIUGNO built the first super-computerised musical instrument. Di Giugno's musical instrument is a far cry from the melodies of the eighteenth and nineteenth centuries.

The impact on the world of Italian opera is too well known to be rehearsed by me. The impact on the world of the works written by Monteverdi and Cherubini, as forerunners of a musical style, is equally great.

But sometimes the influence of opera occurs where it is least expected. It may, or may not, surprise you to know that Italian opera generally, and the music of Cherubini in particular, exercised a very great and formative influence upon Chopin. In his book *Chopin* (Dent, London, 1947), Arthur Hedley (page 59) considers that the debt that Chopin owes to Italian opera in general is 'enormous'.

Opera Houses

• Venice can boast of the first public opera house in the world. This is the Teatro

San Cassiano which opened in 1637 with a performance of the opera *Andromeda* by Mannelli.

San Cassiano continued in use until the beginning of the nineteenth century. Among the city's other opera houses were the Teatro Ss. Giovanni e Paolo and the Teatro San Moise. Its most famous opera house, however, was the Teatro La Fenice which was opened in 1792.

Painting and History of Art

In this field, the contribution of the Italians is so great that it would take volumes to record it. Since, however, I am concerned only with 'firsts', the task is somewhat easier.

●	Perspective drawing was first studied by Paolo UCCELLO in the fifteenth century.

Domenico CAMPAGNOLA (born at Padova) was the first print maker in 1500. At the same time his brother Giulio anticipated by more than 200 years the stipple engraving technique.

●	In 1550 Giorgio VASARI (born in Arezzo) became the first art historian.

His 'Lives' of Italian architects, painters and sculptors provides biographies and anecdotes for all the artists who had gone before him, as well as for his contemporaries. Despite a fertile imagination, his eminently legible account represents compulsory and enjoyable reading for anyone interested in the artists of the Italian Renaissance.

He shows that those whom he describes were well aware of their uniqueness in society and he confirms the high quality of the cultural climate of Renaissance Italy.

It is mainly to Vasari (as well as to Condivi and Giannotti) that we owe the wealth of information about the life of the greatest Italian artist, Michelangelo (born 1475, died 1564, the year in which Shakespeare was born). He is one of the great names of world culture; a painter, architect, sculptor, poet and humanist. Indeed, it has been said that to him are to be traced the Italian Renaissance, the Northern Reformation and the Baroque. There is no doubt that his contemporaries knew that he was a great man and that he would outlive his age. Also, to him we owe what is probably the first recorded forgery in sculpture:

●	In 1495 MICHELANGELO executed a sculptured 'Sleeping Cupid' which is now lost, with the aim of passing it off as an antique. As such, it was re-sold to a high dignitary of the Catholic Church who genuinely believed it to be an object of antiquity. When Michelangelo realised what had happened, he offered to reimburse the money that he had originally received for it.

●	In 1696 Filippo BALDINUCCI (born in Florence) was the first art historian to make full use of original documents.

I distinguish between him and Vasari because Vasari relied mainly on gossip and did not document himself quite so scientifically as Baldinucci.

●	In 1700 Pier Leone GHEZZI (born in Rome) established himself as the first official caricaturist.

I have already considered the matter of whether he was first, or Carracci, or Bernini, or Leonardo. (See page 32).

●	In 1880 Giovanni MORELLI (born in Verona) established the so-called 'Morellian method'. His was a system of direct study which formed the basis for subsequent art criticism and relied on the evidence of the work of art itself. Bernard Berenson was his principal follower.

●	In 1909 Filippo Tommaso MARINETTI (born in Egypt) established Futurism.

It is well known that he published his first manifesto on the front page of the French magazine *Le Figaro* on the 20 February 1909. Of course, French at the time was a language in fairly common use but it is a fact that futurism was born in Milan where Marinetti, despite having been born himself in Alexandria in Egypt, had been living for a few years. Indeed, he wrote: 'Even though I was born in Egypt I am tied to the forest of Milan chimneypots and to its old duomo.'

Pornography (Erotic Literature)

There is nothing new about pornography, as anyone who has visited Pompeii and seen the mosaics there well knows. However, the title of the heading is, in a sense, misleading. The two firsts that follow are in fact masterpieces of literature and not pornography. Only part of Cinzio's book can be said to be capable of being considered pornographic: in my opinion, none of Boccaccio's *Decameron* can.

There are two ways in which the Italians can be said to lead the field in the sphere of erotic literature:

• **In the early fourteenth century Giovanni BOCCACCIO (born in Paris, the illegitimate son of an Italian father and a French mother) who followed closely on Dante and Petrarca, wrote the *Decameron*, which is a masterpiece of earthy, bawdy, funny prose, written in a quiet, understated manner.**

The chapters on putting the devil where he belongs, namely in hell, and on cleaning vats of wine whilst one's wife looks on, have a sauciness and a style which our present-day purveyors of cheaper pornographic rubbish will never be able to imitate, let alone understand.

He had great influence worldwide on writers of short stories who came after him; but as far as England is concerned, his influence went beyond the style of short-story writing, since his themes were utilised in a number of different contexts, both in poetry and in prose. The 'locale' was changed, and the style differed; the descriptions were adapted to the language and to the taste of the reader; but most English writers found something in him that could be put to use in their work. From Dryden to Hazlitt, Shelley to Scott, Keats to Landor, Milman to Lloyd, Shelley to Coleridge. Tennyson to George Eliot, Boccaccio's *Decameron* was topical in nineteenth century England five hundred years after it was written.

Indeed, Boccaccio's stories have a particular charm. His characters are real people, taken from all social classes, masters or slaves of their senses and their passions. Woman is no angel for Boccaccio, but she, too, is quite real. Not fragrant, but vibrant. In fact, Boccaccio's women are quite modern and you could argue that he himself was a pioneer of sex equality.

Surprising though this may sound to Americans or the British, in the field of equality the Italians got there first as well. Let me give you one example.

In his seventh novel of the sixth day, when a woman caught in adultery has to defend herself to avoid death, the following 'cri de coeur' is recorded (my own free translation):

'Laws should be of universal application and made with the concurrence of those who are subject to them; but this does not happen, because (this law) only affects poor women ...; but apart from any other consideration, not only did a woman never consent to such a law, but no woman was ever consulted about it. Therefore, it is a bad law ....'

By the way, the all-male 'jury' acquitted her! But they did so on a different ground

I think, and I shall not spoil your fun by revealing it to you in case you have not read the book.

Boccaccio's espousal of the cause of women ante-dates that of the first 'feminist' writer, Christine de Pisan, by over 100 years. Ardent feminists should also be reminded that in 1772 there was published 'Lana Caprina' or 'Letters from a Licanthrope' which was written by Casanova. This item of information will certainly not make such women happy because, on the whole, women of any kind don't like Casanova. The reason is that they cannot accept that he gave women everything but never his inner being: and all women want to possess the inner man. On the other hand, compared to Don Juan, he was modest in his performances because he boasts only of having possessed about 200 women or, as some authorities have worked out, an average of about 12 encounters every year. But I digress. Casanova, it could be argued, is a very authoritative feminist. For example, he argues that woman has an independence of mind of her own which is unrelated to the functions of her sex and he continues to display his appreciation for them, not only on the physical but also on the intellectual level: a flattering judgement by a born flatterer.

• In 1566 Giraldi CINZIO (born in Ferrara) wrote his 110 *Novelle*.

The first ten deal exclusively with the manners of Italian prostitutes and are a clear attempt to attract the vulgar reader; but they are nevertheless very stylishly written.

Interestingly, although Italians can boast of two firsts under this heading, there is a great lack of erotic literature in Italian apart from some romantic/epic writings in the sixteenth century (Ariosto and Tasso in particular).

Pornography is practically unknown in the Italian literary field. There is only one modern exception, *D'Annunzio*.

If I discount Ovid's *Ars Amandi* because of its antiquity, I find that Italian literature is conspicuously lacking not only in any material of the kind that could be classed as pornographic but especially in any writing that it is even remotely connected with amatory functions or techniques. Apart from the studies of prostitutes in the sixteenth century by Pietro Aretino (see his *Ragionamenti* published in Venice in 1534), and Lorenzo Veniero in *La Prostituta Errante*, and in the nineteenth century by Lombroso, Mantegazza and others mainly in connection with their criminality, there are no major works in the Italian language concerning the subject of sexuality.

It is almost as though there were a reluctance on the part of the Italians to discuss sex in the abstract. It is interesting to note that until the late 1950s, the word 'sesso' (sex) in Italian merely identified in current usage the physical connotations of men and women. The translation to a synonym of 'sexuality' or, even worse, of sexual activity or the act itself, was the result of American influence. One may discuss in Italian the sex of the angels, but one does not 'have sex'. Even in English the word is abused as a matter of semantics.

Italian men may discuss a particular woman or an activity: never sex as a concept. If one feels sexuality, one does not wish and has no need to discuss its theory.

Pottery

• In 1557 Cipriano PICCOLPASSO (born at Castel Durante) wrote the first Treatise on the Art of Pottery. He then published his 'Three books of the Potter's Art'.

• Italians were the first to apply to the Islamic achievement of tin-glazed earthenware ornamentation additional colours and the painting of figures and scenes.

This resulted in the 'istoriato' type of pottery

CAESAR'S CLEMENCY

CLEMENZA DI CESARE

Se è vero, come afferma, ch'è destinato
ad essere un lontanissimo
progenitore di Shakespeare, risparmiamolo!

"Caesar, he claims he is a descendant of
Shakespeare."
"In that case, spare him!"

more especially known as maiolica (or majorica, from Majorca whence the first importations may have come).

Dates and places in this connection seem uncertain. The most that can be said with any degree of accuracy is that the first Islamic earthenware was imported into Italy around the year 1200, probably from North Africa.

It took the Italians almost three centuries to evolve a style which became unique. According to records, the 'istoriato' style started about 1515 in central Italy. The main centres of pottery were Faenza, Urbino, Deruta, Castel Durante, Orvieto, Gubbio and Caffaggiolo. The potters of Caffaggiolo were outstanding. 'Between 1500 and 1530, Stefano and Piero Di Filippo produced some of the most striking maiolica painted anywhere'. (Timothy Wilson, *Ceramic Art of the Italian Renaissance*, p. 86).

Italians also developed the 'sgraffio', namely the technique of incised slipware.

Italian maiolica was exported from the end of the fifteenth century to the rest of Europe. With it, Italy exported also its master craftsmen who travelled to France, Spain and the Low Countries, as well as to the rest of Central Europe, and played a leading role in the establishment of local traditions.

In 1567 they were established in Norwich and from there moved to London, firstly to Aldgate and then to Southwark. The first English pottery factories were set up by Italians. London delftware was extensively copied from maiolica and it is correct to say that 'wherever a national tin-glaze tradition exists, it can be traced back to sixteenth-century Italian immigrants.' (*London Delftware* by Frank Britton, Johnathan Horne 1986).

Theatre and Acting

● **Acting can be said to have started in Italy with the Commedia Dell'Arte in 1545. The Commedia Dell'Arte lasted well into the eighteenth century.**

● **The Commedia Dell'Arte became famous throughout Europe and was the first troupe to go 'on tour.'**

Italian companies, and there were several, went to Germany, France, Spain and England where, with greater or lesser success, they influenced the theatre developments of all the countries they visited.

As regards the theatrical disciplines of mime and pantomime, the Commedia Dell'Arte still continues to influence England to this day: the Christmas panto originated in Italy. Pantomime was already known to ancient Rome but in 1530 it was introduced into Italy as a 'modern' invention by Ruzzante.

● **In 1513 there were erected in the town of Urbino the first three-dimensional structures on stage.**

● **In 1520 Angelo BEOLCO otherwise known as RUZZANTE (born in Padova) organised one of the earliest professional troupes.**

● **To Beolco's company we owe another first, namely the first theatrical contract with its members which listed the discipline which he had set up, the organization of the troupe and the rights and duties of the members.**

● **It was a novelty for the time, although in later years it became common practice.**

● **In 1537 Sebastiano SERLIO (born in**

Bologna) published a work that concentrated on the practical stage of the sixteenth century. He included lighting effects in his analysis.

- In 1584 Andrea PALLADIO built the Teatro Olimpico at Vicenza. This still survives as one of the first and most typical expressions of the architectural style of the period.

- In 1618 the first permanent proscenium was built at the Teatro Farnese in Rome (a temporary one had been built 50 years earlier by Franceso SALVIATI.)

- In 1638 Nicola SABBATINI (born in Pesaro) wrote the first manual for constructing theatrical scenes and machines and was the first to describe systems for shifting scenes about on stage.

- In 1660 Gaspare VIGARANI built in Paris, for the wedding of Louis XIV, the Salle des Machines, the largest theatre in Europe.

- In 1665 architect and sculptor Gian Lorenzo BERNINI (born in Naples) re-established the idea of caricature and introduced it into France.

- From 1605 to 1640 Inigo Jones applied in England all he had learnt about the theatre in Italy between 1596 and 1604. In 1750 the first Italian scene designers were imported into England. From that moment onwards, Italian theatre design, architecture and scenery extended to France, Spain, Germany, Austria and Russia.

- So much for the architecture and design of theatres. As regards the theatrical art itself, the only notable contribution I can recall in recent times by an Italian is that of Pirandello - the founder in effect of the modern theatre - who can be said to have exercised considerable influence upon some English writers, especially Harold Pinter.

(And I am only partly serious about this). In 1918 the first film star was created, namely Rodolfo Valentino (born at Castellaneta, in Apulia).

The product of the US film industry publicity machine, he died young (aged 31) of peritonitis.

Section 3:
Clothes & Dressing Up

Fashions

- The fashion designer first made his appearance in Italy in the early fifteenth century. This coincided with the development of the concept of ideal beauty and the increased importance of the qualities of the female body (more so than ever before). As Francois Boucher observed in his *A History of Costume in the West*, 'in all the Italian States men and women translated this search after formal beauty into costume, thus satisfying their taste for elegance, their passion for colour harmony and their aspirations towards a greater distinction.'

One has only to look at Pisanello's paintings for confirmation of the validity of the foregoing statement.

Not only Pisanello, but also Pollaiolo and Jacopo Bellini created costume models and designed textile patterns. As a result, the role of Italy as a precursor of national costume is of vital importance; in all the Italian Courts, large or small, says Boucher, there was 'a studied pursuit of elegance and a taste for lavish costumes'. Italians made the running. France then overtook them, as Italian influence declined, and as large numbers of Italian merchants and workers took up residence in Lyon, Paris and Tours. But as the 1980s have shown, Italian influence on the world of fashion is once again a force to be reckoned with, catering now for the masses as well as the gentry!

Costume textiles were first introduced in Lombardy towards the beginning of the fourteenth century.

The output of Italy in this field was enormous. Coloured hose, new mixtures of colours, new colours, new mixtures of silk, new linens, laces, fur trimmings, edgings, linings, satins, velvets, taffetas and damasks all became established in Italy, and from there spread to the rest of Europe. At about this time, Woman (a subject we shall return to later) was glorified. Clothes were the concomitant of such glorification - the square cut neckline for women, for example, was an Italian creation, as was fancy headgear, like the Florentine toque. The influence on France was considerable.

With the Spanish domination established by Charles V, costumes became more severe: but the tradition was by then very marked and recorded for posterity in the paintings of Pisanello, Pollaiolo, Jacopo Bellini, Paolo Uccello, Masolino, Benozzo Gozzoli, Carpaccio, Ghirlandaio and Titian.

Lace

• In 1339 the technique of Italian needlepoint lace was first applied in Venice. This 'punto in aria' was the springboard for the use of needlepoint around the world.

Italian mastery of lace making is exemplified by the skills found even today on the island of Burano near Venice, a compulsory stop for tourists. Incidentally, it is not widely known that during the eighteenth century numerous Venetian lace-makers established themselves in England, for instance, in Bedfordshire and in Dorset.

Make-up (Cosmetics)

There is nothing novel in make-up as far as the Italians are concerned. The art of painting the human face is lost in the dawn of history and can be traced back to the Egyptians and Assyrians.

Taking our starting point, however, as the year 1000, it can be said that already in the eleventh century in Italy make-up was worn extensively by women of all classes. The upper class used bright pink, the lower classes used a less expensive reddish colour.

In thirteenth century Tuscany eye make-up was common among upper-class women. The upper lids were lined black and shadowed in either brown, grey, blue-green or violet.

Giambattista Della Porta, (see also under 'Photography' and 'Steam Engines') was the first to provide a recipe for a powder that could be used not only for cleansing the face but also for caring for the teeth. It was made by mixing flowers and herbs with clay and white wine and then burning the resultant concoction to obtain a paste.

• Caterina de MEDICI (see also under 'Gastronomy') is credited with having spread the art of face painting from Italy into France when she insisted on its use at the court of her French husband.

Some products were known by the name of the place where they were manufactured. For example, there was

Venetian Talc (or chalk) for use as present-day Talcum powder and for powdering wigs; and Venetian Ceruse (or rouge for the face).

Spectacles (Eye Glasses)

• These first appeared in Pisa in 1291. Their invention is attributed to one Alessandro SPINA from Florence, a Dominican monk who first used convex lenses to cure myopia.

In 1352 Tommaso da Modena was the first painter to depict spectacles. In 1480, Ghirlandaio depicted Saint Jerome using an eyeglass. (Saint Jerome is the patron saint of the London Guild of Spectacle Makers).

Textiles & Velvet

• The textile industry was born in Sicily in 1130 (despite the fact that the first crepe textiles were manufactured in Bologna around the year 1000 AD). Tuscany followed in 1226; by the middle of the sixteenth century Genoa and Venice had come to the forefront. Later, France took over as leading producer.
Up to the seventeenth century velvet was made exclusively in Italy.
In the Middle Ages, imported Italian velvet was very popular in England for the making of clothes and shoes.
The interplay between Italy and France is historic. Throughout history there have

been a number of fields where Italy has started a fashion and France has taken it over, improved on it and subsequently established itself as master in that particular field. Such interplay is recorded by Shakespeare when he differentiates between the two countries in the *Merchant of Venice* (act 1, scene 2, line 80): 'He bought his doublet in Italy, his round hose in France.'

• In 1884 Gaetano BONELLI (born in Turin) invented the first electric loom.

His was an attempt to provide a cheaper machine than the Jacquard and was based on electro magnets.

Section 4: Communications

Canals

• The first major canal system established anywhere in the world was built in Milan in 1179 and is still known now by the name it had then, namely 'Naviglio Grande' (The Great Navigation Canal).

In 1179, you may remember, other nations were thinking of the Crusades whilst the Milanese were concerned with their amenities.
Much later (in 1496), Leonardo da Vinci was involved in the construction of the famous canal which links the rivers Adda

and Ticino. (Even at this time, most people of northern Europe were no better than uncouth barbarians). The previous year, he had invented lock gates and he used them in 1497 in the form of mitred lock gates on the Milan Canal. (Carter, *Dictionary of Inventions and Discoveries*, p. 98.)

Flying

• Paolo GUIDOTTI (born in Lucca) was probably the first man who actually attempted to fly.

In 1600 he constructed two large wings out of whalebone which he covered in feathers and, having thus converted himself, as he thought, into a bird, he jumped from a great height hoping to fly. He didn't really and although the large wings slowed down his fall, he ended up on the roof of a nearby house and broke a leg.

The desire of man to imitate the birds, at least in the sense of moving about in the sky, ante-dates Guidotti. Long before him, legend tells us that Icarus (and his father Daedalus who flew from Crete to Naples) is said to have made it to the sky but to have been struck down by the gods when carried away by his excitement and conceit. He flew so close to the sun that the wax that kept his feathers together melted: he ended up in the Aegean sea.

• In 1507 at Perugia, Giovan Battista Danti had made an attempt to fly. In 1569 Giovanni Damiano (John Damian) made a further attempt to fly, this time at Stirling in Scotland. Before that, Leonardo had designed a flying machine, a sort of helicopter actuated by a worm screw, as well as a parachute. (See 'Physics', p.118ff.)

Everybody knows both Icarus and Leonardo but not many know of another valiant contributor to 'air travel.' He is Tiberius CAVALLO, who was born in Naples and was admitted to The Royal Society on 9 December 1779.

Cavallo was quite well-known in England as a scientist and spent most of his life in London in little St Martin's Lane.

In 1780 he gave his first Bakerian Lecture at The Royal Society and did so annually for the next twelve years; in this respect he is probably one of the very few, if not the only Member to have given so many such lectures.

The lectures ranged from the observation of meteors to detailed electrical and magnetic studies, as well as to comments on the then most recent development in the field of electricity, namely Volta's plates.

He is to be remembered principally, however, for the lecture that he delivered on the 20 June 1782 under the title 'Common and inflammable airs penetrate the pores of paper', an 18-page dissertation on the lightness of gases. It is recorded at The Royal Society under reference 'L & P VII, Lecture 263.'

It may be interesting to quote an extract from it: 'The experiment was to construct a vessel or sort of bag which when inflated with inflammable air might be lighter than an equal bulk of common air and consequentially might ascend like smoke into the atmosphere.'

He practised with 'some fine china paper' and with different kinds of bladder. The exercise, which he himself called 'a diverting experiment', is significant because it showed for the first time what could be done once a suitable type of vessel was found that would contain nitrogenous gases. This was achieved exactly one year later by the Montgolfier brothers.

The encyclopaedia *Treccani* records Cavallo as an innovator in the field of lighter-than-air gases and studies, as well as in thermo-metrical observations; *Britannica* does not mention him at all. This is surprising because The Royal Society library contains 11 printed works by Cavallo as well as papers that he published in its *Philosophical Transactions*; in addition, it holds 25 manuscript letters and other papers relating to Cavallo.

Another figure who was quite a success in the field of ballooning and who followed closely in the wake of the Montgolfier brothers was Vincenzo LUNARDI.

On the 15 September 1784 he took off in a balloon from London in the presence of 100,000 people. This was treated as an exceptional feat at the time: it was certainly something that London had never seen before. His was the first aerial voyage in Britain in a hydrogen balloon. He flew for a while and then landed in Hertfordshire. He then took off again travelling north-eastwards.

That the event was one of major significance can be drawn from the fact that there is a granite stone at the commencement of Parsonage Lane, North Mymms, (now better known as Whelam Green) in Hertfordshire which commemorates the landing of Lunardi. And a hundred yards down the road from Parsonage Lane we now find 'Vincenzo Close', a quasi-suburban street in the Hertfordshire countryside.

It is interesting that *Britannica* does not mention Lunardi either although he was evidently well known to the English public at the time; indeed to English literature because Sir Walter Scott actually used Lunardi's name to describe something like a balloon in his novel *St Ives*.

Exactly a month after Lunardi, on 15 October 1784, the Frenchman Francois Blanchard made his ascent from Chelsea. Horace Wolpole records having watched him from the window of his round Tower at Strawberry Hill.

- The first night flight in a balloon was made in 1803 from Bologna to the Istrian coast by Count Zambeccari, Dr Grassati and Pasquale Andreoli. (Carter, *Dictionary of Inventions and Discoveries*, p. 16.)

- The first jet aeroplane that flew was designed by Caproni-Campini in 1941. It flew 300 miles. (Carter, *Dictionary of Inventions and Discoveries*, p. 7.)

Hydrofoil (Ships & Biplanes)

- The first successful hydrofoil was built in 1906 by Enrico FORLANINI.

- The first hydrofoil biplane was designed by Aldo GUIDONI in 1911.

Forlanini was a pioneer in aircraft technology. In 1879 he had already designed a helicopter driven by a steam engine, which actually flew. (Carter, *Dictionary of Inventions and Discoveries*, p. 5.)

Libraries

- The first public library was opened in Florence in the year 1571.

The library was built by Michelangelo, and housed the rich collection of books and texts of Lorenzo the Magnificent; it is still in existence today, known as the Biblioteca Medicea-Laurenziana.

The oldest public library in England was founded in 1612 and is to be found in the Great Hall of Lambeth Palace. It is the library of the Archbishops of Canterbury and arose out of a bequest made two years earlier by Archbishop Bancroft.

Motor Cars

After good food, nothing else except clothes and the motor car reflects the taste and the temperament of the Italian nation more effectively. It is not surprising, therefore, that Italy can lay claim to quite a few 'firsts' regarding the development of the 'automobile'.

I do not mean first in racing or in success or in line, although there can be no question that there is a prestige attached to some Italian cars (Ferrari, Maserati, Lamborghini, and once upon a time Alfa Romeo) which is unique.

Italians love motor cars, for they equate them with women. There is an old Italian expression: 'Donne e motori, gioie e dolori', which freely translated means that women are like cars; they both give joy and pain.

In Italy, more than in any other part of the world that I know, the car is the manifestation of the driver. It transmits his taste, his aggressiveness, his manners; it is almost a mirror of his personality. And very few people drive with the same abandonment and panache as the Italians.

It is of course true that Italians drive like madmen, or so it appears to the foreigner with little knowledge of local conditions. It is certainly true that they drive in a selfish manner; and one needs only to be caught in the Rome rush-hour or in traffic in the centre of Naples to realise what a dreadful place both those cities can be in particular circumstances.

And yet, one must often wonder why the number of serious accidents both in Rome and Naples is considerably smaller than it ought to be judging by the way people actually drive. There seems to be an inherent ability in the Italian to control a motor car which I do not think I have seen shared by any other Europeans.

So, what are the facts? The Italians have contributed four inventions in connection with the motor car that are fundamental.

● In 1775 Alessandro VOLTA (born in Como) created the electro-phorus, a device to generate static electricity. He followed this up in 1800 when he invented the first electric 'pile' which was the forerunner of the battery.

Tradition has it that it was Luigi GALVANI experimenting with frogs on the balcony of

his house who made the discovery of 'animal' electricity; and there are drawings that show him, a grey-haired gentleman, examining a number of frogs strung up on a metal wire from one end of his balcony to the other.

I am not certain how reliable this story is, but it is a very picturesque one and as such worthy of being retained if not for its factual accuracy, at least because it makes children so much more interested when they first learn about the discovery of electricity by Volta or Galvani as the case may be.

● In 1802 Giandomenico ROMAGNOSI (born in Salsomaggiore) observed the magnetic effect of electric currents.

● In 1858 the experiments of Romagnosi were followed up by Giovanni PACINOTTI who invented the dynamo (he also happens to have invented one of the very first parachutes).

● In 1884 Giuseppe PIRELLI (born in Como) made the first electric cable.
In 1889 the same PIRELLI made the first motor car tyre.

However, despite all of these discoveries, the early cars did not operate very satisfactorily. Battery, dynamo and tyres ensured that the engine would propel the car forward, but continuity of motion was not guaranteed. This was left to Venturi.
● In about 1800 Giovanni Battista VENTURI (born at Bibiano R.E.) invented the Venturi meter to compute flow volume. At the same time, he anticipated the carburettor.

The carburation system based on the Venturi principle is used in motor cars, airplanes, and wherever motor engines are installed. (He gave his name to the phenomenon known as the Venturi effect, which occurs where fluid flows through a horizontal pipe of varying cross-sectional areas and which results in the pressure of the fluid being least where the cross-section is smallest.)

So, the next time you look at any motor

car - and not only when you look at an exciting Ferrari or an expensive Lamborghini - you might bear in mind that that machine would not be there but for these four Italian firsts.

When you next use the motorway, please remember that:

• The first motorway was the Italian 'Autostrada'. It ran between Milan and Varese, was inaugurated in 1924 and would later connect Turin with Venice.

Newspapers

• The first newspaper was published in Venice in 1563 in order to provide the Venetians with news of the war with Turkey. It thus anticipated the *English Mercury* by 25 years exactly.

To Venice we owe the word 'gazette' derived from the local 'Avviso' or port news, which were also called gazettes because they cost a few cents, the then current coin which was known in Venetian dialect as 'gazeta'.

Incidentally, the oldest Italian newspaper, la *Gazzetta di Parma*, first published in 1735, is still being issued. But it is not the oldest continuously published paper in the world: that record belongs to the *Ordinari Post Tijdender*, a Swedish newspaper first published in 1645, which however became an offical bulletin in the 1970s.

Paperbacks

It has to be said that Allen Lane with his Penguin Books was not the originator of

paperbacks. In this field, too, the Italians laid the foundation stone even though the building did not start until some 300 years later.

• In 1490 Aldo MANUZIO (born at Bassiano) was the first to produce printed editions of Greek and Latin classics.

Manuzio was also the first to issue 'pocket editions' of Latin texts in 'octavo'. These Aldine editions, the first of their kind, started in 1501 and were widely copied.

Between 1770 and 1842 Niccolo' BETTONI from Milan was the first modern publisher to issue popular editions actually equivalent to present-day paperbacks.

Photography

In the fifteenth century Leonardo Da Vinci first set out the principle of a 'camera oscura', thus laying the foundation for the much later development of photography.

The Italian contribution to photography, however, is much greater than some readers might imagine and the debt that Niepce and Daguerre owe Italy is substantial.

• In 1568 Domenico Daniele BARBARO (born in Venice) in his book *Pratica Della Perspettiva* makes the first mention of the application of a lens to thè Camera Oscura elaborated by Leonardo about a century earlier.

The same concept was restated in 1585 by G. B. Benedetti and in 1589 by G. B. Dellaporta.

The chemical aspects of photography, if I may use that expression, had already been mentioned in tentative form by Aristotle.

But the Italian contribution goes further than the 'camera oscura'.

● Ignazio PORRO (born at Pinerolo) was the inventor of numerous optical instruments (e.g., stereogonic telescopes). He revised a number of existing theodolites.

● Porro was a pioneer in the application of photography to topography and, in effect, the creator of aerial photography. Apart from establishing metrophotographic criteria and inventing the photogoniometer, which were later respectively applied and modified by Kappe, he is principally known nowadays as the inventor of the Porro prism, an essential device in optical instruments, particularly in binoculars and telescopes.

By 1854 Porro had finalised most of his inventions, which had to wait until the First World War before they were developed and applied commercially.

Postal Systems

What we have today we owe originally to the Romans, whose public system of communication known as the 'Cursus Publicus' lasted well into the Middle Ages.

The Italian postal system itself was only established in 1862 but it is a fact that:

● In the thirteenth century the Mercantile Corporations of Genoa and Siena provided postal links at fairs which were held from time to time.

Since the early fifteenth century, Italian merchants, both bankers and traders, who came to London had operated a system of deliveries for letters to and from England which during the reign of Elizabeth I, became known as the 'Merchant Strangers Post'. The Italians who ran this service

owned establishments in all the main European cities and, initially at any rate, had practically a monopoly at a time when no official postal system was available to the English public.

The Italians used their own terminology (for example, 'pp' - 'posta pagata' = postage paid; 'pq' - 'per questa' = payment made for this; and many others) and made their own charges (the 'scudo' being a common tariff).

One of the most important Italian families in this field were the 'Corsini'. Over the years, they were variously referred to as 'Cushen' and later as 'Cursen'. Thus, they were the forerunners of the Curzons and, therefore, gave their name to Curzon Street in Mayfair, London.

Printing

● The first map was printed in Bologna in 1477.

● In 1501 Francesco GRIFFO (born in Bologna) designed the first italic typeface used in printing: a far-reaching innovation.

● Also in 1501 Ottaviano dei PETRUCCI (born at Fossombrone) became the first printer of polyphonic music from moveable type. Six years later in 1507 he published the first printed book of lute music.

● The earliest designer of modern typefaces, of which he is credited with many, was Giambattista BODONI (1740-1813, born at Saluzzo). The typeface still in use today continues to bear his name.

● The first manufacturing establishments for producing paper were established in the twelfth century at Fabriano.

This is not to say that the idea was an Italian one; they got it from the Arabs who in turn had got it from the Chinese. What Italians

THE FUNERAL OF REMUS

I FUNERALI DI REMO

Romolo, che inno suoniamo?

Fratelli d'Italia.

"Romulus, which hymns shall we play?"

"'Brothers of Italy!"

(Note: 'Brothers of Italy' is the title of the Italian National Anthem.)

did first, however, was to proceed to produce paper on what one might call an industrial scale. At the same factory in 1286 they first used watermarks for paper identification.

- **The first paper factory was established in Bologna in the year 1200.**

It was operated by machinery which was activated by water, a novelty for the period.

It is a pity that the invention of moveable characters is due to Gutenberg for otherwise Italy could boast quite a few firsts under this heading. In addition to what has been recorded above, it should be noted that in 1472 in Milan Filippo di LAVAGNA printed the first book in Greek type and in 1475 in Reggio Calabria the first book in Hebrew was printed; lastly, the first book in Arabic was printed in Fano in 1514.

- **Gaspare ASELLI's description - made some time in 1627 and published posthumously - of the lymphatic system represents the first medical work to contain coloured 'illustrations'.**

I have a note that the first Cookery Book was published in Italy but have been unable so far to find authoritative backing for it. Its author was a humanist, Bartolomeo SACCHI, better known as 'Il Platina', who in 1457 wrote his *De Honesta Voluptate*, where he recorded Renaissance recipes.

Scientific Societies

- **The first scientific society, known as the Academy of the Lynx (Accademia dei Lincei) was founded in Rome around 1603.**

Galileo contributed an instrument to it which the German entomologist Faber was later to name 'microscope'; and all other European Societies followed the Italian

example.

England's 'Royal Society' united a number of smaller associations and was incorporated by Royal charter in 1662.

The Italian connection with The Royal Society is interesting and for those who wish to pursue it, there is a lecture on the topic by Mary Boas. In 1667, Count Ubaldini became its first Italian member, followed by Malpighi in 1668, G. D. Cassini in 1672 and Viviani, Toricelli's colleague, in 1696.

That same year saw the election of Bonfigliolo, a colleague of Malpighi. Between 1662, when it was founded, and the end of the seventeenth century no less than 10 Italians were admitted; to date, there have been around 90.

The eighteenth century saw a spate of admissions. To record them all would be too cumbersome but the following might be of interest: Scipione Maffei, a tragic poet, was admitted in 1736, the same year in which he received a degree at Oxford; also admitted in 1736 was Francesco Algarotti, a friend of Lady Montagu, who had written a book, explaining Newton's principles 'for the ladies'; in 1782 the Society celebrated a visit by Alessandro Volta, the discoverer of electricity, who gave a lecture on his 'condenser', received a gold medal, met Priestley and Watt and is said to have enjoyed himself immensely, despite the rainy weather. He was made a fellow in 1791.

The Italian connection with The Royal Society is even greater than might first appear. For example, the first item on the first page of the first issue of the Society's *Philosophical Transactions* dated 'Munday, March 6th 1664/1665' is headed: 'An Accompt of the Improvement of Optick Glasses at Rome.'

This first article in an unbroken tradition of publications by The Royal Society, spanning more than three centuries, records the improvements made by Giuseppe Campani to Galileo's telescope by the use of special tooling and recorded in his paper 'Ragguaglio di Nuove Osservazioni.'

Signalling

- In 1551 Girolamo CARDANO (born in Pavia) was the first to use torches to spell out letters.

He worked out a system using five torches that were placed on towers for spelling out letters of the alphabet.

- In 1777 Alessandro VOLTA (born in Como), inventor of the voltaic pile, proposed iron wire signalling lines from Como to Milan.

Steam Engines

- The records show that it was Thomas SAVERY who patented the first commercially successful steam engine in 1698. This is absolutely true, but he got the idea from an Italian.

- It was Giambattista DELLAPORTA, a Neapolitan, (see 'Photography' p.48), who in either 1601 or 1606 first described a steam engine, thus anticipating Savery by nearly a century.

Dellaporta was a very versatile scientist and some of his intuitions, which always resulted in concrete applications, are worthy of note.

- Dellaporta invented the magic lantern projector.

- In 1588, using drawings which originated in Egypt, Dellaporta designed the first incubator.

- Although the kite as such originated in China over 3,000 years ago, the diamond-shaped kite was first described by Dellaporta in 1620.

- To Dellaporta we owe in practice the first electric telegraph.

- In 1558 Dellaporta devised a compass needle telegraph known as the 'sympathetic telegraph'.

According to Carter's *Dictionary of Discoveries and Inventions*, page 133, Dellaporta is also 'credited with formulating the idea of the telescope which was said to have been made in Italy in 1590 before finding its way into Holland.'

Telephones

- In 1871 Antonio MEUCCI (born in Florence) applied for a patent for what was to become the telephone. The application of Alexander Graham Bell was lodged in 1876 and Edison's carbon refinement is dated 1877.

There was litigation in the American Supreme Court between Meucci and Bell and there is no doubt that from the strictly legalistic point of view Bell was entitled to succeed because the provisional patent granted to Meucci had expired in 1873. But Meucci got there at least five years before.

- In 1886 Giovan Battista MARZI (born in Rome) installed and operated for three years an automatic telephone exchange (ten lines) in the Vatican city. Although the number of users was very limited, this was the world's first system of automatic selection. It ceased working in 1890 but nevertheless it anticipated the automatic exchange at Laporte, USA, by six years.

Section 5: Economics, Law & Social Sciences

Banking and Book-keeping

Anthropology

- The forerunner of anthropology (and ethnology) was Giambattista VICO (born in Naples).

Vico was born and died in Naples and had no formal education. He was also one of the first philosophers of history and evolved the theory of historical cycles by analysing the various phases of civilisation and making comparisons between them and the history of the earlier Greek and Roman civilizations. He was hampered by the limited knowledge available in 1720-21 when he wrote his 'Scienza Nuova'. Two centuries later, Oswald Spengler, a German historian and philosopher, was able to operate over a much broader spectrum than Vico.

Like all Neapolitans, he was extremely independent in outlook. He did not get on well with his contemporaries, rather like the earlier philosopher Giordano Bruno who was born in the same area.

Vico's work was practically ignored by scholars for over 100 years. His outspoken radicalism did not help much either and caused problems with the Church. His biography is one of the saddest ever for a man of genius. He was consumptive and also permanently poor.

His work was almost unknown in England until Coleridge became interested in it in 1824. The first known (English) translation of Scienza Nuova was published in 1834.

As you will see from the extent of this entry, Italian interest in this field has traditionally been very high indeed. One fails to understand, therefore, why similar standards are not always maintained nowadays, except perhaps in book-keeping.

Certainly banking in Italy is a complicated process, and until quite recently it was cumbersome and antiquated. However, it is not my personal experience of modern banking that counts, rather the contribution that Italian bankers have made. Let us first consider book-keeping.

Double-entry book-keeping happens to be an Italian invention but what is not widely known is:

- In about 1450 Luca PACIOLI (born at Borgo San Lorenzo) wrote the first book-keeping manual.

It is, however, the Italian bankers of the Middle Ages that deserve most credit.

The best known example of the influence of Italian bankers in England is the fact that Lombard Street is so called. Lombards were Italian merchants who originated not just from Lombardy in Italy but also from many other cities as well - principally from Florence - who, thanks to the support of the Popes and the impetus given to trade by the crusades, formed a sort of 'establishment' for their time, inasmuch as they had a monopoly over money. Not unexpectedly, Florentine bankers were exceptionally rich. It has been estimated that the gross national product of England in the year 1350 was less than that of the city of Florence on its own.

The Florentine names are quite well known: Medici, Ridolfi, Guidotti, Bardi,

Corsini and Peruzzi (there were many others, of course). They started establishing themselves in England towards the end of the twelfth century. To call them bankers, at least at this stage, may be a nonsense since, initially, they were essentially only moneylenders. In the third story of the second day in Boccaccio's *Decameron* - written between 1348 and 1353 - there is an early reference to the three children of Messer Tedaldo who came to London, rented a small house there and began his money-lending business.

Towards the middle of the fourteenth century at least Bardi and Peruzzi had a monopoly of customs and excise, minting money and exacting taxes. (They were 'kicked out' in 1456 but recalled in 1459). It is recorded that the Bardi family had a lease on premises in Lombard Street as early as 1318.

The words *sterling* and *shilling* come from the Italian 'sterlino' and 'scellino' and, as every schoolboy knows, the abbreviation 'LSD' stands for Lire Soldi and Denarii.

But there are a few more names such as bank and bankrupt which come from 'banca' and 'bancarotta', fee that comes from the Italian 'fio' and even on all English bank notes the wording 'Bank of England and Comp. A' appears taken from the Italian 'compagnia' rather than company.

The importance of the Italian bankers in London is also evidenced by the fact that when Sir Philip Sidney, probably the most Italianate Englishman of his time, went to Venice in 1573, he had with him a letter of credit from Vetturelli, a famous Italian banker in London. They were major establishments. The firm of Peruzzi, for example, included more than a dozen other families interested in banking, and had offices in Naples, Bruges, Tunis, and elsewhere.

A similar family business were the FRESCOBALDI, whose representative sat on Edward II's Council.

On what is said to be the negative side of the Lombards' performance it should be recorded that Sir Edward Coke, in his 'Institutes,' accuses them of having brought the practice of homosexuality that was to become entrenched in England, as elsewhere. He based his view on the fact that the word 'buggery' comes from the Italian 'buggerare'. This is a judgement made without considering the facts fully because it ignores the etymology of the word. Whilst it is certainly a fact that the word 'buggerare' found its way into English, French and Spanish, it should be pointed out that in turn it originated in the Italian description of the 'Bulgarian' heretics who later became the Milanese patarines, the object of much criticism in the eleventh and twelfth centuries. Of them it was said that they were the worst possible kind of people who indulged in a number of anti-Christian and strange practices, including sodomy.

Perhaps Sir Edward was being xenophobic; perhaps he was right; who knows.

• **The two bankers Bardi and Peruzzi together lent King Edward III more than 1,365,000 golden florins; which must be one of the biggest loans then ever floated, since it corresponds to more than £500 million today.**

• **Florence is believed to have been the first city to mint a gold coin - the florin - in 1252. (See Ruskin - *Mornings in Florence* p. 56).**

The florin was so called because it bore a floral design.

Many of the English modern commercial financial terms owe their origin to Italy (see 'Law').

• **The Bank of Venice had established the letter of credit in 1171.**

The Italians have left another permanent mark on England in matters of credit. The emblem outside a pawnbroker's shop is no more than a reproduction of the Medici badge consisting of the famous 'palle' which, on a totally different background, enclose the gorgeous ceilings of the cathedral of Pisa. (The Medicis in turn borrowed the design from old representations of St Nicholas of Bari who to this day is considered the Patron Saint of Moneylenders).

Long before Britain acquired its American debt, it had the Florentine debt. I do not recall what happened to the former but it appears that the latter was not repaid. (L. Salvatorelli - *Sommario della Storia d'Italia* - p. 212).

You may recall from the Introduction that the words *fiorino*, *gazzetta* and *zecchino*, all names of Italian coins, gave rise to English equivalents 'florin', 'gazette' and 'sequin' respectively.

It is also worth recalling that the design for the gold sovereign with the St George and Dragon was by the Roman artist Benedetto Pistrucci who also designed the half-crown, the shilling and the sixpence coins. He was Chief Engraver to The Royal Mint and to him we owe also the Waterloo Medal and the Coronation Medal of George IV.

● **The first operational bank providing facilities for its customers was the Bank of San Giorgio, founded in Venice in 1149.**

The Bank of San Giorgio was the result of 18 Genoese citizens of substance lending to the Genoa Municipality the sum of 1300 Genoese lire for a period of fifteen years. This money was needed by the local government to pay for the expenses of its wars against Almeria and Tortosa in the previous two years.

The loan itself was secured by the assignment of certain income from indirect taxation and the concept was applied again in 1150 for similar purposes.

It was dramatically extended in the thirteenth century when shares were issued to those who were lending money to the bank, who thus became the first shareholders in a banking institution.

Private account services started in 1407.

The Bank itself increased its power steadily over the centuries and extended its activities to all the Genoese colonies, especially to Cyprus and to the bases on

the Black Sea, as well as to Corsica. The colonial structure of the Bank of San Giorgio was taken as a model by the British Government when it set up its East India Company.

Chronicles

● **In or about the year 1110 Caffaro Di CASCHIFELLONE (born in Genova) wrote the chronicles of both the first Crusade and twelfth-century Genoa. In 1152 he presented his work to his home city who decreed that it should be kept in public archives. His annals and chronicles were the first recorded history of a township.**

Criminal Associations

● **The first criminal association of the western world became known in Sicily about the year 1000. It was established as an 'onorata societa' but is now known as the 'Mafia'.**

According to Migliorini's dictionary of the Italian language, the *mafia* is 'a secret organization of persons who help one another to make illicit gains, acts of violence and other things forbidden by the law.' If we then look at the etymological dictionary of the Italian language by Battisti Alessi, we find that *perhaps* the word comes from the Arab 'mahja', meaning boastfulness. Of course, nobody knows for certain, but I for one am very unhappy about this attribution because if there is something that a true mafia man will never boast about, it is that he is a mafia man.

I am reassured in this approach by other authors who make the point that the etymology is different and that the word 'mafia' comes from the Arab 'maha', which describes the stone caves where the original mafia men met to plan their deeds or misdeeds.

But whatever may be said about its etymology, we have to take into account the fact that 'mafia' is a comparatively new word: it appears it was practically unknown in Italy until 1862 when it was given prominence in a theatrical work by Rizzatto bearing the title 'I Mafiusi di la Vicaria' which described both the deeds and the mentality which distinguished the mafia in existence at the time.

Today, however, the word 'mafia' has ceased to be distinctive. In the same way that we now use the generic word 'hoover' to describe the carpet cleaning equipment that originally was manufactured by Hoover, we now use the word 'mafia' to describe criminal organizations, whether Italian or not. It is, of course, correct that it was the Italians who established mafia as *the* criminal organization; but nowadays, the word has ceased to have any particularly distinctive connotation that identifies it with Italy.

If the word 'mafia' is a little over a hundred years old, the concept is indeed ancient. Before the word came into existence, the people and the activities that the noun 'mafia' now embraces were referred to as the 'onorata societá' (the respected/ respectable society). There is no doubt that, historically, these two words were used to describe those Robin Hood-type characters who, in a feudal Sicily ruled by cruel barons or distant landlords, acted as just men to redress wrongs.

It is impossible to understand what went on without realising that we are dealing with a desperately poor island, invaded at varying times by Normans, Arabs, Moslems, Spaniards, Austrians, with great landed estates, where the Bourbons ruled indiscriminately and where the feudal

mentality took a hold stronger than in any other part of Italy: a hold which to this day has not been entirely severed.

There were no police, no independent judiciary and, in most cases, no courts of any description: the recourse to other means of obtaining justice or of avenging an injury was therefore inevitable. Those men who had either the ability or the power or the sense of justice to act as such avengers formed the first kind of organization to which the said label of 'onorata societá' was applied in circumstances of which we know little, if anything. There was thus established the kind of mentality and feeling which arose from ancient concepts of chivalry, a great sense of hospitality, the instinctive tendency to assist the weak and to uphold basic concepts of justice, a marked sense of honour in the context of self-respect, even consideration, of a very odd kind, for women, and pride in one's word and one's masculinity.

This way of thinking creates bonds of association and of friendship which are very difficult to break. It ensures that secrets are kept and debts paid. These bonds are described by the noun 'omertá' (I have already referred to it in a totally different context in the Introduction). 'Omertá' is an interesting noun because it is derived from 'omineitá', which is another way of expressing manhood and masculinity and which is associated with pride.

I am only drawing attention to the derivation of 'omertá' because it highlights the male-dominated kind of society which has prevailed over the centuries in Italy. The mafia is obviously a man-oriented society: I have never heard of a woman as a member of the mafia.

The mentality that has developed over 900 years is with us to this day. What I shall call mafia attitudes prevail still in Sicily and will not be easy to eradicate. By mafia attitudes I mean disrespect, if not contempt, for constituted authority, the need to protect oneself and one's family at all costs, a sense of honour and pride, absolute solidarity towards one's supporters and friends, and gratitude for those who have done a good turn to oneself or one's family. Not all these traits are negative; what is negative is their employment towards totally different ends from those for which they were first established; and above all, the abuse of such leanings for the purpose of financial gain.

What we have today is a totally different kind of mafia, it is Mafia with a capital M; and dictionary entries reflect the concept, for they list both names.

It is Mafia with a capital M that is the mafia of money and not of dignity; the Mafia of profit and not of right; the Mafia of organised crime and not of concerted opposition to a repressive regime; the Mafia of dishonour and not of honour.

Criminology

● In 1764 Cesare BECCARIA (born in Milan) published his book *Dei Delitti e Delle Pene* (translated into English as *Crime and Punishments*) which was the first critical study of the criminal law and represented the first systematic statement of the principles that ought to govern criminal punishment.

He proceeded from purely utilitarian principles, propounded a radical reform of both the criminal law and criminal procedure and argued that the purpose of punishment was not retribution but social defence. Torture ought to be abolished and, for practical purposes, he was the first criminologist to advocate the abolition of capital punishment.

He was then only 26 years of age. He also wrote books on economics and he was a keen student of agriculture.

In the years 1768 to 1770 he delivered certain lectures in Milan on economic principles in which he anticipated the thoughts of both Adam, Smith and Malthus.

● Following Beccaria, the Grand Duke of Tuscany, LEOPOLD II, was the first of the European princes to abolish the death penalty and torture.

Economics

● In 1754 Antonio GENOVESI (born at Castiglione), a philosopher and economist, as well as an admirer of Leibniz, was the first to occupy the first European chair of 'Commerce and Mechanics', that is to say political economy, that had been founded by Bartolomeo Intieri.

He wrote in 1765 his *Lezioni di commercio* which was the first Italian work on the subject of commerce.

Genovesi advocated the free circulation of goods, especially corn and, as *Britannica* puts it, his mercantilist view of economics is distinguished by a brilliant analysis of demand, by his high valuation of labour and by his efforts to reconcile free competition with protectionist policies.

● In 1750 Ferdinando GALIANI (born at Chieti), an economist who spent most of his life in Naples and who wrote both in French and in Italian, wrote a treaty on money (*Della moneta*) which anticipated much later work; it was amongst the first analyses of utility and scarcity.

He took as his starting point Locke's 'Considerations on the lowering of interest and raising of the value of money.'

Insurance

NOTE: *This entry should be read in conjunction with the following entry on Law.*

The Italian contribution in this field is considerable; but to understand it one must first look at the historical backcloth against which it was developed.

The fourth Crusade took place at the beginning of the thirteenth century. Venice was the principal city to benefit from this, but Genoa and Florence also expanded considerably in the process. Italy was ideally located to serve as a trading post between the kingdoms of north-west Europe and those of the east. Italian merchants widened the scope of their activities and in so doing looked afresh at relationships such as companies, partnerships and insurance, that were already known both to Greece and Rome. This was the time, however, when a rather fundamental refinement was made to the basic contractual precedents established by the Romans.

The details can be found in Enrico Bensa's *Il Contratto di Assicurazione nel Medio Evo*, written in 1884; Bensa was a Genoese lawyer. Although this is the principal work, it is not the only one.

It is clear, however, that:-

• **The first policy of Marine Insurance for which a premium was paid came into being in Florence about 1319 to 1320.** (F. Edler de Roover, 'Early examples of Marine Insurance' in Journal of Economic History Vol. V, p. 178).

It had been preceded, before the end of the thirteenth century, by the practice in Palermo where a form of loan was established under which the Lender became the shipowner and the Borrower the shipper of goods and the loan itself was repayable on safe arrival. Some authors have looked upon these Sicilian loans as a precedent which is even earlier than the Florentine one previously recorded. Palermo itself was not a principal port at the time - nor, indeed, has it ever been one - but it is to that city that we have to trace the following:-

• **The first genuine Policy of Insurance, drawn in contract form as such, of which there is an extant record, was executed there on the 13 March 1350.**

This policy covered against all risks wheat being carried from Sicily to Tunisia and the premium was about 18 per cent of the value of the cargo (op. cit. p. 183).

Indeed, it is fair to say that some of the wording used in the policies drawn up in Italy at this time, particularly one drawn up in Florence in 1397, were up to the standard of the sixteenth-century marine insurance policies that were adopted in London.

Florence itself, although not on the sea, seems to have been fairly prominent in the field of insurance because on 28 January 1523 it codified its ordinances covering insurance practices and, as has been observed, (see GOW, 'Marine Insurance') the perils enumerated in the Lloyds Policy are listed 'in the same order as in the Florentine Policy of 1523.'

The practice of marine insurance which was thus established by the Italian merchants of the fourteenth century reached the towns of the Hanseatic League. But its journey to London was fairly direct because it was imported into England by the Italian merchants, or Lombards, who resided here.

It is also worth noting that the earliest policies upon which actions were brought in the Admiralty Court (as far as records go) are in Italian. The first one is dated 20 September 1547. This is not the place to embark upon any discussion as to what the Italian wording and hand of these policies proves. Suffice it to record the fact, and to remind the reader that the word 'policy' comes from the Italian 'polizza'.

• Lorenzo TONTI (born in Naples) in 1630, established during his lifetime the concept of what was known as a 'tontine annuity' which he initially proposed to Cardinal Mazarin of France. The concept was followed up both there and in England and forms the basis of life insurance.

Law

The traditional Italian 'disrespect' for law does not arise from any dislike of the law as a concept but rather from an intolerance of authority. It stems from the instinct that exists in every Italian that one should always be very cynical and very critical of authority. It is, in a strange sense, a form of safeguard for the individual which is more appropriate to a true democracy, such as we find in Britain, than to Italy where the democratic process really only began in 1948. But I do not think that this attitude has ultimately anything to do with democracy.

The Italians have taken democracy to heart and even though it is not working quite so well as it should, because it is fairly new, deep down most Italians would like it to succeed; and by Italian standards, it is succeeding. It is neither a British- nor an American-type democracy, nor could it ever be: the country is too different. But one should not underrate its solidity. To look at it from either a British or American standpoint is wrong: political concepts do not transplant easily. Suffice it to say at this stage that in both local and general elections in Italy the percentage of the voting population casting a vote is in excess of 90 per cent. That may tell us something about the Italian democratic process, if by democracy we mean that all people should exercise their right to vote.

What the Italian objects to is the panoply of law enforcement. There is an Italian saying that *Varata la legge, trovato l'inganno* which, roughly translated, means that no sooner is a new law passed than one can drive a coach and horses through it. This saying reflects the attitude to which I have been referring.

However, in order to understand the Italians one must always remember the fact that they were invaded throughout their history. To ensure their survival, therefore, they had to develop techniques for dealing with their invaders. Or put another way, they had to try and be more resourceful and craftier than their overlords. In the present context, I shall ignore the resourcefulness and concentrate on the craftiness.

It is almost endemic in Italy that people want to outdo others. There is no nastiness in this, for it is an instinctive reaction which arises from centuries of experience. But the fact remains that the average Italian is always trying to be clever. There is a well-established expression, *fare il furbo* which can be translated roughly (not literally, of course) as 'I'll show you'. The Italian shows the tax collector how clever he is by not paying his taxes. Since he is not allowed to distinguish between tax avoidance and tax evasion, as the legal system does not recognize the right of the citizen so to order his affairs as to minimise the impact of taxation, the Italian keeps two sets of books. The same approach is reflected in the strenuous efforts made by most Italians to negotiate reductions in the price of anything; whether it be at the market for the price of potatoes or in the shop for that of a dress, one must always try and get a 'special' discount. The special discount relates to the particular ability of the negotiator who will 'show' the sales person that he is better at it than others and therefore will get a greater reduction. The same principle applies again in the network of friends that one establishes, a sort of benevolent 'camarilla', the sole purpose of which is to outdo someone else.

I am exaggerating, of course: there are respectable Italians who pay taxes, who keep only one set of books, who walk into a shop and pay the asking price without murmur, who are not concerned with scoring points off their opponents, who would think twice before being clever at the expense of their neighbours. But the basic mentality and the framework that give rise to that mentality is ever present - hovering, as it were, in the background.

It is an incredibly time-consuming exercise and an absurd waste of resources that could be harnessed to better and, indeed, more profitable pursuits.

In Italy everybody is watching everybody else; the state police watches the military police and vice versa; the managers watch their staff and vice versa; the politicians watch the voters and vice versa. And so on.

That this somewhat negative attitude has also some advantages cannot be denied: but it is an unfortunate fact that very often, because of this approach, the Italian cannot see the wood for the trees, he becomes over-sensitive about certain situations and therefore takes hasty decisions from which he later may have to withdraw, and is incapable of adopting long-term views.

Be that as it may, there is undoubtedly a sense in which the approach of the Italian to law is ambivalent. He wishes to be respectful of it and deep down he knows that he should; but it gives him pleasure to try and wriggle out of it. It is almost a game. It is in fact one of the national pastimes. It is almost a necessity, and all in Italy succumb to it, even foreigners who live there.

But people should not be too misled by what they hear said about the attitude that the Italian has towards the law or by what they see on television in connection with the trials of the Red Brigades, the Mafia and so on. This ambivalent attitude does not apply to more serious crimes and in any event the Italian system of law is on the whole no more objectionable than any other.

Indeed, Italian substantive law is no worse, and in many respects is better, than many other systems of law. It is Italian procedural law which leaves much to be desired and which causes the absurdities and inordinate delays which are so much publicized and which are taken by the ignorant viewer or reader as representative of the Italian judicial system as a whole. They are representative only in the sense that nobody in Italy has so far had the courage to reform dramatically the legal system and to modernize and improve the codes of civil and criminal procedure.

It is regrettably true, as Wendell Holmes has said, that it is in the interstices of civil procedure that justice is to be found. He is quite right. And to that extent, justice is not found very easily in Italy.

But that is a different matter from saying, as I heard said not long ago, that Italians have a hypocritical attitude when it comes to law. I contest this. It is no more hypocritical than any attitude which distinguishes between tax avoidance and tax evasion. In my view this is pure sophistry.

An example of logical inconsistency in English law could be found in the earlier divorce laws. It was then authoritatively stated, to justify the concept of the matrimonial offence, that the courts had to strike a balance between 'the binding sanctity of marriage' and the 'considerations of public policy which made necessary to recognise the fact that two human beings could no longer live together'. What utter nonsense. Repeating an observation of Sir James Fitzjames Stephen - a marriage is either holy and binding forever; or man-made, holy or otherwise, and determinable at will. It is illogical to look at it in any other manner. It must be said, however, that nowadays Italians can no longer complain of such false, Byzantine thinking as I have just mentioned, since they, too, have introduced divorce. There is progress for you.

•   **In 1070 LANFRANC of Pavia brought Roman law to Britain. He was a trusted counsellor to William the Conqueror, apart** from being the first Norman Archbishop of Canterbury, and re-organized the English Church.

But Lanfranc's contribution to English law and legal development went well beyond his official functions as a churchman. Before coming to England, he had been a lawyer in his home town, Pavia, in Lombardy (see 'The Church in England'). Incidentally, the laws of Lombardy were well known at the time inasmuch as they were more progressive than Roman law which had become somewhat fossilised.

Lanfranc was a well known advocate who taught law and forensic techniques to many Normans (clerics or otherwise).

He contributed to Latin becoming the official language not only of the Church but also of the law because the Normans, who had not long taken over, did not yet speak English.

It is to Lanfranc's activities as a lawyer that we owe one of the first recorded English cases, for he took proceedings against Archbishop Odo, who is referred to in the Bayeux tapestry, for the return of Church properties which Odo had appropriated.

That case lasted three days, a record for the time, and Lanfranc was successful. His success increased his already substantial reputation but it also contributed to the establishment of two precedents. Firstly, Lanfranc can be seen as the first barrister on record in England; secondly, he confirmed the position of clergymen as lawyers at the time when there was not a legal profession as such in the country.

It is a sad fact that, as far as I could ascertain, many English lawyers do not know of Lanfranc's contribution and, unless they have made a careful study of Holdsworth or Maitland, they are certainly not aware of the fact that in the twelfth century Italian lawyers successfully practised as barristers in England. Two examples, Vacario and Irnerio, are referred to elsewhere. But there were others, such as Master Ambrose who, with Vacario,

defended Richard de Anestey in his long trial (it lasted about five years). It is believed that, despite his origin, Peter de Mileto was Italian as well.

I find it amusing to reflect on the debt that the English Bar owes Italy; and the more so since, judging by the average barrister's normal behaviour towards, and appreciation for, things Italian, members of the Bar are blissfully unaware of such debt (solicitors have often maintained that members of the Bar are blissfully unaware of many other facts as well ...; but that is certainly a different story).

● In 1146 VACARIO (in English, Vacarius or Vicarius) (born somewhere in Lombardia) was the first teacher of Roman law in England.

● A little earlier, in about 1100, Irnerio had advised Henry V in his fight with the Church of Rome.

● In 1230 AZZONE (born in Bologna) was the first to write systematic 'summae' of Roman law and most of Bracton's writing is derived from him.

(I pause at this stage to remind the reader that if he really wants to pursue the question of the debt that the English common law owes to Roman law he should read Buckland's textbook *Roman Law and Common Law*).

● The main sources of English mercantile trade law are to be found in the trade customs of the Northern Italian cities of the twelfth century.

Commercial law in Italy at that time was fairly extensive. For example, there was a statute of the City of Como dated 1219 (valid until abolished by Napoleon in 1800) which dealt with defaulting debtors. It dealt with them in a somewhat unusual and possibly Italian way because it provided that whenever a debtor defaulted he, dressed solely in a nightshirt, had to publicly beat his backside three or four times on the stone of shame which was set up in a public place. The Latin, for those who enjoy this sort of

THE BEAUTY THAT IS OURS

LA NOSTRA BELLEZZA

Perché l'Italia è così bella?

Perché è sempre stata un popolo di schiavi per rallegrare i quali i tiranni pagavano i migliori pittori, i migliori scultori, i migliori architetti.

"Why is Italy so beautiful?"
"Because it has always been a nation of slaves and in order to keep them happy their oppressors employed the best painters, sculptors and architects."

thing, is quite expressive: *Concusserit seu crolaverit super lapidem broleti cumarum in camixia tantum et ter vel quater dederit de cullo super lapidem publice.*

(I am providing this information more as an item of amusement than of fact but it is recorded in a charming book called *Guida alla Lombardia Misteriosa* published by Sugar Editore, pp 132/33).

• **In the thirteenth century, the first bill of exchange was created in Lombardy by the Lombard bankers.**

I have already touched upon the Lombard bankers who gave their name to Lombard Street. But the bill of exchange was a most significant development and to this same period we must trace its endorsement and discounting as well as the establishment of bankruptcy concepts.

• **The year 1365 saw the first recorded woman judge in Europe, ELEONORA OF ARBOREA, who published a code for Sardinia originally drafted by her father Mariano, another judge, and known as the 'Carta de logu de Arborea'.**

Eleonora was renowned for her love of falconry and one of the first recorded falcons, the 'falcon eleonorae', is named after her.

• **Company law is also traceable to the northern Italian cities.**

The 'compagnia' and the 'comenda' anticipated modern concepts of partnership and limited liability companies.

• **Also in the fourteenth century the Italians invented bankruptcy (the word itself reminds one of 'breaking the Bank'!) as a method of safeguarding the rights of the creditors of a merchant who had failed.**

• **In 1421 the first known patent was granted by the Republic of Florence.**

• **The first known ordinance relating to patents was issued in Venice in 1474.**

• **In 1563 Pierino BELLI (born at Alba) published his book *De re militari et de bello*, the first manual of military law.**

Belli also dealt with the rules for conducting war. He is considered one of the founders of international law, though he never acquired the notoriety of Gentili.

• **In 1588 Alberico GENTILI (born in San Ginesio) wrote his *De Jure Belli*, the first known treatise on international law, as well as his *De Legationibus*.**

I cannot provide an authority, but from my reading I have a record of the fact that in the twelfth century Frederick II of Sicily established the first European system of land registration by creating a 'catasto' (land registry). Land registration, however, was also well known to most of the Italian Communes which had each established their own local registries. These were clearly inefficient and the concern that prompted them was certainly not a guarantee of title, but the more precise and extensive collection of taxes.

Gradually, however, a certain degree of sophistication was reached. It is recorded that in 1428, for example, the city of Florence could boast of five land registries, subdivided into ones for the city, the country, the district, the nobility and, lastly, for aliens.

I should also record the fact that Italians were the first to use the concept of a commercial lien. Although I could find no legal authority to support the foregoing statement, indirect evidence of it can be gleaned from Boccaccio's *Decameron* (Day 8, Story 10) where it is clear that we are dealing with goods stored in a warehouse, a loan of 1,000 gold florins and security for it in the shape of a lien recorded with the custom authorities.

It may be useful to remind ourselves that we were still in the fourteenth century. (A civil lien was already known to Roman law). And where an agent guarantees, at least in part if not wholly, that a customer whom he introduces to his principal will in fact pay, thus becoming a 'del credere' agent, English law adopts almost in its entirety the

Italian wording of the 'star del credere', thus underlining even further the debt owed to Italy.

Finally, although the Common Law developed upon novel and native lines, freeing itself from subservience to Roman law was not easy particularly when it came to terminology. As Maitland has observed: 'How shall one write a simple sentence about law without using some such word as debt, contract, heir, trespass, pay, money, court, judge, jury. But all these words have come to us from the French ...'. And, I add: yes, through French but via Rome!

Indeed, the reliance, both substantive and terminological, of English law upon Latin is fundamental, though taken for granted. The following words, all representing essential concepts, derive directly from Latin:

Alibi, attest, attestation, bail, calumny, camera, challenge, court, contest, culprit, dictum, entail, equity, evidence, indenture, intestacy, intestate, judge, judgement, judicature, judicial, judicious, jury, jurisdiction, jurisprudence, libel, moratorium, onus, perjury, posse, prejudice, right, slander, stipulation, subpoena, testament, testator, verdict.

I have so far been considering only civil and commercial law. But there is another first to be recorded in the sphere of maritime law.

●   **One of the four maritime republics, that is to say Amalfi, (Genoa, Pisa and Venice were the others), set up the first code of maritime law by its Statutes of Amalfi about the year 1000. All the statutes that followed, firstly in Italy and later on in other countries, are derived from the Amalfi Statutes.**

Barcelona's 'Libro del Consulado del Mar', often claimed to be the first medieval maritime code, was compiled in the thirteenth century.

●   **I have already recorded the activities of the Bank of San Giorgio. In the early part of the fifteenth century it began issuing** 'notes' which represented in total or in part the equivalent money deposits it held on behalf of its customers. These notes were the forerunner of the present-day bank cheque.

Statistics

●   In 1300 Giovanni VILLANI (born in Florence) published his history of Florence. It is a study of all that happened in Florence, and to the Florentines, what they manufactured, what money they spent and how they did so. He was one of the first historians and chroniclers and the first one to look at history from the standpoint of economics and statistics. Villani anticipated Holinshed and Stow by two centuries.

According to Villani, in the early fourteenth century Florence was a thriving, wealthy city.

It had 110 churches and countless workshops producing many products and tens of thousands of rolls of wool. Its population was literate, attended schools, was cared for in numerous hospitals, fed itself well and drank much wine. It was politically active, though the two main parties (the Guelphs and the Ghibellines) were constantly at each other's throats.

Time-and-motion Studies

I am sure that the Egyptians would never have built the Pyramids without firm discipline over workers and slaves and without some careful calculation of how long it took to carry out each function. But there is no evidence of any control ever having been exercised over artists and craftsmen - as distinguished from mere manual workers - to get them to conform to pre-established patterns of work and timetables.

This, on the other hand, was done in Italy.

• Filippo BRUNELLESCHI (see 'Architecture' p.30) in 1424 laid down detailed times and systems of work for his masons engaged in the construction of the Duomo at Florence.

Brunelleschi was the first to carry out proper time-and-motion studies, anticipating Frederick Taylor by 450 years.

Brunelleschi even went so far as to control and time each single act of shovelling. As a result, his craftsmen did not like either him or his new methods of building any more than they liked his systems of control. Consequently, in that same year they downed tools and, four years later, 25 of them were sacked: Brunelleschi always meant business.

Section 6:
Folk-lore & Hobbies

Botanical Gardens and Botany

• In 1543 and 1545 respectively the first two botanical gardens in the western world were both established at Padova (the one established in Oxford followed in 1621).

• Andrea CESALPINO (born in Arezzo) wrote in 1583 De Plantis, which was the first botanical treatise to group plants according to their reproductive organs, thus paving the way for the more detailed work of Malpighi.

• In 1671 Marcello MALPIGHI (born at Crevalcore) founded plant anatomy. He was the first to observe the stomata of plants; his treatise on silkworms is considered the first monograph on an invertebrate.

Malpighi also made various important discoveries in the sphere of medical science. (See 'Medicine p.114.')

• In 1592 the botanist Prospero ALPINI (born at Marostica) was the first European to observe and report on the coffee plant. (See 'Gastronomy' p.71.) He was also the first to fertilize dates artificially.

Festivals

Festivals abound in Italy. Whether they are of a religious or historical nature, whether processions or pageants, they are so numerous and so well known that to recall them seems futile.

But there's one somewhat unusual first.

• It is said that in 1625 Benedetto DREI, head gardener of the Vatican flower garden, first invented mosaic patterns in fresh flowers.

Drei's example was followed in many parts of Italy, and abroad: the Italian classic in this respect is the 'infiorata' at Genzano, celebrated on the feast of Corpus Christi. There, flowers, instead of being thrown at a procession, are elaborately laid out on the surface of the street through which the procession is to pass. Acacias, brooms, roses, poppies, with evergreens like box and laurel, are picked the night before and laid out early next morning in sections of the street, each arranged by a different group. The sections then blend into a unit, for all to admire until the procession itself destroys the whole pattern.

Similar deckings of streets with flowers occur in many parts of Italy. (See Thomas Ashby, *Some Italian Scenes and Festivals.*)

Funerals

• **The first designer of catafalques, in 1722, was Giuseppe Galli BIBIENA (born in Parma). He was one of seven members of a family of artists who did all sorts of things including designing scenery for plays and for ballets.**

Apart from the actual catafalques, funerals in Italy are quite a spectacle. I should like to believe that if a deceased gets a very grand funeral indeed, it is because he was dearly loved and will be sadly missed. But I am not sure. Because of the Italian fondness for form, I think a funeral in Italy is very often the equivalent in death of the English debutante ball. Those involved are very keen to out-do one another.

In southern Italy, the tradition is probably stronger. It finds its origins in the Roman 'Preficae' who were paid to go and cry and pull their hair at a funeral.

Funerals aside, the Bibiena brothers were surely the greatest scenographers ever. They dabbled in everything that gave colour or created effects.

One of their best exercises is to be found in the Chapel of the Sacred Heart at Sabbioneta. There, when you look upwards, you see the sky. Well, you believe you do; but in actual fact, the Bibiena brothers painted it on the dome of the chapel so successfully that the first impression is totally deceptive.

The illumination in the same church is

also a great feat, considering that it was carried out over 250 years ago.

• **Sabbioneta is in itself very interesting because it is the first example of a new town, although it was never inhabited.**

One of the first Gonzagas, Vespasiano, in about 1562, pursued one of his many whims whereby he would establish a new town in the province of Mantova that would be a Rome in miniature.

He demolished the existing hamlet and over a period of about 30 years he had erected in its place two palaces, a church, a theatre, a library, a mint and a small printing works.

Vespasiano Gonzaga was an odd character: he could not bear his wife's adultery, and killed her; at the same time he showed extreme tolerance to Jews. In fact, he entrusted the printing works to Jews and encouraged them to come and settle at Sabbioneta.

The place, however, was never quite fully lived in because, before he could complete it, Vespasiano Gonzaga died in 1591. He himself is buried in the Church of the Incoronata and his funeral monument is a life-size statue of himself which is probably the only true-to-life edifice in the whole of the town. The buildings terminate suddenly in fields of corn and the whole affair has qualities almost of a mirage. There is a metaphysical character to the place which, as has been said, reminds one of a De Chirico painting.

Before the countryside took over, about two centuries later the Bibiena brothers complemented the work that Vespasiano set out to achieve. But even though the ducal palace is now open to the public, one derives an uncertain feeling from visiting this 'new town' which is both new and old at the same time.

Vespasiano got Scamozzi to build a small Court theatre at Sabbioneta in 1588. It is still standing and although the furniture has gone, it shows the grandeur of its conception and of the architectural concepts of Sebastiano Serlio whose ideas

Scamozzi applied. It has a novel design in that it consists of a single amphitheatre behind a shallow raked open platform and a horseshoe-shaped bank of seating. It was a design that was to influence Inigo Jones extensively and which paved the way for the Teatro Farnese which would be built about 30 years later at Parma, only 20 kilometres away.

Gaming

• In 1526 Girolamo CARDANO (born in Pavia) worked out the odds on casting dice and was the first to propound the probability theory. He also discovered both cubic and quartic equations. (See 'Mathematics' p.109.)

Cardano, the illegitimate son of a lawyer, published in 1545 his *Ars Magna*, which is a cornerstone in the history of algebra. As *Britannica* records, he was the most outstanding mathematician of his time. In terms of his computation of probabilities, he anticipates Pascal by 100 years. But he was also an astrologer and a physician; and in this latter capacity, he was the first to provide a description of typhus fever. In England, he is known as Jerome Cardan.

• The picture-type playing cards - as distinct from the number cards which are probably a Chinese invention - originated in Italy. The first reference to them occurs in 1299.

These picture-cards were called 'Tarocchi', a word that was later converted into the German 'Tarok' and the French 'Tarot'.

Games, especially card games, are quite popular in Italy. It is no coincidence that the Italians were world bridge champions for nearly twenty years.

Card games are played everywhere in Italy. It is not unusual to find youngsters playing them in the streets or older men outside a bar or an 'osteria', in the same way as Greeks and Turks play backgammon.

They are in a sense part of the Italian scene, although I am not sure to what extent the Italian is temperamentally a real gambler.

Gardens and Horticulture

Everybody knows how successful the Italians have been with the formal garden and the general impact of Italian gardening on Europe is referred to later. For present purposes, suffice it to say that Italy influenced France extensively: it provided the model and inspiration for Louis XIV and gave him an appreciation for gardens like those of Versailles and the Tuileries. Both Marie and Catherine de Medici had taken Italian gardeners to France with them.

When John Evelyn first went to Italy, he was most impressed by the gardens of the Doria family in Genoa, which were very well known for their terraces. Indeed, at first sight he thought that the gardens extended from the sea to the mountains and he so described them.

In 1622 the Danvers brothers started to pioneer the Italian garden in England.

Apart from this general background, there are a number of firsts.

• In 1305 Pietro de CRESCENZI (born in Bologna) who for the previous 30 years had been a judge, and who had retired officially in 1299, wrote his *Liber Ruralium Commodorum*.

De Crescenzi originally wrote the work in Latin. It was translated into Italian in the latter part of the fourteenth century and it was published in 1471. Soon after, it was translated into French and German.

This was the first gardening book, for in it he deals at great length with the size and shape of trees and plants and, above all, garden furniture and statuary.

● **In the fifteenth century the Italians were the first to lay out parterres.**

The approach, based on formal layout, is reflected also in the extensive use made by the Italians at a very early date of arbours or fruit tunnels, i.e. the covering of areas or walks by plants or trees trained over lattice work. Here there was a pioneer.

● **In 1467 a Dominican monk called Francesco COLONNA wrote the *Hypnerotomachia Poliphili*, roughly translated in English as 'The Dream of Poliphilus', which represents the first gardening encyclopaedia.**

Apart from describing elaborate work in the construction of tree tunnels in the book, he deals at great length with landscape gardening, the layout of orchards, woodland, of vegetable gardens, pergolas, garden furniture and fountains, plant utilisation, the use of old stones and the topiary of myrtle and cypress trees.

Any reader of Boccaccio's *Decameron* knows the extent to which gardens are described by him and how in particular he refers to arbours planted with climbers. Obviously Boccaccio antedates Colonna, but to Colonna we owe the systematization of gardening techniques. Colonna's book was beautifully printed by Aldo Manuzio and it is possible that it even antedates the *De Re Aedificatoria* by Leon Battista Alberti (see 'Architecture') which dealt at length with the siting of villas in gardens.

● **In 1545 Daniele BARBARO (born in Venice), was the first to establish a conservatory. He put it to the use of the Botanical Gardens at Pavia; an open fire provided heat during the winter.**

Conservatories were already common features of the Italian Gardens of the Renaissance. A versatile person, Barbaro. He also anticipated the invention of the camera. (see 'Photography').

● **Giovanni Battista CERLETTI (born at Chiavenna), in 1877 was the first to establish at Conegliano, near Venice, a School of Viticulture and Oenology.**

Heraldry

● **In the fourteenth century the Italian lawyer Bartolo da SASSOFERRATO was the first to write about heraldry.**

I must say that I found this 'first' somewhat surprising and slightly inconsistent with the commonly-held views about the history of chivalry.

I had always associated heraldry much more with England and France than with Italy; but it is clear beyond any doubt that Bartolo da Sassoferrato was the first who actually studied it in depth.

In his famous treatise *De insignis et armis*, written in either 1350 or 1356 he propounded the view that anyone can assume a coat of arms at will, as long as it has not already been adopted by another. A similar situation arose quite normally in the use of seals.

Sassoferrato is a very small town not far from Ancona, which is one of the major ports on the Adriatic.

It produced Bartolo but it was also the birth-place of the well-known painter Gian Battista Salvi, otherwise known as 'Il Sassoferrato' who gave his name to a whole school of painters of pictures of the Madonna and Child of a particularly gentle, pleasant image.

Incidentally, his name is not mentioned in the edition of *Britannica* with which we are dealing either under 'Salvi' or under 'Sassoferrato'.

Lotteries

wonder whether it has ever occurred to ou, either when playing the football pools r bingo or even buying premium bonds, hat they all stem from an Italian idea.

In 1530 there was held in Florence vhat is believed to be the first public lottery o have paid out prizes in the form of money, l lotto di Firenze'.

Of course, the gambling instinct is as old s mankind and examples of the use of the oncept of chance to determine events can e found both in the Bible and in Roman istory.

But the Lotto of Florence was an rganised event which represented the tarting point and I suppose we can also ace back to it today's gambling casinos.

There is no doubt that 'Lotto', the Italian lational Lottery, formed the basis of ibsequent games like lotto, keno, bingo, tc. Indeed, on a national scale, Italy would ome first even in modern times had it not een beaten to the post by Australia which ad lotteries as early as the middle of the ineteenth century.

The first National Italian Lottery was reated in 1863; others followed. The Irish weepstake goes back to the 1930s, France llowed in 1933, the Malta Lottery is well nown and in some countries (England, ungary and Malta, for example) even the ame 'lotto' was imported.

It is due to the innate cynicism of the alians, about which more later, that Italy as always been fairly successful in xploiting for economic benefit the eaknesses and foibles of human beings.

Magic

• In 1780, Giuseppe PINETTI (born at Orbetello) established himself as the first stage magician. He was the first to introduce a number of tricks, including the second sight trick ,and he founded the classical School of Magic.

Traditional Tales

• In 1550 Gianfranco STRAPAROLA (born at Caravaggio) published the first known collection of traditional tales under the title *Le Piacevoli Notti*.

Some of Straparola's material was used by Shakespeare and Moliere and his tales were dipped into by all and sundry. However, he was not entirely innocent of plagiarism himself because he had borrowed a considerable number of ideas from Boccaccio.

• At about the same time MACHIAVELLI was also writing novels and developing ideas similar to those of Straparola. Both the ideas of Machiavelli and those of Straparola were also borrowed by John Wilson, John Dekker and Ben Johnson, as well as Shakespeare and Moliere.

A more recent development is Italo Calvino's collection of Italian Traditional Tales published in 1956. There are 200 of them and they echo many themes of 400 years ago.

CHRISTOPHER COLOMBUS

CRISTOFORO COLOMBO

Che vuol dire?

Che stiamo scoprendo la terra
che scoprirà la luna.

"What's he getting excited about?"
"He's saying that we are discovering the land that
will one day discover the moon."

Section 7:
Food & Drink

Gastronomy

In matters of food, the Italians are undisputed masters, and with the exception of the French and perhaps the Japanese most other societies' approach to and appreciation of food is at best crass or inconsistent and at worst appalling.

Of course, I must hasten to add that there is absolutely no authority either in the *Encyclopaedia Britannica* or in any other book that I am aware of to substantiate these two statements: they merely represent my opinion. This is not to say, however, that both are not perfectly true!

Let me try to demonstrate, and, for the sake of argument, let me take the English and the Americans first.

Until the Italians started educating them, the English and the Americans knew very little about good food. There are three principal reasons for this:

(a) The appreciation of culinary expertise is part of a frame of mind and an approach to life which is associated with good wine and good living in a sunny clime and against the backcloth of our Latin civilisation. The former does not exist in either England or the USA and the latter is usually to be found only around the Mediterranean shores in combination with the former.

(b) There is no tradition of cooking in either the British Isles or the USA. If ever there was, which I doubt, it has long ceased to exist.

(c) Good cooking is a cultural and an emotive fact, as well as a physical one. It is born, and it dies, within the family, and is a labour of love. It is taught by mothers to daughters and it represents the distillation of all the teachings and remarks by whomsoever spends most of her life in front of a stove. It is not learnt from a book, any more than it is learnt by part-time mothers/wives. Cooking, like looking after a family, is a full-time occupation which cannot be left in the hands of anyone, male or female, who has already spent some eight to ten hours in an office or has been busy at some other job. People who get home in the evening after a full day at work are tired; they do not want to cook, though they might just want to eat.

If they have to prepare a meal, theirs is not a labour of love but of hasty necessity. They cut corners, they lose their critical sense, their touch, and, above all, their own appreciation for what they are doing.

Where the housekeeper is out at work there can be no real cuisine. Hence the ready-made, pre-packed, pre-cooked, pre-frozen so-called food which has no taste, no style and no freshness. It suits those who buy it, who end up by getting exactly what they deserve.

Good cooking is a full-time occupation: there is no escape from this axiom. And where there is no family to warrant total commitment, there is no good cooking.

Inasmuch as the family (and extended family) has ceased to have any real significance in England and America (for the most part), there cannot possibly be any appreciation of good food there. The tragedy is that the family is being demolished in Italy as well; but that is a different story. However, when that happens, the consequences will be exactly the same: canned spaghetti and a couple of tablets!

- **In all matters of food the Italians have given a lead.**

I have watched with increasing amusement over the past 10 to 15 years the number of recipes for Italian food that have emerged on the back of pasta or cheese packets or elsewhere, which have all been copied direct from Italian cookery books. I can think of at least three so-called English authorities on cooking, the bulk of whose recipes - proffered not only as Italian recipes, but as their own advice - have been abstracted in their entirety from the leading Italian books on cooking by Pellegrino Artusi and Ada Boni.

The spread of Italian restaurants in London has obviously contributed to a greater appreciation of the fine things in life by the English but the standard of Italian cooking outside Italy and particularly in England is not always constant.

In actual fact, it is not Italian cuisine that the English public is being accustomed to, but a cuisine which has been adapted to suit it to local requirements and to make it more acceptable to the local palate.

Italian cafes, restaurants and other food establishments variously named, some abusive of the Italian language, have sprouted like mushrooms throughout London over the past 20 years. They are usually opened by people whose only claim to Italian cooking is that they have an Italian name. (Sometimes they are not even opened by Italians!) They have no gastronomic education, and little taste. It is as though a butcher had determined that merely because he knew how to handle a knife he should become a surgeon. It is true that there are some surgeons who are butchers but I know of no butchers who are surgeons. By parity of reasoning I know of few Italians here who know anything about the real art of Italian cooking.

The reader will have gathered that I feel very strongly about this aspect of the so-called cultural education that present-day Italians have been imparting, in matters of cooking, not only to the English and Americans but to the world at large. The standards of true Italian cooking are not being maintained abroad, save in very few cases.

It is difficult enough to maintain them in Italy where we have an appreciative and

highly critical public; it is expecting too much that they should be maintained wherever the public is undiscerning. This is not to say that Italian food establishments in England are not good, or do not offer value for money. They are, and they do, but they reflect falling standards and have had to adapt to local requirements and availability of produce. This is inevitable: in fact, it is a mark of Italian inventiveness that surprisingly good results are still achieved.

On the optimistic side, there is no doubt that the lead that we have over all other nations, France included, is great. In fact, I believe it is so great that we have ample justification for being conceited in this context. I suppose we feel as Red Rum's jockey must have felt when he won the Grand National for the third time: supreme in the field.

It is difficult, however, to disabuse people of the notion that the French are better. The use of language is significant: the English refer to French cuisine, but to Italian cooking. The nuance is not great but is very significant. I still feel that the Italians have greater imagination with food. Why this should be so I endeavour to explain later.

Meanwhile, suffice it to say that it is too easy to ascribe the reason to the Mediterranean climate. Spain and Greece enjoy the same climate as Italy, but food in the former is, to put it mildly, barely adequate except in Cataluna and in the latter good cuisine is non-existent. What makes the food enjoyable in Spain and Greece is the sun and not the technique of those who prepare it.

In Italy on the other hand there is not only the sun but also a gastronomic tradition which goes back at least 400 years.

●   **In the Renaissance, Italian cooking was the turning point in the development of gastronomic excellence. Italy influenced France intensively.**

●   **It was Catherine de' MEDICI who brought Italian cooking to France when she**

married Henry II of Navarre and took with her to France a retinue of Italian cooks.

Italian supremacy has been established since that time and has continued uninterrupted. It is not so much a matter of Parmesan cheese, known in England since the fourteenth century, or Parma Ham, known since the seventeenth century, or indeed, Bologna sausages being the best in the world. (For the sausages, you will find the observation in Boswell's Life of Dr Johnson for Saturday, 9 May 1772.)

Nor can we ignore the debt that the world owes to Italy when it comes to ice-cream. How many Anglo-American makers of ice-cream would not exist but for the recipes provided by Italians and the use of Italian names, for example, 'Neapolitan', 'Tartufo', 'Cornetto' and 'Cassata'.

And how many other nations are indebted to us when it comes to food? One example only, namely salami: it was an Italian chestnut-vendor called Piazzoni who taught the Hungarians how to make salami. He is credited with founding their salami industry, which is now fairly substantial, in the year 1850. But our contribution goes beyond simple inventiveness; it goes deeper than the mere product. It is rather a question of the enjoyment that the Italian derives from his expertise in making something out of comparatively simple ingredients. This is the ability and the ingenuity of the Italians when it comes to food, and it is not shared by any other people I know except the Chinese.

Apart from any other consideration, this excellence is not limited to the taste of the food, or to its presentation. It goes beyond that, to its substance.

Our dieticians and doctors, who seem to change their minds as quickly as the wind changes direction, have now told us that we can only improve our chances of survival if we change to the Mediterranean diet. They have told us that carbohydrates are not fattening and are indeed necessary; that olive oil is better than butter, margarine and other fats; and that we should increase our intake of pulses, vegetables and fresh fruit. I must say, I knew this when I was very young; my mother taught me and it is what the Italians have been doing since at least the days of the Romans.

● **The fork for dining was invented in Italy in the sixteenth century. It came into use in England about 100 years later.**

Finally, since at least in the eyes of the Mediterranean people one cannot separate good food from good coffee, it should be recorded that it was the Venetians who introduced coffee to Europe. Coffee appears to have originated in Abyssinia and thence spread by the Arabs to the Balkans, Spain, India, North Africa and Turkey. The Venetian traders are credited with having been the first to introduce coffee to Italy round about the year 1615.

Coffee was already known to the Europeans by then.

● **In 1592, in Venice, Prospero ALPINI, a botanist at Padua University, published the first recorded description in the western world of both the coffee plant and the drink in his treatise The Plants of Egypt.**

Seven years prior to that publication, Gianfranco Morosini, who had been a governor of Constantinople when it was part of the Venetian empire, had reported to the Venetian Senate on the Turkish habit of drinking coffee. In fact, it is believed that he was himself the first importer into Venice of coffee berries.

● **Venice also claims another first, namely the establishment of the first coffee house in the western world in 1645.**

The habit of drinking coffee, firstly for medicinal purposes and later on for pleasure, spread very quickly in Venice and coffee houses proliferated. The famous 'Florian' cafe was established in Piazza San Marco in 1720; the equally well known 'Pedrocchi' coffee house followed in Padua in 1831 and gradually coffee houses became established in all major Italian cities.

The spread of coffee throughout Europe

was very rapid. The first London coffee house is said to have been established in St Michael's Alley, Cornhill, under the sign of 'Pasqua's Head' in or about 1652, although the first coffee house in England was opened that same year in Oxford by a Jew.

Also towards the end of the seventeenth century, more precisely in 1689, a Sicilian nobleman by the name of Francesco Procopio Dei Coltelli (Lit. 'Procopius of the Knives'), from Palermo, opened the first coffee house in Paris which was appropriately called 'Cafe de Procope'. The establishment very soon acquired notoriety.

● **The first espresso coffee machine was invented in 1946 by Gaggia of Milan. It was in Naples, in 1800, that pasta was first mechanically produced and the first factory of pasta so manufactured was built at Sansepolcro in 1827 by Buitoni. Alcohol was first distilled at the Salerno School of Medicine in the year 1000. Large-scale production of alcohol, however, is recorded for the first time at Modena in the thirteenth century.**

Ice-cream

I thought this heading should be put in on the one hand because, as is common knowledge, there is very little to beat Italian ice-cream and on the other because any westerner who reads this would expect some connection to exist between the Italians and ice-cream.

From the historical standpoint, however, the Italians themselves got there first only in the sense that they continued what the Romans or the Chinese had done. Water ices in fact were already known to the Romans.

● **The recipe for milk ices originates in the Far East. It was recorded by Marco POLO during one of his travels in China and was brought back to Europe by him.**

We are told that Charles I of England was particularly appreciative of the milk ices prepared by his Italian cook, Mireo, and it is claimed that his Italian wife, Enrichetta Maria Medici, and her said cook introduced ice-cream into Britain.

● **In 1896 Italo MARCIONI, an Italian immigrant to New Jersey, USA, created the first ice-cream cones.**

There is no doubt, however, that the Italians did turn ice-cream making into an art.

Leaving aside Mireo, the association of Italians with ice-cream comes naturally. And this must be based on the factual recognition that particular techniques of ice-cream making, especially from Naples and Sicily, have been the foundation of the later manufacture of ice-cream on an industrial scale.

There is something exceptionally sensual about ice-cream. It is addictive almost in the same way as smoking or drinking; but it does not have the same drugging effect. Indeed, it seems to me that the effect of tobacco is primarily chemical and only secondarily sensual; that of alcohol is primarily psychological and again only secondarily sensual. In the case of ice-cream, however, one's sense of taste determines the addiction.

It is interesting that poets and writers seem exceptionally fond of ice-cream. Both Goethe and Stendhal praised Italian ices; our own Leopardi waxed lyrical about Neapolitan sorbets. Whether Dickens liked it or not I am not sure, but in his *Pictures from Italy* he records the extent to which the locals partook of ice-cream practically the year round.

I am not so enthusiastic about ice-cream myself but I am told by those in the know that its present large-scale production, which originated in the USA and was later exported to all countries, Italy included, has deprived us of the pleasures that Goethe and Stendhal obviously enjoyed.

Section 8: Living Style

Aesthetics

- Aesthetics (or the study of beauty) as an art was founded in 1903 by Benedetto CROCE (born at Pescasseroli). In his *Estetica*, Croce establishes the link between intuition and expression. Jenkins and Dewey followed on.

- In 1553 Gaspare TAGLIACOZZO was the first to make artificial noses, thus establishing himself as the forerunner of a very popular development in the modern world, namely plastic surgery.

Animals

You may be one of those people who believes that Italians are not too fond of animals; for example, they shoot birds indiscriminately and eat grilled sparrows greedily.

You are quite right, they are not. Do not be misled by the fact that at Crufts in early 1986 the top prize went to a charming Italian lady breeder; it was a one-off. Nor should you be misled by the fact that it is now very popular in Italy to have dogs around the place: they are used mostly as guard dogs and in choosing them people are concerned more about their wealth and possessions and rather less about any affection they may have for animals.

This is understandable. Italy has been until recently, and still is in many areas, an exceptionally poor country. In poor countries, people do not have enough to feed themselves: hence they cannot spare food for their animals. If the animals perform a useful function, then they are cared for; if not, they are disposed of.

Indeed, the animals themselves become food for their keepers. To an Italian an animal, like nature, is merely ancillary to man. Man is the centre of all activity and animals and plants only serve his purpose.

From this follow the many uses to which animals have throughout our history been put as a result of erroneous or superstitious beliefs; snakes and mice killed for their special properties, or, as was done at one stage, dogs cooked in a saucepan in order to cure rickets. Most animals have throughout Italian history been considered as having some special properties.

These beliefs are common to most primitive people. In Africa, for example, they think that the horns of rhinos and the tusks of elephants have aphrodisiac properties.

There is no sentimentality in the way an Italian looks at animals; particularly in the south, the animals themselves appear to be different. They are thinner, neglected, they look haggard and old; ultimately, they are neither cared for nor fed.

You need a romantic outlook on life to be truly fond of animals and economic pressures are not conducive to a disinterested approach to our four-legged friends in particular. In case you are in doubt, may I remind you that on the 18 February 1986 all British newspapers reported the complaint of The Royal Society for the Prevention of Cruelty to Animals that the number of cases of cruelty to animals in Britain had gone up by one-third in the previous year. In 1985, according to the RSPCA, 64,678 complaints were investigated (as against 47,362 in 1984).

In 1985 there were 2,112 convictions for cruelty to animals, a post-war record (in

1984, there had been 1,889). Is it a coincidence that our standards of living dropped in the same period?

I am not trying to blind you with statistics nor am I advertising myself as someone who does not love animals. I have two German shepherd dogs, three cats and a number of other domestic animals, so I record the above with sadness. But poverty and love for animals do not always go hand in hand.

The Italian approach to animals is somewhat ambiguous and I think it stems not only from the poverty of the country but also from its cynicism. Animals do not serve a terribly useful purpose unless they work.

I agree, the Italians who believe this are totally mistaken. And I can already hear the protests of animal lovers of Italy that the picture I paint is wrong.

It may be, but it is the picture that I paint. I am comforted in it by the fact that I cannot find many writings in Italian literature that relate to animals and even though the Patron Saint of Italy, St Francis of Assisi, talked to the birds, he was a saint and, according to his preaching, hardly an Italian.

I am reminded of a poem by Trilussa in Roman dialect in which he describes a beggar who approaches the President of the Italian equivalent of the RSPCA for alms and is told that that Society only cares for animals; whereupon he takes off his cap and, pointing to his hair, suggests that in that case the Society ought to care for 'such poor little animals'. Crude, cynical and typically Italian.

You may be wondering what facts of significance relate to this topic. I can find only two, and they are not much to boast about:

• In 1738 Antonio FRANCONI (born in Udine) standardized the diameter of the circus ring at 13 metres, which is exactly what it is today.

• Franconi was also the first lion tamer and the first person to exhibit trained canaries in a circus.

Franconi came from a noble Venetian family and fled to France when he was accused of murder for having killed an opponent in a duel.

He was a famous trick-rider of horses and was assisted by his two sons, one of whom, Victor, established the first open-air Hippodrome in Paris.

The Franconi circus tradition greatly influenced American circuses, especially Barnum.

Calligraphy

• In 1430 POGGIO established the formal minuscule type of script.

• In 1437 Niccolò NICCOLI (born in Florence) invented the type of writing known as 'antico corsivo', a forerunner of the Italic script.

These inventions are very much in keeping with the Italian fondness for form. Indeed, this fondness is one of our basic failings.

It is quite a respectable approach to life. Even Dante, at one stage in his Divine Comedy, complains not so much about what was done but of the manner in which it was done to him ('E il modo ancor m'offende').

The Italians' fondness for form, however, is not entirely negative. It has resulted in the acquisition of an aesthetic appreciation for things, particularly those things with which we have a close association, as it were. This trait is a distinguishing feature of Italy. Things may be empty inside, but they always look pretty outside. For example, Italian medieval armour was the most handsome then manufactured, and acknowledged to be so by many writers, but not the most resistant. In modern times, some Italian motor cars have beautiful lines but rust away quickly.

The examples are very numerous. I shall not labour the point too much, for it hurts sometimes to have to acknowledge one's failings. But this is the reason why Italians are so fond of clothes and on the whole take very great care about their appearance, men and women alike. This may not be such a bad thing after all; as Byron puts it 'Don Juan, Canto XIII stanza XXVIII) '... and to be well drest will very often supersede the rest.'

(The) Church in England

A somewhat unusual heading, but it is a fact that the Church in England owes its structure and its first Archbishop of Canterbury to two Italians, namely Anselmo of Aosta and Lanfranc of Pavia.

• **In 1070 an Italian cleric, Lanfranc (born in Pavia in 1005) was appointed (rather than consecrated) the first Norman Archbishop of Canterbury. He reformed, re-organized and systematized the English Church assisting William The Conqueror in maintaining his fullest possible independence from Rome.**

• **In 1093 Anselmo, later a saint (born in Aosta in 1033) followed Lanfranc as Archbishop of Canterbury. He was the founder of scholasticism and the originator of the ontological argument for the existence of God.**

Lanfranc had moved from Pavia to France to teach Roman law and there he became head of the Benedictine Monastery at Bec in Normandy. William chose him as adviser and he became the first Norman Archbishop of Canterbury. Norman, in the sense that he followed William the Conqueror; but he was Italian. He was a very good organizer and was the first to state that the Archbishop of Canterbury prevailed over all the other Bishops in

England, a supremacy which is maintained to this day. His most important task, however, seems to me to have been to ensure that whatever directives the then Pope Gregory VII issued (Gregory VII was a great reforming Pope) should be diluted before they were applied in England, assuming they were going to be applied at all, a matter as to which Lanfranc had his own opinions.

Anselmo, who succeeded him at Canterbury as he had followed him at Bec, was not a lawyer but a theologian and philosopher. He was a great thinker and came into conflict with William the Second, though he came to terms with his successor, Henry, whose daughter he married off to the King of Scotland, quite usefully and intelligently.

I was taught at school that St Anselmo of Aosta was a philosopher but I had never realised that both he and Lanfranc had played such a big part in England's history.

From far away Italy they brought the knowledge of Roman and canon law, as well as up-to-date theology and philosophy.

They were not looked upon as foreigners but as Normans but were fully absorbed into the system and were amongst the first Italians to become Anglicised.

Anselm in particular was a political churchman, who felt no compunction in bending the rules of the Church for reasons of State. For example, he caused Edgar's daughter, Edith - when she married Henry I - to change her name to Mathilda, a more Norman name, and he conveniently disregarded the fact that she was a nun. Dynastic reasons had to prevail.

But Lanfranc and Anselm were not quite the first, for they had been preceded in their posts by Augustine of Canterbury, a Roman Benedictine prior, who was consecrated first Archbishop of Canterbury in the year 598. I have not spent too long on him for, as you will recall, I am only dealing with events after the year 1000. Even so, it is useful to remind ourselves that the first Archbishop of Canterbury, the founder of the Christian Church in England, was an Italian. (*Britannica* Volume I page 649), and the founder of the greatest of the religious orders, St Benedict, was also an Italian.

Civic Amenities

• In 1276 the city of Genoa started the construction of its harbour jetty consisting of two docks; this was a gigantic feat of engineering for those days.

• In 1295 Genoa built the first aqueduct of the modern era.

• By 1300 Venice had consolidated its base on sea and mud.

• By 1300 the streets and squares of most towns in Italy were paved by flags. The streets of London and Paris at that time were still unpaved and muddy. Indeed, it is a fact that many side streets in St James's, London, were not even paved until about the middle of the nineteenth century.

And you will recall that even earlier than that, in 1179, Milan had built the first canal in the world.

• In 1335 the first public striking clock was made and erected in Milan. It was placed on the bell tower of the nearby church of San Gottardo by Azzone Visconti.

By the eighteenth century, Milan could also boast cornices and balconies that jutted out from the walls of buildings to protect passers-by from the rain, as well as the first tin-plate guttering, which was collected in surface water drains. Its streets were paved with granite stones and were always kept clean.

Milan provided another first when, a hundred years ago, the Galleria Vittorio Emanuele II was opened. It is a glass-roofed area of streets with shops, offices, cafes and restaurants, which was to be copied throughout the world, particularly in Nort America. There, these covered areas ar known as 'malls' and I am informed tha there are more than 25,000 of them.

Elsewhere, they have become arcades courts or precincts. But as far as I kno none of them has been able to imitate th style of the 'Galleria', which stands as a firs in a class of its own.

In 1785, for the first time, Milan street had a name shown on a tablet at th beginning of the street. This was a initiative of Count Wilzeck who at the tim was the Austrian plenipotentiary. At th same time he insisted that all houses shoul be numbered and that oil lamps should b positioned at all street corners.

Milan was at the forefront also in different context. Ever since the thirteent century horse-drawn carriages had bee popular. In fact, the first travelling wago known as a 'cocchio' was manufactured i Italy in 1288.

Initially, the 'cocchio' had no suspensio but by the sixteenth century this had bee remedied and it is recorded that whe Isabella D'Este was a guest there she wa astonished by the fact that Milan could boas of no less than sixty carriages drawn b four horses and hundreds drawn by two This should be compared with what wer on in Paris at the same time, for at the Cour of Francis I, there were only thre carriages: one for him, one for Diana (Poitiers and one for a courtier of his wh was somewhat overweight.

The Italians were the first to protect th travellers in such conveyances by applyin windows to carriages; this was done in th early part of the seventeenth century.

Towards the end of the seventeent century the first public bath houses wer established in London, contributing t improved hygiene at least amongst th better off. They were known as 'bagnios', mis-spelling of the Italian word 'bagno since they were copied from Italy. The soon became places of corruption and vice some of them, if not most, high-clas brothels.

Finally, one can go back to Venice and treat as a civic amenity, for such it certainly was, the construction of the sea walls that protect the town (the 'murazzi').

Conceived initially in 1716, they were completed in 1782, work having started about 37 years previously at an enormous cost. The walls were badly needed because the previous defences were of wood and had to be constantly replaced, apart from the fact that they were not very efficient.

The 'murazzi' are nearly 20 feet high and over a foot thick at the base, built of marble and stone. They are a great feat of engineering and of effort, the crowning glory, in building terms, of the Venetian era. To this day they continue to perform the function for which they were undertaken. The 'Queen of the Sea' became extinguished as a power when Napoleon invaded Italy in 1797: but the stones linger on as a memorial to Venetian determination, resourcefulness and wealth.

• (More a private amenity than a civic one). The first brick hearth with a chimney breast and flue was constructed in Venice in 1227.

• The process of water chlorination on a large scale - effectively to stem an epidemic of typhoid - was first used at Pola in 1896.

Clocks and Watches

It is almost a contradiction in terms to say that the Italians have made any contribution to time-keeping because on the whole, as far as Italians are concerned, time does not exist. Their lack of punctuality is proverbial. It is not discourtesy; it is not lack of consideration; it is not even poverty in the sense that one may not possess a time-keeping piece. I have never known what it is and I should welcome hearing from anybody who could explain it.

It is far too easy to say that the influence of the Spaniards in Southern Italy, coupled with that of the weather, makes people indolent, if not lazy; since they cannot move fast, they will always arrive late. But I find that a rather facile explanation because in my experience this lack of punctuality is to be found all over Italy. The position is better, of course, in the north, in the sense that people are more punctual there. But the reason why they are more punctual has nothing directly to do with the weather, rather with their approach to business. People in business have a different value of time and do not wish to squander it.

But the reason is surely deeper. I believe it is to be found in the basic disregard which the average Italian has for other human beings. This disregard, coupled with the fact that Italians on the whole resent discipline and object to authority of any kind, has resulted in Italians being considered as highly individualistic persons. (They certainly are in many senses but in many others they also like to conform.) In fact, Italians have always been most impressed by the precision and punctuality of the English. Nothing but extraordinary praise is lavished by all the Italians I know upon the ability of the English to organize Royal events or parades or military tattoos, etc. The Italian would like to be able to do it, but he can't. It is interesting that one of the events about which the Fascist regime boasted almost above any other was that Mussolini had made trains run on time in Italy. In fact, this was considered a much more important and significant result than even the elimination of malaria from the Pontine Marshes.

In lavishing such praise upon their ruler for 22 years the Italians were acknowledging that he succeeded in getting them to do something which was almost contrary to their nature, namely to be punctual.

Elsewhere, I have already recorded the fact that the first public clock was erected in Milan in 1335 and the first astronomical clock in 1364.

- In the early part of the fourteenth century Jacopo DE' DONDI (probably born in Cremona) created the first clock moved by weights. He was a member of the same family as Giovanni DE' DONDI (see 'Astronomy'). The whole family was renowned for its clock making and commonly referred to as the 'Dondi dell'orologio'.

- Horology was born in northern Italy. Already early spring clocks existed there in 1482. Italian horology influenced the world but, after 1500, was eclipsed first by Germany and then by France.

- In 1335 the first automatic striking clock was installed in the belfry of the chapel in the Visconti Palace in Milan.

Leonardo was the first to illustrate and describe in 1490 a fusee for clocks, although fusees were known since about 1405.

- In 1704 the first jewelled watch was designed by Niccolo' FACIO.

Clubs

Generally speaking, Italians are often envious of the English, or the British as the case may be. Some envy them their monarchy and their history, others their Empire and their traditions; some are appreciative of the Mother of Parliaments, others wish they could enjoy the same civic sense and efficient bureaucracy. But all are united in envying the British their clubs: these are something that the Italian has never had.

It is true that in Italy one has the Club Nautico, or the Round Table, or some other association; but there are few, not quite so exclusive nor quite so welcoming as in Britain. In Italy, the English word 'club' is used to describe them, thus showing where they originate, but it is pronounced 'klab'. The reason for the comparative scarcity of clubs in Italy is that, on the whole, Italians are not what Dr Johnson called 'clubable' men (the *Concise Oxford Dictionary* prefers 'clubbable'), nor do they in any sense adopt the view of Addison that clubs are 'a natural and necessary offshoot of men's gregarious nature'.

It all follows from the fact that the Italians are much less gregarious than the English. Real club life could only exist in its inception and conception in England and not elsewhere.

We are taught that historically English clubs followed from the coffee houses that became established in the seventeenth century. But there were reasons why clubs became established in England to the extent and in the manner which has lasted until the Second World War. These reasons included the desire to be together with people of the same class and taste, as an outlet for conversation, as a place to drink at any time of day, as an escape from the female sex, for the reassurance provided by the continued presence of people from the same school and background whom one knows and trusts, the haven of tranquillity thus established, the ability to use smoking and billiard rooms (today, of course, it is snooker), the need to belong to a group for company or support, a genuine liking for one's fellow men, a sense of loyalty, the camaraderie of sport and, where appropriate, the political affiliations that distinguished White's from Brooks or the identification with particular strata of society like the Athenaeum and the Garrick.

All these are perfectly proper and sensible reasons why English club life became established as a male preserve. Clubs not only provided meeting places where views on society and on politics could be voiced privately, and exchanged freely, they also ensured conformity: conformity both of dress and of thought. Of course, there were leaders of dress, like Brummel, and leaders of thought, like Pitt. But the dilution of individual traits was great and the blackballing system was such as to ensure that nobody was admitted who, because of his schooling, background, family connections and attitude, would not make a jolly good fellow and not become one of the boys.

Thus clubs represented one of the major sources of strength of English society: namely, its ability to provide uniformity, to absorb and permeate, to bind together, to reinforce patriotic feeling and unity and, where necessary, to anglicise.

The requirement that individuals should conform to English manners, thought and attire, if not to Shakespeare's language, is manifested in the subtle but inexorable prescription that if strangers do not anglicise their names - as Francesco Bianco did when he became Francis White - they should at least change the Christian name to an English one. Thus Giuseppe Bonomi (architect 1739 - 1808) becomes Joseph Bonomi, Antonio Genesio Maria Panizzi becomes Sir Anthony Panizzi, Giovanni Caboto is turned into John Cabot and more recently, Giovanni Battista Barbirolli becomes Sir John Barbirolli, Carlo Forte is first Sir Charles Forte and then Lord Forte, Paolo Girolami (Chairman of Glaxo plc) becomes Sir Paul Girolami. Examples abound.

But in the case of males-only clubs, I think that Italians would find them boring. I for one can think of nothing more dreadful than having lunch or dinner or even a chat surrounded only by tailored suits. I suppose an Italian would prefer to see the warm face of a woman who displays an attractive smile and is well dressed: that is for most of us a pleasant experience. It shouldn't be believed for a moment that such a view is solely the result of a normal sexual inclination: on the contrary, it is purely a form of aesthetic appreciation. After all, is it not the case that women dress largely to

impress other women?

Be that as it may, the Italians do envy the English their clubs. More than once I have been asked by Italian visitors whether they could be taken to a truly English club. I am also aware of the pride with which some Italians - and I know more than one - make known their membership of White's or Brooks, and so on. As far as they are concerned it is, they believe, proof of their respectability and of their acceptance in British society since they are admitted to the 'sancta sanctorum'.

Whilst this reaction is understandable, I would suggest that it is totally misconceived in today's world. Most clubs are now run by committees whose assessment of candidates is on the whole reasonably superficial: provided there is a suitable introduction with adequate bank and other references, it is unlikely that an otherwise respectable member of the community would be turned away: gone are the days of blackballing, in most instances.

Present-day reality is that clubs have ceased to be havens of tranquillity where members, all of the same social strata, all of the same scholastic or university background, all of equal traditions, attire and taste, could meet in peace to discuss the political and social events of the day.

But what, you may well ask at this stage, has all this to do with the Italians?

Let me tell you.

• **The first English club, White's, was founded by an Italian, Francesco Bianco.**

This fact is recorded in the first *History of White's*.

Compiled by the Honourable Algernon Bourke of 39 St James's Street, London in 1892, this limited edition publication in two volumes (with betting book from 1743 - 1878 and a list of members from 1736 - 1892) was published by Waterlow & Sons Limited of London Wall. The document provides a full history of White's Club from its inception as the Chocolate House founded by Francis White.

Let me quote an extract from page 13.

'At the enlarged premises, White carried on the business of the Chocolate House until his death in 1711. He was buried in February of that year in St James's Church in Piccadilly and his Will shows that he was a man of some property.

'This document, executed in 1708, begins in the impressive manner usual in Wills at that time and states that the Testator is "weak and infirm in body but in sound disposing mind and memory (thanks be given to Almighty God for the same)". From it we learn that White left four children, minors, and a widow, Elizabeth, but that the rest of his connections were settled in Italy. Thus there are legacies to his sister, Angela Maria, wife of Tomaso Casanova of Verona, and to "my aunt, Nicoletta Tomasi", also settled at Verona. *It is possible that White himself was an Italian or of Italian extraction.* It is not unusual for foreigners settled in England to assume an English form of their patronymic. White may have been some Bianco or Bianchi ....'

The author goes on to say that White probably decided to take advantage of the reputation which one or two countries had established in England for their cooking.

I think the author is being unnecessarily cautious. It is *possible* that White came from Outer Mongolia, or Transylvania. As Euripides put it, it is possible that what we call death is in effect life and what we call life is really death.

But given the foregoing statements that the author himself makes, it is obvious that White was Italian: if he had come from Outer Mongolia or elsewhere his sister would not be called Angela Maria nor would his aunt be called Nicoletta Tomasi, nor would they all be living in Genoa or in Verona.

One wonders whether the psychological reluctance of the Honourable Algernon Bourke to acknowledge that White was Italian induced him into what I consider a Freudian slip, namely the use of the adjective 'possible' instead of 'probable, when he should have used in reality no qualification at all.

It is well established that Francis White was in fact Francesco Bianco or Bianchi, who was born in Verona (the home town of his sister and aunt) and who had decided to make a success in this country at a time when the drinking of coffee was spreading. (See *Royal St James's* by E. J. Burford, Robert Hale, London 1988, page 131, as well as *White's - 1693 to 1950* by Percy Colson, Heinemann, London 1951, page 16.)

In his Will White refers to himself as 'Gentleman', that is to say, a man of means, and his estate must have been substantial, judging from the size of the legacies. (For those who wish to know more, a copy of his Will is obtainable from the Public Records Office, London.)

He was probably the first of many Italians to make a good living in England out of catering to the general public.

There is no doubt that club life in England began with the establishment of White's, a London institution which antedates the Bank of England by one year, since White's Chocolate House was founded in 1693. White's Club soon developed into a gambling den where huge sums of money were ventured, mainly at faro. For example, on 21 February 1775, Sir John Bland lost £230,000 at one point (though he recovered most of it). (See *Selected letters of Horace Walpole*, edited by W. S. Lewis, Yale University Press, 1973, page 61).

Who would have imagined that the oldest and probably most respected club in London, from which most others took their cue, was founded by an Italian? But then facts which elicit amazement, astonishment and disbelief is the recurring theme of this book!

Contraception

The modern methods of contraception, all prompted by the feminist priority that woman rather than man should be in control of the birth-giving function - thus, it is commonly believed, becoming at long last emancipated from her slavery to man - have greatly contributed to the spread of sexually-transmitted diseases. This was apparent even before the latest AIDS scare. It can hardly be a coincidence that at the same time crimes of violence against women and young girls have increased dramatically.

There must be a moral somewhere in this situation: perhaps one should not divorce the function of procreation from that of pleasure; perhaps, at the very moment that the parties determine that the act of intercourse should have as its primary aim their mutual enjoyment rather than the essential, natural life-giving finality for which it was developed, the act itself ceases to be of any real significance by eliminating the risk of pregnancy and by transforming the woman from the cradle of humanity she has always been to a receptacle of dubious enjoyment for multifarious partners; perhaps, at that very same moment, man ceases to consider woman as the potential mother of his children and looks upon her in the same way as he would an object or tool by which he can more efficiently pander to his pleasures; perhaps Marie Stopes did not, after all, quite understand the consequences of her insistence that woman should be mistress over her own body; perhaps we are none of us masters of our bodies anyhow, but mere tools in the hands of nature; perhaps society will one day determine that women should decide once and for all whether to be givers of pleasure or fountains of life, classing them, helping them, taxing them and treating them accordingly. To do so would certainly make relationships between the sexes clearer.

But I digress - again!

Let me get to the fact that I wish to record. I shall not say that methods of birth control were invented by an Italian because it is not the case. The oldest recorded medical recipes to prevent conception are to be found in Egyptian papyri. Ancient Greece

and Rome, as well as Islam, were well aware of contraceptive techniques. But it is to an Italian that we owe the invention of the condom.

● **At some time in the sixteenth century Gabriele FALLOPPIO (born in Modena) designed a medicated linen sheath for use by the man. (See 'Medicine' p.114.)**

In 1564 Falloppio published in Padova his book *De Morbo Gallico* where the use of sheaths made in Italy of fine linen, and later of isinglass and the caecum intestine of the lamb, was recorded (V. Havelock Ellis *Sex in Relation to Society* - 1921 Edition, p. 599). Casanova, according to his memoirs, used Falloppio's condoms about a century later. Not too successfully, though, for Casanova - if his memoirs are to be believed - had nine bouts of venereal disease of some sort or other; but they did not seem to trouble him unduly. He appeared to look upon them more as a war veteran would his battle scars.

'Cave Luem,' my biology teacher used to say, which roughly translated means 'Watch out for syphilis'. Nowadays, I suppose we would say 'Seek some aid to prevent AIDS'. Nothing changes, really.

May I add that I am old enough to recall the days when brothels existed in Italy (we closed them down in or about 1949, following the example of France that, first amongst western countries, had closed them down in 1946).

Feminists had campaigned for the dignity of woman. I consider that such dignity is more debased nowadays by newspapers, TV and magazine pornography than it ever was in the days when a particular kind of behaviour was catered for and controlled.

I am sure that there was very much less venereal disease in Italy in the days when brothels were run in supervised form by the State, than there is in the last decade of the twentieth century, when contraception of the more progressive and liberated kind has become freely available to all.

Finally, I cannot resist the temptation of

CONFESSION

CONFESSIONE

Io sono onesto.

Non si preoccupi, vedrà che ci sarà
un'amnistia.

"I am an honest man."
"Don't worry, there will soon be an amnesty."

mentioning one thought that recurs as a result of contraception and it is this: I wonder how southern Italians now manage when they go looking for a wife. Let me explain.

It has long been an established practice in southern Italy that what was called a woman's honour was of fundamental importance. People killed for it and people searched for it long after it ceased to be a normal commodity.

The average southern Italian would not as a rule marry a girl who did not reach the marital chamber inviolate. He must have wondered at the custom reported by Marco Polo about the Tibetans, namely, that in that country no-one would marry a virgin on the principle that a wife is worth nothing if she has not had intercourse with other men: there, the more she has known, the more appreciated she is. But perhaps southern Italians have not read *Il Milione* because the search for virginity is a well-established feature of their mentality (or rather, was) and is the result of a number of causes and traditions, some practical, some religious, of which the following may serve as examples.

The principal reason, I believe, is that the male looked upon the woman as a chattel. Not for nothing we have in Italy the saying 'choose your wife from the same places where you choose your oxen'. The equation of woman with a thing is perfectly clear. An interesting analogy is to be found in the purchase of cars: on the whole - and I appreciate that this is a generalisation of the type that I have tried to avoid - Italians have not, until very recently, been inclined to buy second-hand motor cars. They prefer them new, in the same way as they prefer their woman to be new.

The second reason is the basic selfishness of the Italian male. Selfishness perhaps is too harsh a term: I suppose he feels the defloration of his wife provides the same sensation as the climbing of Everest for the first time. There was nobody there before him.

This is an understandable reaction, no matter how unpopular it may be with feminists.

The next reason is possibly a rationalisation of an instinct, but it is that a woman who has not had previous sexual experiences is less capable of analysing the ability or otherwise of her partner. This not only makes it easier for the man because his performance is subject to less stringent standards and criticisms, but it also provides greater peace of mind for the woman since she cannot miss what she has never had; and to that extent it may, although it need not, even strengthen the marital bond.

There is also the question of hygiene. This is now widely discussed throughout the world but it has always been very much at the forefront of people's minds in Italy, especially in the south. Apart from syphilis, which is inherited, I think I am right in saying that until the advent of AIDS, there were no other sexually-transmitted diseases that could be passed on by a woman who had not previously had intercourse with other men.

These are some of the reasons: there may be others. But I have little doubt that all of them have contributed to the creation of a culture which has imposed virginity. A culture which has drawn a very clear dividing line between the woman who will be the mother of one's children and the woman who will merely provide a sexual diversion; a culture that recognised, until after the Second World War, that human frailty had to be catered for by a particular type of woman in a particular type of establishment: hence the comparative success of the brothel in Italy. A culture that has attributed to the Italian mother an importance which has resulted in her being venerated well beyond any limit imposed by her own limitations as one. And this type of culture has been reflected in Italian art and literature generally. The distinction between sacred and profane love is an often repeated motif which proceeds from a clear-cut assessment of humanity and its weaknesses. As has been observed so many times, the Italian has a tendency to put motherhood on a pedestal.

As I have remarked, I feel sorry for the southern Italian male. I heard it said recently by one of them that the gospel should now be adapted to say that it is easier for a camel to go through the eye of a needle than for a virgin to be found in Italy at the altar. Which brings to mind the joke about the Sicilian boy who, just after the marriage ceremony and before departing with his bride for their honeymoon, is seen by his male friends busily painting a particular part of his anatomy with green paint. When asked by them what he is doing, he replies in all seriousness: 'If she looks even mildly surprised, I shall kill her.'

Cryptology, Cryptography & Cryptanalysis

They were known to all ancient people; the Greeks and the Romans used ciphers extensively.

Modern cryptography, however, was born in Italy. By the thirteenth century the Papal State had already begun using ciphered correspondence. The 'Fibonacci' system which was set up in 1202 is now used extensively in all ciphers (see 'Mathematics'.) Indeed, it is amazing to consider that even today espionage depends on a form of arithmetic first evolved by an Italian more than nine centuries ago. (If you are in any doubt about this statement, see *Spycatcher*, Viking 1987 Edition, page 179.)

• In 1379 Gabriele de LAVINDE (born in Parma) published the world's first manual on cryptography.

Lavinde's manual is still available in the Vatican archives. It is fairly elementary.

• In 1411 Luigi PASINI (born in Venice) established his own cipher.

Refinement came in 1470 with the publication by Leon Battista ALBERTI of his book *Trattati in cifra*, which was followed in 1563 by Giovanni Battista DELLA PORTA' own treatise on the same subject.

• In 1474 Sicco SIMONETTA set down for the first time rules of cryptanalytic procedure.

Dictionaries

• In 1502 Ambrogio CALEPINO (born in Bergamo) compiled the first dictionary.

Calepino's dictionary was so popular that at the time, and for many years thereafter the word 'calepin' in English was used as a synonym for dictionary.

Diplomacy

Italians are not always good strategists, but on the whole they are exceptionally good tacticians. In a negotiation where diplomats are brought in, the strategy is already laid down for them; they are left to deal with tactics. That is why I think Italians have always been successful diplomats.

In addition, there is the question of manner and suavite. There is also the lack of dogmatism and the ability to see a number of sides to each argument Furthermore, a healthy dose of cynicism is essential. All these are qualities which, generally speaking, the Italians have in abundance.

Finally, for a diplomat, the Italian has an outstanding virtue because on the whole he will never really, in any negotiation, slam a door shut in the face of his opponent. He will certainly push it hard, but he will always leave a little bit of it open. And that I think is fundamental for a diplomat worth his salt. Indeed, one can think of a number of present-day politicians and leaders whose careers might well have developed much more successfully had they adopted a less dogmatic and doctrinaire approach to their dealings.

The Italian bankers who were so successful in London in the fifteenth and sixteenth centuries must have been born diplomats in any event to survive. One thinks also of all the clerics sent out from Rome by the Church to different parts of the world.

● In 1588 Alberico GENTILI (born at San Ginesio) wrote the first known treatise on international law, the *De Jure Belli*. He had spent some time as a Professor of Law at Oxford and in this book he deals generally with the finer points of war and peace.

● Prior to that, in 1585 Gentili had written his *De Legationibus* which, based on his lectures at Oxford, was the first text book on diplomacy. He dedicated it to Sir Philip Sidney whom he considered the ideal Ambassador.

● The first diplomat ever to be on record (and here I am ignoring the numerous Venetian ambassadors and spies) was Guido BENTIVOGLIO (born at Ferrara) who in 1607 went to Flanders as the first accredited papal nuncio.

Education

Nobody can accuse us of not having been at the forefront in the establishment of educational institutions even though, ironically, we may have failed to educate ourselves properly. For example, no matter where they were founded, all universities stem from the colleges of students and teachers that became established in Italy at the beginning of the eleventh century. That is to say, long before any other country ever thought of the concept of 'education'.

● **There is no doubt that the oldest university in the world is that of Bologna.**

According to the Italians, and to Volume R - X - page 1004 of *Britannica*, it was founded around the year 1000. But *Britannica* seems to be in some doubt about it because in Volume 6, page 337 and in Volume R - I - page 131, it claims that Bologna University was founded in the year 1158. But I don't suppose this matters very much.

● **Paris University was founded 22 years later, in 1180. There then followed the University of Perugia which was founded in 1200. This was closely followed by the University of Vicenza which was founded in 1204. Cambridge followed in 1209, the University of Arezzo in 1215, Padova in 1222, and Oxford, finally, in 1229.**

Padova is interesting because, contrary to some of the other Italian universities, it soon became known for its very liberal tradition ('patavina libertas'). For example, Protestants were unmolested there and the only other city in Italy which at that time was so liberal, at least as regards religious thinking, was Venice (which, however, did not have a university until much later).

● **The University of Naples and that of Salerno were both founded in 1224, Vercelli in 1228, Ferrara in 1264, Florence in 1321 and Pavia in 1362.**

I must not ignore Scotland and Ireland and I should add that the University of St Andrew was founded in 1412 and that of Dublin in 1591, as can be verified under the same reference as for Cambridge and Oxford.

(There is a great deal to be said about the first medical school at Salerno but that is provided under 'Medicine'.)

- In 1400 Pietro Paolo VERGERIO wrote the first significant exclusively paedagogical treatise and contributed to the development of humanism at Padua University.
- One of the first acknowledged educators was Guarino BARZIZZA.
- In 1444 the architect Leon Battista ALBERTI published his *Trattato della Famiglia* which was the first manual on family life.

Alberti's book deals with marriage, marital harmony, the education of children, the economic resources of the group and the citizen's duties to his family and to the State. It is not good reading for exasperated feminists although I suppose even they would be prepared to make allowances for the fact that it was written over 500 years ago. He is clearly a misogynist but then, perhaps, so are, deep down, the Italians, even though they may not readily admit to it.

- In 1894 Maria MONTESSORI (born at Chiaravalle AN) founded the Montessori method which, as most educators know, is still in use today.
- The first encyclopaedia ever to be compiled is ascribed to Domenico BANDINI in the fifteenth century.
- Bandini's encyclopaedia did not have an index. The first compiler of an index for encyclopaedias was Antonio ZARA in 1614.

Gemstones

- In the early seventeenth century Vincenzo PERUZZI (born in Florence) was the first to cut diamonds to make brilliants, by inventing the 58-facet form.
- In 1669 Nicola STENO was the first to note the regularity and constancy of facial angles of crystals.

In 1694 Averami and Targioni fused a diamond at the focus of a burning glass.

Glass

The glasses of Venice are particularly well known and no visit to Venice is complete, it is said, without a short excursion to the island of Murano.

- Colourless glass was first achieved by the Venetians.

In the year 1000 AD or thereabouts the Venetians first developed their glass-making techniques. They later moved out to the island of Murano, either to avoid causing fires on the mainland or to keep their techniques more secret and safe.

In 1530 they first developed their 'cristallo'-type glass, which some twenty years later they allowed on patent to dealers in Belgium.

The success of Venice in this field prompted many to try and steal its secrets. A number of Venetian workers were enticed away to foreign countries, including England where the Duke of Buckingham employed them in his glass works.

Lighthouses and Lighting

- The 'Lanterna' at Genoa was probably the first lighthouse of the modern world (apart from the lighthouse at Alexandria in Egypt, which was built in 285 BC and was visible for over 40 miles).

- In 1603 the first investigation of luminescence (by studying barium sulphate) was made by an Italian cobbler called Vincenzo CASCARIOLO (born in Bologna).

The Cascariolo research is a classic instance of the versatility of the Italian people. Here we have an ordinary cobbler who goes to the trouble of investigating luminescence. The Italians, in fact, will turn their hands to anything and will improvise on anything. We often make a mess of it but sometimes we have flashes of real inspiration. And herein lies the genius of the Italian people.

In the case of Cascariolo, he found near his home town white stones of barium sulphate and synthesized from them a material which, after exposure to the sun by day, glowed at night. He was an alchemist as well as a cobbler and it may be that he thought that he had found at last the philosopher's stone that would enable him to turn things into gold. He had not: all he had found was the mineral barite.

Illumination of public buildings was also fairly well developed in Italy at an early date. Certainly by the beginning of the nineteenth century, the technique of using reflectors was well established. In one of his 'Letters to his Parents' - 24 June 1845 - Ruskin records a celebration at the Ponte Vecchio in Florence where apart from 'the arches of the bridges all lighted around and the innumerable boats gliding about with lamps', he found the illumination of the cathedral dome and of the Palazzo Vecchio 'very noble because of the use by the locals of lamps with strong reflectors to throw the light on the walls.'

But long before that, Goethe (*Italian Journey*, 30 June 1787) had remarked on the spectacular illuminations in Rome to celebrate the feast of St Peter and St Paul. It was, says Goethe, 'like a scene from fairyland'; the spectacle of St Peter's colonnade and dome outlined in fire prompted him to suggest 'that nothing like it could be seen anywhere else in the world'. The brilliance of the lighting was so great that 'the moonlight was eclipsed'.

Manners

- In the year 1513 Baldassarre CASTIGLIONE (born at Casatico MN) wrote *Il Cortegiano*. It was a book that was to have an enormous impact upon England. It was the first book of manners but it also dealt with the relationship between the courtesan and the prince and it was used by young members of the English establishment until the days of Edward VII as their bible on manners.

Thus states the *Encyclopaedia Britannica* more or less paraphrased by me. But the contribution of Baldassarre Castiglione goes beyond that.

He had visited England when Henry VIII had made the Duke of Urbino (the town in which Castiglione lived) a knight of the most noble order of the Garter. One wonders whether he could ever realise when he was here, what impact he was going to have.

Henry VIII knew Italian and spoke it and was very keen to maintain close contacts with the Italian Courts of the Renaissance. Apart from his disagreements in religious and political matters, he seems to have got on quite well with the Italians. His son Edward had an Italian riding master and Elizabeth was taught Italian at an early age; it was an Italian, Polidoro VIRGILIO, who wrote a history of England for him and was rewarded by being made Archdeacon of Wells Cathedral. It is suggested that his *Anglicae Historiae* were absorbed in Holinshed's *Chronicles* and as such contributed quite a lot of material to Shakespeare who relied upon the latter publication.

But there is no doubt that at this particular time there were many Italians in London,

MUSSOLINI DOGMA

MUSSOLINI A DONGO

Eccolo lì, voleva fuggire travestito da tedesco, è un vile!

Già, ma siamo un popolo che, di questo vile, ha avuto paura per vent'anni.

"There he is, the coward, he wanted to escape by dressing up as a German."
"That may be so, but what about us — a people who has been afraid of this coward for 20 years."

whether artists or craftsmen, secretaries or Court musicians, writers, doctors and even lawyers. As we shall see later, at or about the same time as Castiglione's *Il Cortegiano* appeared, there was published Machiavelli's *The Prince* and in the same general period there was started the course of training for English gentlemen, or otherwise, namely the grand tour to Italy. It did not start initially as so grand a tour as it became later in the eighteenth century but the Italian universities were well known; and it was part of the curriculum of good breeding that English gentlemen should spend a few terms at one of them, thus acquiring the polish and refinement for which Italy was in those days held in the highest esteem.

That in so doing they should acquire also the bad manners of the Italians is not surprising; it is impossible to copy only the good without being tainted by the bad of any culture. The ideas and morals that some of these English gentlemen brought back provoked scandal to the extent that the English adopted the saying which originated in Italy and not in England, namely that 'The Italianate Englishman is the devil incarnate.' I am sure that is an exaggeration; I suppose all it shows is that it is a mistake to ape others. (Lord Burghley said that in Italy young men would learn nothing but pride, blasphemy and atheism.)

Certainly, however, by the time Roger Ascham wrote his book *The Schoolmaster* (Constable 1935) Baldassarre Castiglione was only too well known.

Ascham wrote between 1563 and 1568. To show how much impact Castiglione had at the time let me quote an excerpt from what Ascham has to say in *The Schoolmaster* about *Il Cortegiano*:

'Which book, diligently followed, but one year at home in England, would do a young gentleman more good than three years travel abroad spent in Italy.' (p. 66)

Ascham was in a difficulty. He did not object to what Castiglione said, because all that Castiglione says is admirable. But he certainly did not like Italy.

Another example: 'Italy now is not that Italy that it was wont to be; and therefore now not so fit a place as some do count it for young men to fetch either wisdom or honesty from it.' (p. 72) I suppose the same is true even today...

On the other hand, this attitude of Ascham's is probably understandable because he hated popery and therefore he hated Italy. How he could possibly reach the conclusions he did about Italy as he had only spent 9 days there (p. 83) escapes me.

The Schoolmaster is divided into 'books'. The first book deals with the bringing up of youth and the second with the ready way to the Latin tongue. He then spends 86 pages to vilify Italy but 80 pages to praise the Latin tongue, almost as though you could have one without the other.

But he certainly did not like Italy. (p. 83):

'I was once in Italie my selfe; but I thank God, my abode there was but ix daes; and yet I sawe in that little tyme in one citie more liberti to sinne then euer I heard tell of in our noble citie of London in ix yeare.'

Nor was he alone in criticising the all pervasive Italian influence on the England of the sixteenth century. One cannot help recalling that Shakespeare himself - who as we shall see later, owed much to Italy - had to complain about the slavish acceptance of Italian culture. (See *Richard II*, Act 2, Scene 1, Line 21: '...proud Italy, whose manners still our tardy apish nation limps after, in base imitation.') The fame of the Italian courtiers is recorded elsewhere by Shakespeare. For example, he says in *Cymbeline* (Act 1, Scene 1, Line 103): 'Your Italy contains none so accomplished a courtier to convince the honour of my mistress.'

The Italian puppet theatre was beginning to take over in London. About one century later, in 1662, *Pulcinella* made its London debut, and stayed to this day in the title of the magazine 'Punch'.

● **In 1550 Giovanni Della CASA (born in Mugello) wrote *Il Galateo*, the first etiquette manual.**

This book became quite well known in England but it never acquired the popularity of nor did it have the same impact as *Il Cortegiano*.

• **The handkerchief was invented in Italy during the Renaissance.**

• **Eau-de-Cologne was invented by Giovanni FARINA. He was born in 1685 in southern Italy and in 1709 he settled in Cologne in Germany where he reproduced certain experiments that he had been carrying out in his home town of Reggio Calabria. He based the scent on the essence of bergamot.**

The art of creating perfumes goes back a long way in history. Nobody can claim that the Italians were first in developing perfumes because that would not be true. But there is certainly one additional first connected with perfumes, and that is a literary one.

• **In 1548 the Florentine Agnolo FIRENZUOLA, a monk (who had received dispensation from his vows), and a man of letters, wrote the book *Dialogo Della Bellezza Delle Donne*, a discourse on the beauty of women.**

In it he provides for the first time full descriptions of what he considered to be the ideal Renaissance Beauty and he establishes himself as the first writer of a manual on beauty. According to him, the classic Tuscan gentlewoman had a white face, fair hair, ebony eyebrows and thin, short eyelashes.

Her eyes were carefully painted, her ears were touched up in the colour of pomegranate seeds and her cheeks had a slight vermilion paint applied but, as he says, not too much.

Rouge was to be used discreetly, particularly on the mouth; the intention was not to make the mouth too sensual a part of the body. It was left to Casanova to describe in rather more sensual terms the need for women to apply lipstick liberally to heighten men's desires.

The Medici tradition in Florence encouraged the arts but also fashion styles; men of the period, as appears from a well-known painting by Bronzino, were known to pluck their eyebrows in the feminine manner.

Finally, the Medici family were great supporters of the perfumery industry. With funds advanced by the Medicis the Dominican monks of Santa Maria Novella established in 1508 what was to become one of the most celebrated perfumeries in Europe. Their 'spezieria' was located in the cloisters of the church where rooms were open to the public, each containing different products, some of which were made from plants and herbs grown in the garden annexed to the church itself. It must have been almost an inconsistent sight to see the monks as apothecaries.

And to conclude under this heading, it should be noted that the umbrella is recorded as having been in use in Italy as early as 1578 (Carter p. 179). Its first mention in England occurs in a comedy by Ben Johnson in 1616.

Section 9:
Politics & War

Atom Bomb

• In 1934 Enrico FERMI (born in Rome) developed the theory of beta radioactivity.

• In 1942 FERMI elaborated mathematical statistics for atomic phenomena, discovered neutron-induced radioactivity and directed the first controlled nuclear reaction, which was really the heart of the modern reactor, thus becoming the father of the atom bomb.

● In 1942 FERMI also gave his name to the neutrino and in 1950 was made a Fellow of The Royal Society.

On the campus at Chicago University there is a monument to him with a plaque indicating the spot where he first split the atom.

It is interesting to find such a major contribution by an Italian to what ended up by being the most powerful weapon ever used in war.

Although it is true that Leonardo and Galileo helped their masters to develop machinery of attack and defence, it is a fact that Italians on the whole are not enamoured of war. This is not so much because Italians lack discipline or courage; it is much more because their cynicism prevents them from believing with sufficient conviction in any particular cause to the point where they are forced on the one hand to run the risk of losing life or limb and on the other of being distracted from their main pursuit, namely the enjoyment of life and the pursuit of pleasure.

Bureaucracy

It is hardly surprising that it was founded in Italy where it has become a curse upon the country.

Italian bureaucracy is accused of being inefficient and corrupt. It is, of course, both, but that is easily explicable.

It is inefficient because too many incompetent people are recruited who have to justify their existence in their posts. They are all poorly rewarded and therefore easily open to corruption. The mentality of officials is medieval.

However, it is clearly not the case that bureaucracy is corrupt only in Italy. It is patently corrupt in Italy; it is latently corrupt in other countries.

As I have said before, the corruptibility point is merely a function of one's general appetite and the amount of food that is available to one's family. It is quite easy to do a job without having to insist that bribes should be offered when one is in a position of power, so to say, or if one has enough to eat. It is easy to be honest when your wallet is full of bank notes. Not so easy to be generous, because wealth often engenders meanness. But certainly, the temptations are fewer when one is not too badly off or, put another way, the point at which one yields to temptation becomes more difficult to achieve.

Corruption is universal and it produces the same results wherever it operates.

There is corruption which is brought about by monetary inducements and there is social corruption; the former is fairly widespread in Italy, the latter is perfectly normal in England. It is surprising what an Oxford or Cambridge or equivalent education, the right accent, membership of the right school or club or freemasonry, can achieve in England that money cannot; and some perfectly respectable bureaucrats here would consider themselves affronted if offered monetary inducements who succumb daily to the blandishments of an accent or to membership of the right club.

In England there is the old boy network; in Italy it is the poor boy network. Corruption occurs everywhere; it is merely dressed up differently. What, however, is thoroughly objectionable about corruption in Italy is that it has become a way of life. Everyone expects everyone else to be corrupt; and corruption is proffered quite openly, as though it were the most natural thing in the world.

● 1390 can be taken as the date of origin of bureaucracy in the western world. It was invented by Gian Galeazzo VISCONTI at his Milan court when he created a special class of paid clerks and secretaries for various departments of his court. They kept ledgers regarding income, expenditure and taxes and dealt with his correspondence.

Politics and Power

- The political writer 'par excellence' was Niccolo' MACHIAVELLI (born in Florence, 1469). He is the founder of political and analytical science in Europe. He popularised the concept of state in his book *The Prince* and took state sovereignty for granted.

No-one influenced the arts of politics and of government to a greater degree than did Machiavelli. His outspokenness was a fundamental teaching for leaders of all time.

He was responsible for the popularisation of a theory, which he never really meant, that the end justifies the means. As a result, his name has ever since been used in a pejorative context which has been associated with Italy. Contrary to popular belief, he was in fact a patriot and behind his cynicism his heart beat for a united Italy.

- Machiavelli's work was continued by Giuseppe GUICCIARDINI (born in Florence) but, although they were both Florentines, they did not have very much in common.

Guicciardini had no patriotic heart. He did however have one great merit: he was the first historian who, in his *Storia d'Italia*, considered his country against the backcloth of what was happening in the rest of Europe. No other historian before him ever looked beyond national boundaries.

- Gaetano MOSCA (born in Palermo) elaborated the concept of a ruling minority present in all societies - whether military, priestly, oligarchic or aristocratic (whether by wealth or by merit).

Mosca proceeded from the premise that majority rule was, in reality, a fiction. His main work (*Teorica*) published in 1925, was seized upon by Fascists who failed to understand the points he was making.

Another first, but one can take little pride in it. In the 1920s Mussolini began talking about his 'ferocious, totalitarian will'. This was a phrase that was coined to represent a new kind of tyranny in which the State was everything and the individual nothing, compared to which the tyrranies of the past faded into insignificance.

The new political creed proceeded in theory from support of the masses who, instead of being enlisted to support democracy, were indoctrinated with concepts of tyranny.

Because of Italy's historical background (and although Mussolini could not be taken seriously - his ability to be both a bully and a clown was a serious handicap in the historical context) Fascism became quite successful there and represented the inspiration and the model for totalitarianism throughout Europe. The list of people who followed it is long: Dollfuss in Austria, Pilsudski in Poland, Horthy in Hungary, Salazar in Portugal and Franco in Spain. But in its most original form totalitarianism settled in Nazi Germany and Bolshevik Russia.

- In 1957 Enrico MATTEI (born at Matelica) was the first to negotiate separate oil treaties with Third World countries.

He founded the Italian National Hydrocarbon Agency, ENI, and the petrol company AGIP, represented by the six-legged dog breathing fire on a yellow background which must be well known to anyone who has travelled through Italy. Whether his death in 1962 in a plane crash was an accident or not remains a question mark.

AGIP were the first petrol company in Europe to provide a comprehensive range of services at their petrol filling stations and more particularly to endeavour to maintain a high standard of cleanliness in their toilet facilities. The standard thus set has been imitated ever since, as have the bar, restaurant and motel facilities that Mattei originated.

According to Luigi Barzini (*The Italians*, Penguin 1964, p. 141) the political cartoon is attributable to an Italian. Barzini discovered that in the middle of the fourteenth century the Roman tribune, Cola di Rienzo, had pictures painted on walls to make political points.

Trade Unions

• **Trade Unions were founded in Italy during the Renaissance with the establishment of the 'Arti' and the 'Confederazioni' of the principal Italian cities.**

I have been unable to find any authenticated record of strikes (lawful or unlawful by modern standards) during that period.

But there was a first 'go-slow' in Florence in 1424 when the masons employed by Brunelleschi on the construction of the Duomo complained about his methods of building and the fact that he was a hard task-master. (see 'Architecture' and 'Time and Motion Studies'.) In 1428, for example, he had no qualms whatsoever about dismissing 25 master masons who objected to the new work practices that he planned to introduce.

Treaties

• **In November 1190 the first recorded peace treaty ever concluded by England**

was with Tancred, King of Sicily. It was a Charter of Peace with a foreign power that took effect immediately and was intended to last forever.

Although it is by no means a first, it is interesting to note that on 15 May 1367, another treaty was entered into by England with Italy. Here, the term 'Italy', of course, is a misnomer, since Italy did not become a political entity until 1870. The treaty, in fact, was with Milan and related to the marriage of the Duke of Clarence with Princess Violanta of Milan.

War

It is my firm belief that taken as a whole, the Italians are less warlike and less feudal than most other people. For twenty-two years Mussolini tried to inculcate into them a more militaristic spirit, but failed. Fascist Italy had the 'Cubs', the 'Balillas', the young 'avant-garde' members of the Fascist party. The uniforms might have been pretty and enjoyable, but the spirit wasn't there. The Italians are too resentful of authority and their historical development has made them highly suspicious of military power.

Machiavelli called all foreigners 'barbarians'. Our culture was such that all these barbarians who invaded us failed conspicuously to imbue the Italian spirit with their love of war and of chivalry. Feudal life and feudal hierarchies did not become settled in Italy at any time. As a result, the country was able to move out of the darkness of the Middle Ages faster than any other people in Europe.

The drawback, assuming it to be a drawback, was that when it did so, Italians were politicians, artists and scientists, but not soldiers. Our armies never meant very much.

If anything, Italians are sailors, but not soldiers. The four maritime Italian

Republics (Pisa, Genoa, Amalfi and Venice) made an enormous contribution to sailing, discoveries and politics. The next time you sun yourself in the Balearic Islands you may care to remember that Pisan sailors occupied them as far back as the year 1115. They had been preceded as conquerors by the Carthaginians (Mahon in Menorca takes its name from the Carthaginian General, Mago) and by the Romans.

As is commonly known, Venice left its mark throughout the Mediterranean, particularly in Cyprus and Crete and most notably in Heraklion, Rhethymnon, Chania and, to a lesser extent, Ierapetra in Crete.

Machiavelli, who knew the Italians well, in ending his The Prince complained that they were intolerant of authority and could not fight well together. He said: 'Look at the duels and the combats between a few, how the Italians are superior in strength, in skill, in inventiveness; but when it is a matter of armies, they do not compare. All this because of the weakness of the leaders. Those who are capable are not obeyed. Everyone imagines he is competent'. (I am quoting from George Bull's translation of The Prince in the Penguin Classics Edition.) It is the very last sentence of what has been transcribed that is so revealing.

Even so, we have had some bright ideas:

• In 1326 Rinaldo Di VILLAMAGNA (born in Florence) developed the 'Bombarda', the first metal cannon that fired iron bullets.

A Florentine ordinance of that same year represents the earliest unequivocal evidence of the existence of such a weapon.

By definition, the 'bombarda' presupposed the existence of gunpowder at that time, for its explosion propelled the 'bomba', or projectile. If, which seems unproved still, the Chinese invented gunpowder as they claim, they did not use it in weapons before the Italians. However, it must be admitted that this still remains a contentious issue.

• In 1450 Bartolomeo COLLEONI (born at Salza BG) invented the gun-train.

• In the fifteenth century pistols were first manufactured in Pistoia, hence their name. There is also a later (1540) attribution of this invention to the gunsmith Camillo VETTELLI, also of Pistoia.

• In 1475 Bartolomeo COLLEONI pioneered artillery tactics by getting artillery to fire from the rear through gaps left by the infantry.

• In 1512 Niccolo' TARTAGLIA (born in Brescia), the mathematician, originated the science of ballistics.

• In 1550 the Viceroy of Naples, the Duke D'AVALOS, worked out the concept of calibre.

• In 1588 Agostino RAMELLI (born at Maranza) wrote a book describing all sorts of machines that could be used for war-like purposes.

Ramelli had a successful army career as engineer-in-chief to the Duc d'Anjou, later Henry III of France, for whom he designed equipment.

His inventions ranged from pumps, derricks and sawmills to continuous bucket conveyors and even an amphibious armoured vehicle. All his machines used water power and he elaborated on the conversion of rotary to reciprocal power, and all were meant for military use. Not all his ideas could be put into practice, as most of them were well in advance of his times and no tooling was then available for the kind of fine work that they necessitated. Nevertheless, his work Le Diverse et Artificiose Macchine, represents a landmark in technical publishing.

In 1588 Ramelli described a new roller mill and that same year, together with Veranzio, mechanised bolting mills.

A wire link-type driving chain was also first mentioned by him.

• By 1495 a blow-gun known as 'Cerbottana' was in use in Italy. In 1605 Leonardo invented the airgun, thus allowing his compatriot, Bartolomeo Crescenzio, to design a much more powerful weapon with a stronger spring.

- In 1750 Duke Alfonso the Second D'ESTE invented the gun case.

- In 1835 Giovanni CAVALLI (born in Novara) developed rear-loading guns and rifled barrels.

- In 1846 Ascanio SOBRERO (born in Turin) discovered nitroglycerine.

- The first military application in aeroplanes of Marconi's wireless system occurred in September 1915.

On that occasion Marconi and his life-long friend and colleague Luigi Solari (who had helped Marconi in the development of a more efficient Coherer) fitted the then still elementary Marconi apparatus to an Italian two-seater military bi-plane in which Solari flew as radio operator, communicating with Marconi who remained on the ground.

Section 10:
Sport & Travel

America

- Italians discovered America and gave it its name.

We were all taught at school that America was discovered in 1492 by Christopher Columbus and that it was named after Amerigo Vespucci who followed him in 1497 and who made known to the world the fact that it was not the Indies, but a new continent.

We are now told that it is possible that what we were taught at school was not correct and that, just as Shakespeare was an Italian, or a Russian, America had been discovered previously by the Venetians or the Vikings, or some 10,000 years ago, by migrant Asians.

We are finally told that even in the event that it was Columbus who discovered America, he was not an Italian but he was a Jew; or a Spaniard; or a Spanish Jew.

For the sake of what follows, however, I shall assume that he was an Italian born in Genoa and known as Cristoforo Colombo who, after sailing from Spain in three little ships made available to him by the Spaniards, discovered America. When he set out from Palos, he did not mean to discover America because he was looking for a through sea route westwards to the Indies. It could be said that, like all Italians, he did not really know what he was doing even though he had the benefit of the use of a compass, invented by another Italian (Flavio Gioia), who had got the idea from the Arabs.

It does seem to be a national failing of the Italians that they make great discoveries without always realising exactly the implications of what they are doing and, even though they may understand the significance quite well, once they have made the discovery they cease to be interested.

I have, of course, the greatest respect for Christopher Columbus, whoever he was. The next time I am in Pavia I shall certainly go to the university library there and stare at his ashes; that is where the Italians claim they are preserved. I know that there is an alternative claim that they are to be found in the Cathedral in Santo Domingo: who knows? The Spaniards maintain that his remains are to be found in Seville Cathedral where he was initially buried in 1506. They admit that in 1536 his bones were removed to Santo Domingo from where they travelled firstly to Havana Cathedral and thence to Santiago De Compostela, ending ultimately in Seville Cathedral in 1902.

FLAVIO GIOIA

FLAVIO GIOIA

Dò la bussola al Paese che più
spesso la perderà.

**"I'm busy discovering the compass for the country
that will most often lose its bearings and direction."**

Archaeology

• The first fully documented tomb robber (would you believe!) was Giovanni Battista BELZONI (born in Padova). He started his career as a tomb robber in 1817 on the 'instructions' of the British Museum. He discovered the tomb of Seti The First, stole the obelisk from Philae (only to have it taken away from him at gunpoint by the French) and provided more than two dozen principal Egyptian antiquities for the British Museum.

Indeed, most of what is best in the Egyptian Galleries of the British Museum (the Young Memnon, the Pharaoh's Queen from Abu Simbel, the Figures of Sekhmet, the Head of Thothmes The Third, and the statues of Ramses The First) were all stolen from Egypt by Belzoni.

He can be said to have laid the foundations of the English school of Egyptology; he certainly established a worldwide interest in Egyptology which has lasted to this day. His father was a barber; he himself started out in life playing in fairs and fairgrounds as a pantomime giant and as a conjurer. A typical, larger-than-life Italian character who died young at the age of 45 and whose work, if one can put it that way, is extensively described in Stanley Mayes's book *The Great Belzoni* (Putman, London 1959).

He was throughout his life much concerned about plagiarism. But Belzoni was not to be defeated: he carved his name in permanent fashion on anything he found and wherever he went.

You will be reminded of him if you visit the Sir John Soane Museum in London, for on display there is the Sarcophagus of Seti The First which Belzoni obtained for Sir John Soane, a patron of the arts, who is said to have been so delighted with it that as soon as it was installed in his house he gave a party for all his friends to celebrate the event; the party lasting three days. We were in 1817, approximately 3,137 years after the burial of the Pharaoh.

A few years before Belzoni had embarked upon his plundering, another Italian, Gian Battista Lusieri - an illustrator and painter - had been employed by Lord Elgin to take possession of the metopes from the Parthenon, then under the control of the Turks.

The task was handled much more carelessly by Lusieri than by Belzoni and history has still to decide whether Lord Elgin was a lover of Greece and of its antiquities, who only acted out of the best possible motives, or whether, in taking possession of what clearly did not belong either to him or to Britain, he was abusing his position as His Majesty's Ambassador and displaying the well-known acquisitiveness of the English in the artistic field, putting it into practice with the help of an Italian.

If, as appears to be the case, taking possession of the Elgin Marbles in 1801 was the result of bribery of the local Turkish officials (at that time, Greece was under Turkish occupation) there is little doubt that when the committee of the House of Commons in 1816 awarded Lord Elgin the sum of £35,000 for his efforts by almost the narrowest possible majority (82 votes in favour, 80 against) they were swayed by considerations more of an acquisitive than of an historical and artistic nature.

This is not an unusual approach by the British, or the Americans for that matter, to antiquities.

• Italians can also boast the first archaeologist on record: Ciriaco DE PIZZICOLLI, known to the English as Cyriacus of Ancona, where he was born.

De Pizzicolli was a merchant who travelled extensively and who in the first quarter of the fifteenth century summarised his travels in southern Italy, Greece and Egypt in his 'Commentaries'. There, he records inscriptions on monuments, makes drawings of them and annotates the artefacts which he either found or collected. All later archaeologists and classicists owe him a great debt.

Bowling

• The Italian game of 'Bocce' was a precursor of bowling. Played initially in the Italian Alps about 2,000 years ago, it consisted of the under-hand tossing of stones. It was then exported to Germany in the form of bowling at pins where it was developed around the third and fourth century AD.

Canada

• The groundwork for the British claim to Canada was laid in 1497 by an Italian, Giovanni CABOTO. He is otherwise known as John Cabot, a name which may lead a number of people to believe that he was British. He was not. He was born in Genoa. His son Sebastiano was born in Bristol, England, and both of them led the earliest English expeditions across the Atlantic.

It was Giovanni Caboto who discovered Newfoundland and indeed who anticipated Columbus by reaching this part of the new continent first. He was sailing in a British ship but he was at heart a Venetian, so much so that when he touched land it is said he dug into the soil a standard with both the British flag and the rampant lion of St Mark. (Sir Humphrey Gilbert later claimed Newfoundland for England, in 1583).

It seems to be the destiny of Italians that they are not appreciated in their own country. Columbus sailed in a Spanish ship, Caboto in a British one and a number of other Italian sailors rendered service under the British flag. Filippo ALBINI had been in

the service of King John and Leonardo PESSAGNO in that of Edward II and the two brothers Oberto and Niccolo' USODIMARE had been in the service of Edward III.

Marconi had to come to England to conclude his experiments with radio waves, as did PONTECORVO with his genetic engineering.

Marconi and Caboto are associated in a different sense for the Canadians. In 1901 Marconi received the first Transatlantic wireless radio signals from Poldhu in Cornwall on Signal Hill, at St John's, Newfoundland. The spot is next to Cabot Tower, a monument to Caboto.

Fencing

• Rapier fencing was invented by an Italian.

• The two acknowledged masters of the technique of fencing with light sabres were Giuseppe RADAELLI and Italo SANTELLI.

Domenico Angelo was a famous fencing master who spent quite a while in London in the eighteenth century. He is recorded as having lived at No. 3 St James's Place, SW1 from 1758 to 1762 and as having had a quite high-class clientele.

Horse-riding

• In 1550 Federico GRISONE (a Neapolitan) published *Gli ordini di cavalcare*, in which he attempted to combine Greek principles with the requirements of mounted combat.

• At about the same time Giovanni Battista PIGNATELLI (also born in Naples) cooperating with the said Grisone laid down the practice and principles of horse-riding which were to be developed three centuries later by the Spanish riding school at Vienna.

● In 1895 Frederico CAPRILLI (born in Livorno) revolutionised the mechanics of locomotion and created the forward seat position which is now in universal use. It was his pupil, Piero Santini, who popularised Caprilli's new idea.

Map-making

The Italian contribution to charting the various ports and inlets of the Mediterranean started in the eleventh century and the first consolidation of that work found its outlet in the so-called 'Portolan' charts. (See 'Travel and Exploration'.)

● The first real maritime map was made in Italy towards the end of the thirteenth century and it was known as the 'Carta Pisana'.

It was so called not because it was made by Pisan sailors but merely because it belonged to a family from Pisa. According to researchers, it was almost certainly drawn by a Genoese. It is undated.

● The first dated map (1311) belongs to Pietro Vesconte who was also a Genoese.

These maps were used by all Italian sailors (Pisan, Genoese, Venetians and Neapolitans) and the accumulated experience was obviously extensive. It is recorded that Venetians traded with London from Italian ships as early as 1240.

Mountain-climbing

There is little in the old authors about the subject. Apart from minor references in Herodotus and Thucidides, it is the Latin writer Sallust who records the first attempt (in the year 106 BC) to climb a mountain.

In his history of the Longobards, Paolo Diacono records the first *failed* attempt to climb the Rocciamelone mountain which is 3,537 metres high and stands in the Alps near Susa in Piedmont.

The first historical document on mountain climbing is to be found in Petrarch's letter to Father Dionigi (*De Rebus Familiaribus* IV). Petrarch himself in 1336 climbed the Ventoux mountain which is 1,912 metres high.

But the first recorded, successful attempt to climb a mountain over 2,000 metres occurred in 1358.

● In that year, Bonifacio Rotario D'ASTI climbed the Rocciamelone mountain which has already been referred to, thus becoming the first recorded mountaineer to climb over 2,000 metres.

● A much more recent first should also be recorded here. The first person in the world to have climbed all the world's-8,000 metre peaks is an Italian (from the north), Rheinhold MESSNER. He was also the first to climb Everest alone.

River Nile

I have already recorded the thefts of antiquities by Belzoni (see 'Archaeology'), but there is another first by the Italians which is associated with the River Nile.

• In 1856 Romolo GESSI (born at Constantinople) was the first to study the Nile. He is known more especially for having served under General Gordon and for being the first man to circumnavigate and map Lake Albert in Uganda.

Sailing & Boating

• In 1300 the first boat race was run in Venice.

Italians were from the very inception of their history, competent and innovative sailors. Indeed, it can be said that as a rule Italians have always made better sailors than soldiers.

As history shows, the four republics of Genoa, Venice, Pisa and Amalfi at one stage ruled the Mediterranean in the same way as five or six centuries later Britannia ruled the waves.

This is hardly surprising: Italy's coast line is very long indeed: it is about 2,600 miles if one only considers the mainland and over 5,000 if the Italian islands are included. And all of it is within the cradle of civilisation, the Mediterranean.

Throughout its history, Italy, until the nineteenth century, relied almost exclusively on its ports as outlets for trade or points of communication. The conformation of the country to the north, protected to some extent by the Alps, reinforced this reliance. As will be pointed out later on, the Italian side of the Alps is much more difficult than any of the other sides, with the result that the exit from Italy through the Alps has always been more arduous. This explains the comparative ease with which Italy was invaded at regular intervals.

On the other hand, apart from the raids by the Normans, the Saracens and the Arabs, and also excepting the Allied landings at Pachino and Anzio during World War II, the Italian coast-line has never represented a major point of invasion. On the contrary, it has represented a point of escape and a trading post. This may help to explain why the naval tradition in Italy is strong, the military is weak.

• The compass was, according to tradition, discovered by Flavio GIOIA (born at Amalfi) in 1302. (Columbus is said to have used it when he sailed to America in 1492). In turn, it is said that Gioia got his idea for the compass from the Arabs.

• By the mid-twelfth century Genoese ships had two decks and the best sails were made in Genoa.

Hence the term 'Genoa sail' to describe a particular type of quality sail. Related terms are the 'Genoa lead block' and the 'Genoa' car.

Genoese and Venetian sailors set examples which the English mercantile and war fleets followed. It is said that the first ships that sailed up the Thames as far as London were Italian. (For examples of Italian sailing expertise used in England see 'Canada').

• In 1584 Fabiano MORDENTE (born at Saluzzo) wrote his first work, *Il Compasso et Riga*, where he describes his invention of the eight-point compass.

• In 1591 Bartolomeo CRESCENZIO (born in Rome) - a naval officer for the Pope - wrote *Il Proteo Militare* in which he illustrated a kind of nautical instrument which improved on Gioia's and which was in effect the precursor of the precision compass invented by Galileo.

• In 1602 the same Crescenzio drew a 'Portolan' chart in which he showed with extreme clarity and for the first time all the inlets of the Mediterranean suitable both for sailing ships and for oar vessels.

The ship's capstan was already known to Columbus who referred to it as a 'cabestante'.

Travel and Exploration

- In 1271 Marco POLO (born in Venice) started on his journey to the East. He was the first great traveller and explorer and wrote the first travel book (*Il Milione*), in French. Niccolo and Matteo Polo had started out ten years before him.

Marco Polo belonged to a Venetian family of merchants and diplomats and as a result of his travels, after his father and uncle had left with him on their second expedition to the Court of Kublai Khan, the ruler of Mongolia and China, he was away from home for a total of 25 years. With his father and uncle he spent nearly 17 years in the service of Kublai Khan.

His book made an enormous impression at the time and it alerted Europe to the existence and importance of the East. Its writer, however, remained throughout his life very much a merchant and a traveller: he records more than he comments or moralises.

- In 1300 or thereabouts the 'Portolan' charts created by Italian sailors were the precursors of maps and harbour guides.

- In 1291 the brothers Ugolino and Vadino VIVALDI circumnavigated Africa, and are said to have anticipated Columbus by reaching America; other members of the same family founded the first trading posts of the western world in India during the fourteenth century.

- Francesco Balducci PEGOLOTTI (born in Florence) was the first writer of books that, in addition to describing places and trade routes, also provided glossaries of foreign terms, the names of market places and a description of imports and exports of the various regions involved as well as generally giving information on marketing. His principal book was called *Pratica della Mercatura*.

- In 1492 (Christopher COLOMBUS discovered America. (see 'America' p.97.)

- In 1497 Amerigo VESPUCCI (born in Florence) followed and had America named after him.

- In 1497 Giovanni CABOTO discovered Canada. (see 'Canada' p.100.)

- In 1338 a Franciscan Friar called Giovanni dei MARIGNOLLI (born in Florence) became, after Marco Polo, the second great world traveller. He was the first to stay at the Court of the Mogul Emperors and become a notable traveller to the Far East.

- In 1524 Giovanni da VERRAZZANO (also born in Florence) explored the coasts of North America and was the first European to sight New York (where a bridge is now named after him).

- In 1537 a Jesuit Priest by the name of Alessandro VALIGNANO (born at Chieti) travelled extensively in Japan. He was the first to do this. His travels extended to the Far East generally and there he introduced Christianity. He was a forerunner of and assistant to Matteo Ricci who specifically introduced Christianity to Japan.

- In 1582 another Jesuit Priest, Matteo RICCI (born in Macerata), an early visitor to China, was the first to gain entrance to China's interior which at that time was closed to foreigners. He was a pioneer in his attempts to foster understanding between East and West.

Section 11:
The Sciences

Astronomy

When considering the following facts please bear in mind that the unique contribution to astronomy by Galileo is covered separately under the head 'Physics'.

● In 1364 Giovanni DE DONDI created the first astronomical clock which, in addition to the time, showed the phases of the moon and the signs of the Zodiac.

● In 1636 Francesco FONTANA made the first drawing of the planet Mars.

● In 1666 Francesco CASSINI (born at Perinaldo) was the first astronomer to identify the Polar Caps of the planet Mars.

● In 1666 Giovanni SCHIAPARELLI (born in Savigliano) established the Mercurian year of rotation.

● In 1666 Giovanni Domenico CASSINI (born at Perinaldo) discovered what is known as Cassini's Division as well as four of Saturn's moons. He was the first to record zodiacal light. He studied Jupiter and Mars and discovered the four satellites of Saturn known as Japetus, Rhea, Thetis and Dione. He became a Fellow of The Royal Society in 1672.

● In 1728 Francesco BIANCHINI (born at Verona) who also studied the moon and discovered three comets, was the first to measure the rotational period of Venus as 24 days.

● In 1801 Giuseppe PIAZZI (born in Valtellina) discovered the first minor planet known as Ceres (Neptune 2.8).

The work that Piazzi carried out between 1790 and 1800 represented attempts in the main to measure the parallax of heavenly bodies: it was of fundamental importance.

As Mari Williams has observed ('Notes on some records of The Royal Society', volume 37, 1982/83, pp 83-100): 'It was the beginning of more than 30 years of interest in parallax throughout Europe, culminating in the production in the late 1830s of acceptable values.'

Piazzi himself had been preceded in his studies by a compatriot, Eustachio Manfredi, who in the 1730s had made an extensive study of stellar positions whilst he was Professor of Astronomy at Bologna University.

● Giovanni Battista DONATI (of Pisa) was the first to observe the spectrum of a comet in 1864.

● In 1849 Angelo SECCHI (born at Reggio E.) made the first survey of the spectra of the stars and was the first to suggest the classification of the stars according to their spectral type. His was a precursor of the Harvard classification of stars (incidentally, he gave his name to the Secchi Disc used to measure water transparency). He also described the chromospheric layers viewed at the limb of the sun (the spicules) as a 'burning prairie'.

This is a poetic description for a scientific phenomenon (Encyclopaedia Britannica, Volume 17, page 804) especially considering that he was no poet, but merely a Jesuit priest. As such he was elected Head of the Pontifical Observatory at the Collegio Romano. (In 1856 he became a Fellow of The Royal Society.) He worked there for nearly 30 years, during which time he examined almost 4,000 stars. He was the first to use photography to obtain a picture of the solar eclipse of 1851.

- In 1861 Giovanni Virginio SCHIAPARELLI (born at Savigliano) discovered the asteroid Hesperia. In 1877 he discovered the 'canals' on Mars.

Schiaparelli called the markings he had seen 'canali', a word which was erroneously translated into English as canals instead of channels, thus giving rise to speculation that intelligent life existed on that planet. In 1866 he had discovered the connection between comets and meteorites. He was Director of the Brera Observatory in Milan for 38 years (1862 to 1900) and was elected to The Royal Society in 1896.

Autopsies

- The first post-mortems were carried out at the first Medical School of the western world, which was founded in Salerno in 1221.

- Mondino dei LIUCCI (or de LUZZI) is credited with having carried out the very first autopsy in the western world in 1315. His work was carried on by Guido da VIGEVANO, who, apart from being a doctor, also wrote a treatise containing drawings of men working what is believed to be the first known crankshaft inside a vehicle.

You may recall that at about this time France was waking up from its medieval slumbers, as a result of the policies of the successors of Charlemagne, especially Philip Augustus and Louis VIII and IX; Germany was recovering from the extinction of the Hohenstaufen dynasty whilst the Hapsburgs had not yet established themselves fully in power; and England was beginning to reap the benefit of foreign chivalry and foreign clericalism, by which it had progressed under the Normans and the early Plantagenets.

Barometer

- The barometer was invented in 1641 or thereabouts by Evangelista TORRICELLI (born at Faenza). (See 'Physics' p.119ff.)

Biology

- In 1627 Gaspare ASELLI (born in Cremona) observed for the first time the lymphatic system. He described the 'venae albae et lacteae'. (see 'Medicine'.)

- In 1680 Giovanni Alfonso BORELLI (born in Naples) demonstrated that muscular contractions are explicable in physiological and chemical terms. He was the first to determine how muscles are contracted on impulses travelling down the nerves from the brain.

- In 1684 Francesco REDI (born in Arezzo) set out for the first time the germ theory of infection. (He was a writer and a very famous humorous poet in his spare time.)

Redi's scientific interests, well apart from his literary ones, were quite catholic. For example, he was a keen student of vipers. After extensive observations he found conclusively that their poison originated not in their teeth or their tail as had been commonly believed previously, but in a bladder-type container that covered their teeth.

His studies on vipers and his conclusions are quoted on page 160 of Volume 1 of the *Philosophical Transactions of The Royal Society* in the form of a report to that society by a French author who commented on experiments carried out by Redi which had not yet reached England and who states in turn: 'There is no place left for doubting after so authentick a testimony.'

• In 1685 the same REDI demonstrated that maggots came from the eggs of flies and set up one of the first experiments with proper controls.

• Agostino BASSI (born in Lodi) was the founder of the parasitic theory of infection, which he developed in 1835 studying silkworms.

• In 1728 Giovanni Maria LANCISI (born in Rome) - who wrote on influenza, cattle plague, malaria and cardiac pathology - was the first modern hygienist.

Lancisi was the first to use the expression 'aneurysm of the heart' which has sadly become so topical in this age of heart trouble. He also described in detail the part played by mosquitoes in spreading malaria.

• In 1830 Giovanni Battista AMICI (born in Modena) discovered the sexual process in flowering plants. (He also built the Amici Prism for prismatic spectroscopes.)

Amici had started work on the general aspects of fertilisation in plants in 1823. In 1846 he identified the female agent in these processes, paving the way for the refinements brought both to his studies and to his techniques by cytologists more than 50 years later.

• In 1873 Camillo GOLGI (born at Cortena) (PV) commenced his studies of the nervous system and discovered the silver nitrate method of staining nerve tissue. He also identified the Golgi nerve cell, the Golgi tendon organ as well as the Golgi apparatus. Finally, he studied malaria and was made a Nobel Prize Winner in 1906.

Golgi's work was truly revolutionary. From his discovery of the nitrate impregnation staining method (1873) to that of the nervous tendon spindle (1888), on to the division of tendon cells by 'arborescence' in 1898, his contribution to medical science was exceptional.

• In 1903 Adelchi NEGRI (born in Perugia) discovered the Negri bodies in cytoplasm that are diagnostic of rabies.

• In 1938 Guido PONTECORVO (born in Pisa) discovered the process of genetic combination in fungus, opening the way to probing the nature of gene action and deserving the name of 'father' of genetic engineering.

Chemistry

• Nitric acid was first produced from saltpetre and alum in Italy in 1150.

• In 1350 gold wire was first made in Italy.

• In 1805 BRUGNATELLI was the first to gild silver coins.

• In 1811 Amedeo AVOGADRO (born in Turin) formulated his hypothesis that elemental gases are groups of atoms and elucidated the number of atoms in a given volume of gas.

Avogadro was the first to propound the theory that, given the same circumstances of temperature and pressure, equal volumes of all gases contain equal number of molecules. His was 'a brilliant conception ignored for 50 years'. (see *Biographical Dictionary of Scientists*, ed. Pitman, London, 1969). He laid down the fundamental method of chemical formulae.

His discovery is sometimes attributed to Ampere who, to his credit, admitted Avogadro's paternity of it.

• In 1836 Roberto PIRIA (born at Scilla di Calabria) discovered salicylic acid by the oxidation of salicylic aldehyde present in a fairly common herb known as meadowsweet (Latin name 'spiraea ulmaria').

Fifteen years after that, Gerhardt discovered acetylsalicylic and he and Piria paved the way for the Germans Rolke and Lauterman to create aspirin.

It would be nice to think that the very name of this medicament comes from Piria, but I believe that to be a coincidence: all that has been done is that the Latin name 'spiraea' has been turned into aspirin.

Even so, the next time you take an aspirin, you might spare a thought for Piria who is not normally given credit for his discovery.

• In 1850 Francesco SELMI (born at Vignola Novarese) published the first systematic study of inorganic colloids.

• In 1858 Stanislao CANNIZZARO (born in Palermo), as part of a process of rehabilitation of his predecessor, gave the first representation of Avogadro's hypothesis.

Cannizzaro became a Fellow of The Royal Society in 1889. The name may be familiar to some Londoners. 'Cannizzaro House', now an hotel and formerly the home of the Sicilian Duke of Cannizzaro who lived there in the eighteenth century, can be seen lit up at night across Wimbledon Common.

• Helium gas was first discovered on earth in 1882 by Professor PALMIERI.

• Giulio NATTA (born at Imperia) invented polypropylene in 1954. It was first marketed throughout the world by Montecatini under the brand name of 'Moplen'. He also discovered polymers in 1957. In 1963 he was the Nobel Prize Winner for Chemistry.

Contagious Diseases

• In 1530 Girolamo FRACASTORO (born in Verona) was the first westerner to describe syphilis.

He was mistaken inasmuch as he did not believe that it came from America and called it the 'French disease'; but I suppose his mistake is understandable because the plague that had started in Naples in 1495 was spreading throughout Europe on an epidemic basis and he may have believed that it came from there and that the French were responsible.

He thought at one stage it also came from the air and suggested that it be cured with quicksilver.

He was quite a character because he wrote a whole book on it in rhyme (by the title *Syphilis sive de morbo gallico*).

• Fracastoro was the first to study epidemiology and is credited with being its founder. He propounded the germ theory of disease and anticipated Pasteur by 300 years. (He also anticipated Copernicus by postulating the planets revolved spherically around a central point, in his work 'A Single Centre of the Universe', published in 1538).

Fracastoro was a very influential humanist, apart from being a famous physician, and, with Copernicus, had studied at Padova University. He anticipated Leibnitz and his 'monads', when he established his 'semina' as primary philosophical concepts similar to atoms - thus giving the idea to his compatriot Bruno.

• In 1546 Fracastoro wrote the first textbook ever on contagious diseases, where, for the first time, he correctly identifies infection as the passage of minute bodies from the infected person to another.

Fracastoro must surely be one of the greatest names in Italian science. All that he said and did in 1530 is extraordinary and I am sure that one would be hard put to believe it were it not for the authority of the *Encyclopaedia Britannica*, Volume 12, page 109.

ITALIANS FIRST!

108

Geology

- In 1760 Giovanni ARDUINO (born at Caprino Veronese) was the first to classify rocks and to establish bases for stratigraphic chronology by defining the four major layers of earth as primary secondary tertiary and quaternary. He also pioneered the use of fossil and chemical methods to determine the age of rocks.

Geometry

- In the early seventeenth century Girolamo SACCHERI adopted the 'reductio ad absurdum' argument on Euclid's axioms.

- In 1646 Evangelista TORRICELLI (born at Faenza) described the asymptomatic point 'O'.

- In 1728 Guido GRANDI (born at Cremona) analysed the rhodonea curves.

Hydraulics

- In 1630 Bruno CASTELLI and Evangelista TORRICELLI founded modern hydraulics.

- Castelli was the first to measure running water with a water meter.

- In 1680 Domenico GUGLIELMINI (born in Bologna) studied rivers and was the first to understand the equilibrium between water and the resistance of the river bed to flow. He was the founder of the Italian School of Hydraulics.

- In 1762 Paolo FRISI (born in Milan) wrote the first engineering textbook, 'A Treaty on Rivers and Torrents'.

Longevity

- Luigi Alvise CORNARO (born in Venice) - one of the many members of the well-known Venetian Corner family - wrote in 1558 *Della Vita Sobria*, the first treatise on how to live to be 100 years, as he thought he would. He died aged 99 and wrote it when he was aged 83.

By profession Cornaro was an architect and he was the first to import the Romanic Renaissance style to northern Italy. It is likely that he knew and influenced Palladio.

But he also dabbled with good results in hydraulics, agriculture and land reclamation. Above all, however, he was best at building villas.

He maintained that the key to a long, healthy life is sobriety in everything, but particularly in food. He found that members of his generation ate far too much.

He was himself fortunate in more respects than one. He was successful, he had money, he lived well; he had two homes. The one where he spent most of his time he had designed himself and was very comfortable, cool in the summer and warm in the winter. He ate and drank exclusively products from his own land. It was easy for him to lead a healthy life. But well apart from the healthy life he led, he certainly displayed great will-power.

As he says: 'I have carefully avoided heat, cold and extraordinary fatigue, interruption of my usual hours of rest, excessive venery, making any stay in bad air and exposing myself to the wind and sun.' He limited himself to 12 oz of food a day.

His house was situated in the most beautiful quarter of the noble and learned city of Padova and was 'very convenient and handsome.' He also enjoyed many days' stay in his villa by the river Brenta. (The Brenta Canal - for a canal it is, more than a river - runs from Padova to Venice and on or by it are to be found some of Palladio's best works, from the Villas Cornaro and Capra to La Malcontenta and La Nazionale, some of over 4,000 villas that were built in this part of Italy at the very time that the Venetian Republic was declining.)

Cornaro's philosophy was that up to the age of 50, one might allow oneself to deviate from the norm. But 'After 50, our lives should in everything be governed by reason which teaches us that the consequences of gratifying our palate and our appetite are disease and death.'

Correct he might have been about the wisdom of self-restraint, particularly in food, but I believe he is important for a totally different reason. I think it can be fairly said that he anticipated the concept of food allergy. For example, he remarks that he had applied himself diligently to discover what kinds of food suited him best. In so doing he found that mature wine upset him, but new wine did not, that pepper could properly be replaced by cinnamon and that different foods affected different people. Of course, he was not saying anything very new: 400 years before Christ, Hippocrates had mentioned the fact that there were certain people who showed intolerance for specific constituents of their physical environment. In Roman times, Lucretius, the author of De Rerum Natura, was the first to use wording the modern equivalent of which is 'One man's meat is another man's poison'.

It is a fact that before the word 'allergy' was invented, essentially in the nineteenth century, it had long been recognised that there were some of us who are made ill by eating, drinking, inhaling or sometimes even touching things which most others take in their stride.

But Cornaro was the first modern writer who actually elaborates the concept in the sense that he builds a whole philosophy of life or, perhaps more accurately, an entire way of living upon the fact that some foods suited him and others did not.

It is interesting to note that the 1975 version of the 15th Edition of the Encyclopaedia Britannica only mentions him in passing as an architect at Volume III, page 154 and at Volume XIII, page 932. The 1978 version of the same edition does not mention him at all.

Mathematics

• In 1202 Leonardo da PISA, otherwise known as Leonardo FIBONACCI (the son of Bonacci), wrote the first book ever on mathematics. It was called the Liber Abaci, a book he revised in 1228 and dedicated to Michael Scott. In it he set out the sequence of numbers thenceforth known as the Fibonacci Sequence, which has proved to be inexhaustible and formed the basis of all future number games. He also introduced Hindu-Arabic numbers into mathematics.

Although written in 1202, this book was not well known until after 1450, when it was printed by Luca Pacioli and brought to the knowledge of the general public.

• In 1494 Luca PACIOLI, a monk, who established the 'Lucas sequence', published his Summa de Arithmetica Geometria Proportioni et Proportionalita.

• At about the same time, BRUNELLESCHI (born in Florence), the famous Florentine architect, applied mathematics to his principles for the use of perspective in building.

• In 1510 Scipione del FERRO was the first to find the solution to cubic equations.

- In 1512 Niccolo TARTAGLIA (born at Brescia) was the first to find the solution to quartic equations.

Tartaglia is said to have got his surname from the Italian verb 'tartagliare' which means to stutter because, according to tradition, when he was young, he received an injury to his lips by French soldiers who at that time were invading his home town of Brescia. He was a versatile man. In 1543 he published the first translation of Euclid in Italian.

In *Nuova Scienza*, which he wrote in 1537, he dealt with the theory of gunnery, applying mathematics to it. His interest in artillery was so great that in 1546 he wrote and dedicated to Henry VIII a whole volume on artillery and fortification.

He determined the rule for dividing a number into two parts such that the continued product of the numbers and their difference is a maximum. (see *Biographical Dictionary of Scientists*).

- In 1540 Ludovico FERRARI (born in Bologna) was the first to find an algebraic solution to the quartic equation and he competed publicly with the said Tartaglia to solve the cubic equation.

- In 1545 the formulae for cubic and quartic equations were put forward for the first time by Niccolo TARTAGLIA, Ludovico FERRARI and Girolamo CARDANO.

- In 1635 Bonaventura CAVALIERI (born in Milan) fashioned the geometry of indivisibles. The Cavalieri theorem takes its name from him and it involved the use of logarithms. He anticipated both integral calculus and the modern theory of calculus, and exerted profound influence on the later studies of Leibnitz and Newton.

- In 1640 Evangelista TORRICELLI (born in Faenza) was the first to find the length of the logarithm spiral. He is the inventor of the barometer.

- In 1678 Giovanni CEVA (born at Mantova) established the geometric theorem known by his name. It concerns lines intersecting at the common points of a triangle.

- In about 1670 Pietro MENGOLI was the first to analyse convergence and divergence.

Mengoli determined certain features of the harmonic series before Jacques Bernoulli and also produced a series of logarithms. 'His definition of definite integral is similar to that propounded by A. C. Cauchy 100 years later.' (see *Biographica Dictionary of Scientists*.)

- In the year 1700 Girolamo SACCHERI (born in Sanremo) was the first to develop hyperbolic geometry.

- In 1712 Iacopo Francesco RICCATI gave his name to the equation otherwise known as a second-order equation.

- Luigi LA GRANGE (born in Turin) was the first to apply mathematical criteria to mechanical sciences. In 1761 he was recognised as the greatest living mathematician. In 1788 he published his major work, *Mecanique Analytique*, which, ignoring completely metaphysical concepts, provided a review of mechanics of the past 200 years.

- In 1799 Iacopo Paolo RUFFINI (born at Valentano) showed for the first time that there is no algebraic solution to the general quintic equation.

- In 1857 Enrico BETTI (born at Pistoia) wrote the first book on topology and gave the first exposition of the theory of equations which was later to be developed by the Frenchman Galois.

- In 1860 Luigi CREMONA (born at Pavia) originated graphical statics, the study of forces in equilibrium, using graphical methods.

- In 1868 Eugenio BELTRAMINI (born in Cremona) observed for the first time the correctness of Lobatchevsky's postulates in Euclid's geometry.

• In 1880 Gregorio RICCI (born at Lugo) developed absolute differential calculus, called after him Ricci Calculus. He also created the first systematic theory of tensor analysis.

• In 1885 Giuseppe PEANO (born at Cuneo) established the Peano axioms as a series of geometrical calculus and mathematical logic.

• In 1890 Ernesto CESARO (born in Naples) developed the theory of divergent series.

• In 1900 Vito VOLTERRA (born at Ancona) created functional analysis. He was elected to The Royal Society in 1910.

• In 1908 Ernesto ZERMELO gave the first system of axiomatic set theory.

• In 1917 Tullio LEVI-CIVITA (born at Padova) developed the notion of parallel transport and together with Cumbastro Gregorio Ricci was the first to formulate absolute differential calculus (otherwise known as tensor analysis). Levi-Civita was elected to The Royal Society in 1930.

• In 1930 G. TONELLI (born at Gallipoli), L. CESARI and E. DIGIORGI were the first to study multiple integral surfaces.

Medicine

• In 1221 the first medical school of the western world was founded in Salerno. It was licensed by Frederick II of Sicily in 1224, the same year as the university was founded.

At some time between 1175 and 1230 Ruggero of Salerno, otherwise known as Ruggero Frugardo, wrote his treatise on surgery, probably the first textbook on surgery ever compiled; its editor was Guido d'Arezzo. It was, of course, written in Latin but a copy of it translated into Anglo-Norman French is in the possession of Trinity College, Cambridge.

The book contains many expressive drawings and shows the techniques used by doctors at that time, either in preparing potions or in viewing the ailments of their patients. It dominated European surgery techniques until the Renaissance.

• The first post-mortems of the western world were carried out in Salerno by Mondino de' LUZZI and Da VIGEVANO.

The School was already in existence before the above date for there seems to be evidence that it was considered as 'ancient' three centuries earlier. It continued to be well known until about the sixteenth century.

A number of medical students flocked there from all parts of the world. The principal purpose was to obtain a diploma from the Salerno School which entitled them to practise their profession in every country of Europe.

Patients, too, came from all over, including soldiers who had taken part in the crusades; in fact it was the practice to give the crusaders a 'vade mecum' before leaving - a sort of aide-memoire of what they should do when they were no longer in touch with their doctor. This 'vade mecum' is in Latin but there is an amusing English translation of it made by Sir John Haryngton which was published in London in 1607. Haryngton himself is connected with Italy in a different way because in 1591 he translated the *Orlando Furioso*. (A man of some versatility, since he had also invented the water closet in 1589.)

This is not the place to go through the various rules which, according to the School of Salerno 700 years ago, were supposed to keep one healthy. By modern standards, some read a little bit strangely; but one of the principal ones is a rule of conduct of universal application, namely that the best medicine consists in a mind that is happy, rest and food in moderation. ('Si tibi deficiant medici, medici tibi fiant haec tria:

mens laeta, requies, moderata diaeta' which is cheerfully translated by Sir John Haryngton as 'Use three physicians; first Dr Quiet, next Dr Merryman, and Dr Diet'.)

There are also a few gems of a different kind which have now been rediscovered as part of modern medicine; for example, that if one had too much to drink the previous night, a drop of the same stuff first thing in the morning would redress the balance (I am told that a number of cures for allergies acknowledge this principle); or that plums are very good for you and for the system, as our grandmothers knew only too well; or that the herb sage is excellent for most ills, as are nettles, hyssop, watercress, and leeks.

●   In 1275 Guglielmo Da SALICETO, who was a major surgeon, wrote the first treatise on surgical anatomy.

●   In 1315 Mondino Dei LIUCCI (or de LUZZI) is credited with having carried out the very first autopsy, as we have already recorded (see 'Autopsies').

●   In 1552, Bartolomeo EUSTACHIO (born at Sanseverino) laid his claim to posterity through his (unpublished) book *Opuscola Anatomica*. He is now known generally because of the tube in the human ear which bears his name. But he did much more.

●   Apart from the fact that he was the first to describe in scientific form anatomical variations, Eustachio did much work on muscles, showing their nerve supply, on the brain and on the sympathetic system.

●   Eustachio was the first to describe the thoracic duct and the azygos vein, thus anticipating Jean Pecquet by a century.

Eustachio also made extensive studies of the larynx. Many of the concepts that he established were developed more fully by others, especially by Vesalius.

We now come to the father of modern medicine, namely, Matteo Realdo COLOMBO (born in Cremona).

●   In 1540 Colombo was the first to describe clearly the pulmonary circulation. He thus anticipated Harvey who acknowledged him as the discoverer of pulmonary circulation.

●   Colombo was also the first to describe the mediastinum, the pleura, the peritoneum, and the action of the heart, namely its two phases of systole and diastole.

●   Alvisio LUIGINI (born in Udine) spent some time on venereal diseases and particularly syphilis and was effectively the first to write more than one book about it.

●   In 1566 he wrote his *De Morbo Gallico* which was a summary of world knowledge and techniques of treatment for syphilis and in 1599 his *De Lue Venerea* treatise on V.D.

●   In 1573 Costanzo VAROLIO (born in Bologna) published in Padova his study on the optical nerves. He gave his name to the Varolio 'bridge', the transverse part of the brain, and was the first to teach that when dissecting the encephalus one had to start from its base.

●   In 1561 Gabriele FALLOPPIO (born in Modena), who was the most illustrious of the sixteenth century anatomists, studied particularly the ear and the genital organs. He discovered the tubes that now bear his name and was the first to name the vagina, the placenta, the clitoris, the palate and the cochlea. He invented the condom.

●   In 1622 Gaspare ASELLI (born in either Pavia or Cremona) discovered lacteals, namely the lymphatic vessels that serve the small intestine, which he described as 'white and milky veins'.

Aselli also made an extensive study of the digestive system and in particular of the absorption of the food in the mesentherium. He laid down the foundation for those studies which the Frenchman, Pecquet, was to develop more fully.

●   In 1668 Francesco REDI (born in Arezzo) was the first to question the spontaneous origin of living things by his experiments with maggots and flies on rotten meat, firstly in the air and then away from it.

• Lorenzo BELLINI (born in Florence) was the first to describe the excretory tubes of the kidneys (still known as Bellini's tubes).

Bellini was only 19 years old when he made this discovery in 1662 - three years later he described the human organs of taste.

• Marcello MALPIGHI (see also 'Botanical Gardens & Botany') made a number of major contributions to medical science.

In 1661 Malpighi discovered the capillary vessels which connect arteries and veins; he also described in detail the structure of the human lung, brain and spinal cord.

As a result of his discoveries, his name is associated with the epidermis (the Malpighi layer), the spleen (the Malpighi corpuscles) and the kidneys (the Malpighi tufts).

He studied in detail both red blood corpuscles (which he first found in the lungs of a frog using a microscope) and the cells of muscles as well as the structure of secreting glands. He discovered the papillae of the tongue and the cortex of the brain.

The depth of knowledge he developed as to the fertilization of eggs and the development of the chick can be gauged from the very beautiful drawings that are preserved in the archives of The Royal Society where seven of his papers were published in the *Philosophical Transactions*. The first true Italian scientist, Malpighi was admitted as a Fellow of The Royal Society on 4 March 1668. (The first Italian to become a member of The Royal Society beat Malpighi to it by just 3 months; he was Count Carlo Ubaldini about whom, however, nothing seems to be known.)

• MALPIGHI was the first to use the microscope for detailed analysis and study.

• Santorio SANTORIO (born in Capodistria) was the first to employ instruments of precision in the practice of medicine.

In 1614 Santorio published his *De Statica Medicina*. This represented the first systematic study of basal metabolism. Well ahead of his time, his instruments were not introduced until a century later and the implications of his research were not realised until the nineteenth century.

In 1670 for the first time he attempted to cure TB sufferers with transfusions of blood of mutton. (see entry under 'Physics'.)

• Giovanni Guglielmo RIVA (born in Asti) was the first to carry out blood transfusions.

• In 1700 Antonio Maria VALSALVA (born at Imola) discovered how air pressure on the pharynx can cause the Eustachian tube to open. This is the same reflex of which we are too well aware when we fly.

• In 1714 Bernardino RAMAZZINI (born in Carpi) was the first to publish a systematic account of trade diseases.

• We now come to the father of modern pathology (the description, as the previous one for Colombo, is not mine; I am using the words of the *Encyclopaedia Britannica*), namely Giovanni MORGAGNI (born at Forli).

Morgagni revolutionized medicine by his thorough studies and teaching of the human body.

He was the greatest pathologist of the eighteenth century and his world-wide fame resulted in his being elected to The Royal Society in 1722.

Morgagni discovered the so-called pockets of the larynx, he made extensive studies of the urethra, he was the first to identify the anterior cervical muscles and the nodules of the arterial valves of the heart. His analysis of the human body and its organs, consequent from his numerous dissections, was much more thorough even than that of Leonardo. In one of his publications dated 1761, Morgagni described 700 post-mortems.

It has been said that if the totality of his anatomical discoveries had, in fact, been named after him, about a third of the parts of the human body would bear his name.

His interest ranged from the organs of procreation to the fluid of the cornea of the eye but, above all, he was a great teacher and a very active person who was still busy at work when he died aged 89. His contribution to human wellbeing is very great indeed.

• Lazzaro SPALLANZANI (born in Modena), a priest and a biologist, showed for the first time that spermatozoa were necessary for the reproduction of mammals. He established animal artificial insemination and in 1776 laid down the technique of sterile cultures. He was the first to show that the tissues use up oxygen and give off carbon dioxide.

Over 200 years ago, and well in advance of modern scientific developments of the past few years, Spallanzani contributed profoundly to the question of whether spontaneous generation of life exists. He was elected a Fellow of The Royal Society in 1768.

• Spallanzani was the first to determine the pressure of the blood.

• In 1835 Filippo PACINI (born in Pistoia) discovered the corpuscles of the digital nerves that are nowadays known as Pacinian corpuscles.

In 1852 Pacini began studying the pathology of cholera and shortly thereafter he identified the vibrios of cholera as bacteria.

His contemporaries, however, did not attach much significance to what he was doing. It was left to R. Koch in 1884 to identify finally the bacillus of cholera and to earn a Nobel Prize for doing so.

• In 1850 Angelo RUFFINI (born at Arquata del Tronto) described the endings that are known by his name in nerves, ligaments, joints and subcutaneous tissue.

• Cecilio FOLLI (born in Modena) was the first to describe the anatomy of the inner ear.

• In 1851 the Marquis Alfonso CORTI (born at Gambarana P.V.) was the first to describe a fundamental part of the inner ear which is now known as the organ of Corti.

• In 1889 Carlo FORLANINI (born in Milan) devised the first pneumothorax to cure congenital tuberculosis.

• In 1896 the sphygmomanometer was invented by an Italian doctor, Scipione RIVA ROCCI.

• In 1937 the first applications of electro convulsive therapy were elaborated by two Italian doctors, Ugo CERLETTI and Lucio BINI as a treatment for schizophrenia.

Metallurgy

• In the sixteenth century Vannoccio BIRINGUCCIO (born in Siena) wrote the first book on the subject.

Biringuccio was particularly interested in the application of metal fusion techniques to cannons and other weapons and he wrote what is probably the first book on such applications, namely his *Pirotechnia*. He described in detail the mining and industrial techniques of his day.

He was also among the first to provide cannons with ornamentation (scrolls, figures, etc.) and in 1540 was the first to make mention of boring machines for cannon.

Nobel Prizes

Italian performance as far as winning Nobel Prizes is concerned is indifferent, if not poor. To date, we have a total of 14 prize winners.

Compared to Britain which has 80 and to the United States of America which has 148, Italy's results are not so impressive. I would make two observations:

1.   The Swedish Institute and the Nobel Foundation started awarding their prizes in 1901. By then, most of the spade-work in the fields of universal knowledge had already been done by the Italians. In all fairness one may ask the question 'How many prizes would Italy have got if the Nobel system had come into operation in the year 1001 instead of in 1901?'

2.   No Nobel Prizes are awarded for mathematics. It is conceivable that under this heading Italy might have picked up a further three prizes. Even so, I suppose that what the following list shows is that the Italians of the past centuries were much better than those of the twentieth century. Evidently, quality is deteriorating.

•   The following Italians won Nobel Prizes:

1906 Giosué CARDUCCI - Poetry (born at Petrasanta)

1906 Camillo GOLGI - (Cytology) - Medicine

1906 Ernesto MONETA - Peace (born in Milan)

1909 Guglielmo MARCONI - Physics (Radio) (born in Bologna)

1929 Grazia DELEDDA - Literature (born at Nuoro)

1934 Luigi PIRANDELLO - Literature (born in Agrigento)

1938 Enrico FERMI - Physics (born in Rome)

1957 Daniele BOVET - Physiology (synthetic curare) (born in Neuchatel)

1959 Salvatore QUASIMODO - Poetry (born at Modica RA)

1963 Giulio NATTA - Chemistry (born in Imperia)

1975 Eugenio MONTALE - Poetry (born in Genova)

1984 Carlo RUBBIA - Physics (born in Gorizia)

1985 Franco MODIGLIANI - Economics (born in Rome)

1986 Rita LEVI-MONTALCINI - Physiology (born in Turin)

Philosophy

•   In or about the year 1535 Giordano BRUNO (born at Nola) was the first to represent the universe as infinite. His ideas were 'picked up' by Galileo, Kepler and William Gilbert.

•   In 1565 Bernardino TELESIO (born at Cosenza) was the first philosopher and natural scientist to adopt empirical criteria, to object to the practice of making generalisations without providing concrete data, as had been done by a number of the Greek philosophers, especially Aristotle, and to move over to the evidence of the senses rather than of primary theoretical concepts, thus anticipating both Sir Francis Bacon, who called him 'The first of the moderns', and his two compatriots, Campanella and Bruno (both from the south of Italy) as well as Thomas Hobbes.

None of the above-mentioned Italian philosophers can truly be termed great. In his *History of Western Philosophy* Bertrand Russell does not mention any of them. This is understandable in respect of Bruno, who was most unpopular in England when he stayed there; it may be understandable also for another reason, namely that not all Bruno's works have been translated into English. I wonder whether Bertrand Russell read Italian?

HENRY MOORE EXHIBITION IN FLORENCE

LA MOSTRA DI MOORE
A FIRENZE

La parte più bella di questa scultura è il
foro attraverso il quale si vede la cupola di
Santa Maria del Fiore.

"The best part of this sculpture is the hole in the
middle through which one sees the dome of Santa
Maria."

But to ignore not only him but also Campanella and above all, Telesio, seems stretching Italophobia somewhat too far. Indeed, it is also interesting to observe that the only Italian 'philosopher' whom Russell records, (apart from St Thomas Aquinas, St Augustine and Galileo), is the political philosopher Machiavelli. No criticism of that, but one wonders what the rationale was that caused him to omit Bruno, Campanella and Telesio and to include, for example, Byron.

That the Italians have not made a greater contribution to philosophy is somewhat surprising. Philosophizing seems to suit us. There is also a contemplative element in some of our thinking that, especially in the south of Italy, must be derived from the Arabs directly. Nevertheless, there is an explanation.

On the whole, as I shall be mentioning in greater detail later on, Italians are realists. As they themselves defy categorisation, they abhor classification and systematization. They are only interested in practical solutions: their resourcefulness dictates this.

In a strange way - and I know that by saying this I shall contradict all that the English (and probably most of the rest of the western world) have ever believed about the Italians - we are doers rather than thinkers.

This is why Italians have never really been too interested in philosophy. Philosophy, or love of knowledge, is by definition a theoretical science. It teaches us to make an effort to understand what goes on around us, what are the causes of our thinking and of our behaviour, what is the reason for our existence, whether God exists, etc. Although it may have practical applications, it is not in any sense a practical science.

When it comes to the reality of life, one needs a concrete approach; one needs a concrete science that will enable us to improve our lot, to learn new techniques, new methods, in substance to change the world about us.

And in this, as becomes more apparent under the heading 'Physics', Italians have been leaders. The practical importance of science was recognised by Leonardo, Galileo, and many others. True, for Leonardo, more in connection with war than with everyday life; true, for both him and Galileo because both of them had to justify their existence to their pay masters. But even so, this shows that scientists/ philosophers like Galileo and artists/ scientists like Leonardo had, like other Italians, their feet firmly on the ground.

The same practical approach also explains the Italians' lack of patriotism, a topic which I shall also return to later. The great Italian hero is not Mazzini. I know that we are all taught at school that his contribution to Italian political emancipation and to the repulsion of the Austrian yoke is great. But his thoroughly honourable, stirring cries of 'God and country', 'thought and action now and forever' never really meant very much to the Italians even when they were first uttered. The Italian revolutionary movement, as all historians have observed - in common with most revolutionary movements - was inspired by a small group of intellectuals. We have never been able fully to understand Mazzini's austerity and his capacity for suffering, nor I suppose, cynically, his appeal to thought.

The Italian national hero is Garibaldi. He donned a red shirt and, in defiance of authority, with little official support, if any, and with even less apparent chance of success, he went to free the kingdom of the two Sicilies. There was adventure, there was resourcefulness, there was the 'locus classicus' of the Italian way of doing things, 'alla garibaldina'; for what that really means is: without necessarily thinking the matter out, impulsively, relying on one's heart and one's instinct.

I do not mean to sound critical. Reliance on one's heart and instinct is, to me at any rate, the greatest virtue in life: 'rationality' be damned!

The use of language is significant. Italians

pray to emulate the behaviour of Garibaldi; nobody ever suggests that they should do things 'alla mazziniana'. If and insofar as we refer to Mazzini at all as representative of a particular style or manner, we do so when considering his beard and sideboards, but certainly not his spirit.

In the final analysis, all I am doing here is drawing a distinction between theory and practice, between Mazzini and Garibaldi. Ultimately, those who do things have little need to discuss them. Those who have things have even less need to broadcast the fact. Those who know things do not go around clamouring about their knowledge.

Be that as it may, it must be admitted that in philosophy we have not contributed much. Perhaps it is because in essence we prefer not to be rational.

Physics

This section includes such diverse ideas or discoveries as diving, incubators and electricity. There is no real causal connection between them, but it was a matter of convenience to encompass them all under a single heading.

I must confess that in compiling the Physics entries I experienced my greatest surprise. I remember that when I was still very young and studying in Rome the then Fascist government had caused to be published a book entitled *Da Leonardo a Marconi* which listed all the achievements of the Italian people in the artistic and scientific world. Regrettably, my recollection of it is limited to the two names of the title and I had never realised until I embarked upon the present exercise how noticeable the Italian contribution has been in the scientific field. I began to appreciate it a little more when trying to ascertain what had been done in the fields of chemistry

and medicine. But when I came to physics I was very pleasantly surprised.

There are, to my mind, four Italians whose names stand supreme in the world of knowledge and art. They are in order of seniority: Leonardo Da Vinci, Michelangelo, Galileo and Verdi. They represent what is best and most noble in Italy and, in particular, Leonardo and Galileo have made a contribution to science which can never be equalled. This is not to minimise the scientific impact of the three subsequent Italian Nobel Prize-winners, namely Marconi, Fermi and Rubbia. But when you consider Leonardo or Galileo, you are almost referring to something superhuman. Because of this I have listed their contributions separately.

However, before we get to them, consider the following facts:

• **The first recorded application of a cam in the western world occurred in a fulling mill on the River Serchio in Tuscany roundabout the year 1000.**

• **In 1420 Giovanni da FONTANA sketched jet propelled fish, birds and rabbits. He proposed the use of jet propulsion for measuring water depths and air heights.**

• **Seventy-five years later Francesco DI GIORGIO designed jet-propulsion petards on wheels and floats.**

• **In 1490 Francesco DI GIORGIO described a ball and chain centrifugal governor.**

• **The true theory of the rainbow was explained by Antonio DE DOMINIS in the sixteenth century.**

• **Also in the sixteenth century Geronimo FABRIZZI was the first to apply mechanical principles to the anatomy of muscular movements.**

LEONARDO DA VINCI (1452-1519)

LEONARDO was the first man to:

• **Work, experiment and design on diving. For example, he actually designed a diving tube.**

• **Analyse the rectineal propagation of light.**

• **Design a screw-operated printing press and a machine for cutting screws.**

• **Sketch spur, bevel and worm gears.**

• **Design roller bearings.**

• **Study fluid-flow engineering.**

• **Design the first porous hygrometer.**

• **Elaborate a 'camera oscura'.**

• **Carry out underwater exploration.**

• **Design a gas and a water turbine.**

• **Design a flying machine.**

• **Lay the foundations of photometry.**

• **Design a multiple crossbow.**

• **Draw a repeater-type of gun.**

• **Design a parachute.**

• **Design a bicycle.**

• **Develop a rope-making machine.**

• **Design a retractable undercarriage.**

• **Evolve explosive bullets for firearms.**

• **Describe a submarine.**

• **Sketch the first tensile-testing machine.**

• **Devise a hand-saw for cutting marble.**

• **Sketch a disc-grinder and internal and external grinders and polishers.**

Leonardo's genius was of a unique nature, his imagination equally so, his curiosity boundless. He could take the same trouble over the human body as he did over the drawing of a leaf or a rock. His interests were so wide-ranging as to be almost frightening. They ranged from making wax impressions of the interior of the human brain to drawing fairly accurately a womb with an embryo inside. His concern with causation and the way things work is exceptionally modern: his confidence in his ability to understand anything ran counter to the then teaching of the Church. Whether considering why leaves are arranged in a particular manner on a stalk or what the effect was of the movement of the wings of a dragonfly, in anticipating to some extent both Copernicus and Galileo, he pioneered studies on the nature of sound and light, hydraulics, optics, meteorology, the use of air as a source of power and innumerable war machines. I have already recorded his contribution to the building of the canals in Milan, which he designed. Water and air seem to have fascinated him. His approach to aerodynamics has still not ceased to puzzle modern scientists. Over five centuries ago, his contribution to the development of gliders, parachutes, the helicopter and retractable landing gears and wheels is such that one can only consider him truly unique. It is impossible to compare him with anybody.

GALILEO GALILEI

Galileo was born at Pisa in 1564 and died at Arcetri in 1642. In fact, Galileo was born more or less on the day when Michelangelo died and died in the year that Newton was born.

Galileo was the founder of modern mechanics and experimental physics. Most students remember him for re-stating in scientific terms the argument as to whether the sun rotated round the earth or vice versa, but he did much more. He was a great astronomer and a real scientist and his list of firsts is truly outstanding:

• **Galileo was the first man to construct and use a telescope.**

- He was the first man to consider the implications of the movements of a pendulum. In 1583 he discovered that the oscillation period of a pendulum is virtually independent of the amplitude of its swing.

- He was the first to state informally the principles embodied in Newton's first two laws of motion. (Effectively, he discovered that acceleration, which was previously believed to be circular, occurred in a straight line).

- In 1604 he proved the law of uniformly accelerated motion (thus disproving Aristotle who had stated that heavier bodies fell faster than lighter ones); he was the first to prove that air has weight.

- He was the first to discover and observe the four satellites of Jupiter.

- In 1610 he was the first to observe that the planet Mars was not, as had previously been believed, round.

- He anticipated the law of inertia.

- He invented the lens and the microscope.

- He set out the law of freefall.

- In 1610 he observed Saturn and started his study of the phases of Venus which spread over many years.

- He was the first to establish the law of parabolic fall, although studies on the theme were made before him by the mathematician Bonaventura Cavalieri.

- He was the first to establish the concept of energy.

- He was the first to analyse the principle of odds when playing dice.

- In 1610 he explained sunspots, which he had discovered, as solar phenomena.

- He was the first to carry out a controlled chain reaction.

- He revised and improved Leonardo's hygrometer, which was later to be improved again by Francesco FOLLI.

- In 1592 he invented the thermoscope, forerunner of the thermometer.

There is no doubt that Galileo was one of the greatest Italians who ever lived and that the debt that the scientific world owes him is enormous. Again, what did his compatriots do to him? The Church banished him to Arcetri and in 1633 he had to recant. Italian schoolboys are taught that even after he recanted he kept saying *Eppur si muove* (and yet it moves) referring to the earth, and maybe he did say it. But for practical purposes he was treated in such a manner that his recantation marks the end of scientific development in Italy for about 200 years.

He had the ability to combine theory with practice. In fact, he studied projectiles for his employer, the Grand Duke of Tuscany, and was able to show that, apart from air resistance, a projectile's actual velocity would remain constant. His discoveries enabled Newton to restate the principles of gravitation.

Galileo had considerable influence during his own lifetime. In 1611, for example, there appeared the first published poem of John Donne under the title 'An Anatomy of the World'. It was a disturbing poem which was directly inspired by Galileo's demonstration that the world was no longer the centre of the universe. This caused John Donne to remark that the world was 'All in pieces, all coherence gone'.

Two further contributions are also sometimes attributed to Galileo, but I believe them to be doubtful. One is that he discovered that the Milky Way consisted of a multitude of separate stars and the other is that he invented the pendulum. As regards the former, it is possible that this was believed before him and as regards the latter there is the argument that its inventor may have been the Dutchman Huyghens. In the circumstances, I have not recorded either as a first.

So much for the great firsts. Now to some lesser ones:

● A bucket-type dredger was patented in 1561 by VENTURINO of Venice.

● Prior to that, in 1551 Girolamo CARDANO, who was also a mathematician, had invented the universal joint or cardan shaft as well as the gimbal suspension.

● In the sixteenth century Francesco MAUROLICO, a great optical mathematician, preceded Kepler in many of his ray reflection theories.

● In 1612, Santorio SANTORIO (born in Pavia) elaborated Galileo's thermoscope to invent the first medical thermometer.

Santorio was the founder of the modern study of metabolism. He spent most of his life weighing himself and the products of his body, attributing great importance to the individual's pulse rate. At a time when watches had no seconds hand (and probably no minutes hand either) he devised (1602) a method of measuring the pulse not by its rate but by its strength and rhythm. He devised a machine called a pulsimeter.

He was quite technically minded, since he elaborated machines to weigh the human body and its discharges, he did work on hygrometers and even designed a device for bathing a patient in bed.

● In 1641 FERDINAND THE SECOND, Grand Duke of Tuscany, developed the first sealed-in liquid glass thermometer by replacing water with wine vinegar. He also developed one of the first chicken incubators.

● In 1644 Evangelista TORRICELLI created his 'Tube', the first barometer, later to be refined by Pascal.

Viviani, a Fellow of The Royal Society (1696), himself an engineer and mathematician of repute, assisted Torricelli in this work.

Torricelli was the first man to create a sustained vacuum. He was a great mathematician (his is the famous theorem bearing his name that deals with the speed of water); he was an expert on fluid motion and also studied projectiles.

In 1640 he succeeded in grinding telescope lenses which came near to optical perfection.

● In 1660 G. A. BORELLI (born in Naples) and V. VIVIANI first measured the velocity of sound by the cannon flash and sound method.

● In 1660 Francesco Maria GRIMALDI (born in Bologna) discovered the diffraction of light.

Grimaldi made it clear that 'light was propagated by reflection, refraction and diffraction.' He was also a good physician and was the first to observe the weak sounds produced by muscle contractions. But he remains particularly well known for his fundamental experiments in the field of optics.

● In 1664 the said G. A. BORELLI was the first to suggest the idea of a parabolic path for heavenly bodies.

● In 1664 Giuseppe CAMPANI (born at Castel San Felice) established himself as a technician in lens production. He improved on Torricelli's method and refined the grinding of lenses to such a degree that he managed to build telescopes that were better than those built by Huygens. It was Campani who supplied G. D. Cassini with the telescope that enabled Cassini to study the rotation of Jupiter and Mars and to discover the four satellites of Saturn.

● In 1770 Luigi GALVANI (born in Bologna) experimenting with frogs discovered electricity as a form of energy, thus anticipating the voltaic pile by 30 years.

● In 1801 Giuseppe PIAZZI (born in Valtellina) discovered Ceres - the first of the smaller planets. In 1804 he became a Fellow of The Royal Society.

● In or about 1810 Giovanni BECCARIA (born at Mondovi) discovered the electrical stimulation of muscles.

- In 1838 Angelo SECCHI (born in Reggio E.) was the first to apply the spectroscope to the study of stars.

- In 1820 Macedonio MELLONI (born in Parma) discovered that heat rays are also light rays and in 1832, with Leopoldo Nobili, he invented the thermo-multiplier. He became a Fellow of The Royal Society in 1839.

- In 1824 Ignatio LEMENI invented the mechanical wine press operated by rollers or cylinders. Hand-operated presses were known to the Egyptians, who used a wooden type with two screws.

- In 1853 Eugenio BARSANTI (born at Pietrasanta) and the Marquis Carlo Felice MATTEUCCI (born in Ravenna) deposited at the Florence Academy of the Georgofili a report on what is considered the prototype of the internal combustion engine.

In the report, Barsanti and Matteucci refer to a 'chamber' where 'there is to take place the ignition of the mixtures of gases, the expansion force of which activates at each stroke of the camshaft which is at its bottom.' I know that priority for this claim is attributed to Otto Van Langen at the Paris Exhibition which took place three years later. But I think that the seminal idea was Italian.

- In 1858 Giovanni PACINOTTI (born in Pisa) invented the dynamo which was patented ten years later by the Frenchman Gramme. (Pacinotti also developed one of the first parachutes).

Britannica ascribes the invention of the dynamo to Gramme, but Pacinotti got there at least five years before Gramme. Siemens called Gramme's claim to Pacinotti's invention a 'usurpation'.

- In 1875 Augusto RIGHI (born in Bologna), who was Marconi's teacher, discovered that Hertzian waves are also light waves.

Righi was Professor of Experimental Physics at the University of Bologna and was elected to The Royal Society in 1907.

- In 1889 Galileo FERRARIS (born at Livorno) discovered alternating current.

- In 1866 Felice MARCO patented his principle of electric generation by water power.

- In 1894 Arturo MALIGRANI invented the phosphorous 'gettering' process to assist in creating a vacuum in electric lamp bulbs.

- In 1898 Ernesto STASSANO invented the arc electric steel furnace.

- In 1914 EMANUELLI invented the first oil-filled electric cable of the high-tension type.

- In 1897 Guglielmo MARCONI (born at Bologna) registered his patent number 12039.

Marconi had started work quite young but after his experiments at Pontecchio he, like many Italians, found that he would be more appreciated abroad. Acting probably at the suggestion of his teacher Righi and certainly of his mother, a Scotswoman from Eire, he came over to England and established the historical radio station at Poldhu in Cornwall from which on the 12 December 1901 he transmitted signals to St John's in Newfoundland, Canada. Marconi also invented the directional aerial.

The rest of the Marconi story and the ramifications of his inventions, including the discovery of short waves and the applications of Marconi's principle, above all to its uses in war - especially Radar which he anticipated in 1934 and 1935 (W. P. Jolly - *Marconi* - Constable 1972, page 266), is recorded elsewhere. But it can fairly be said that it was Marconi who laid the foundations upon which the whole system of modern communications was built.

- Emilio Gino SEGRE (born in Tivoli) was the co-winner in 1959 of the Nobel Prize for Physics.

Together with three other physicists at the University of California at Berkeley, USA (Chamberlain, Wiegand and Ypsilantis) he produced technetium, that is to say, the first man-made element not found in nature. In 1940 he discovered astatine and a little later Plutonium 239.

PART 2:
THE DEBATE

CAESAR LANDS IN BRITAIN

CESARE SBARCA IN BRITANNIA

Chi è questo straniero che viene a rompere
il nostro Splendido Isolamento?

"Who's this damn foreigner who's coming to ruin
our Glorious Isolation?"

1.

The Italian Impact on England

Much has already been written concerning the effect that Italian culture has had upon Britain (but England in particular) in so many different fields, including poetry, painting, architecture, landscape gardening or whatever. I decided that my approach, therefore, should be a practical, non-academic one with a view to demonstrating on the one hand how the English react to us and on the other that in the cross-fertilization of ideas that is inevitable in life, the usual two-way flow of influence between Italy and England has accrued to the benefit of the latter. This is not to say that the benefit has been only one way; but the impact of the Italians upon England has been greater and more beneficial than the reverse. And it has been quite substantial. I propose to provide an overall picture of that impact.

After all, it was an Italian who 'discovered' England, an Italian who brought it Christianity, and an Italian who taught it manners (Julius Caesar, St Augustine and Baldassar Castiglione respectively).

When Julius Caesar invaded Britain in 55 BC he established two firsts, one for Rome and the other for Britain. He annexed a new province, thus extending the boundary of an already impressive empire and he brought Britain out of pre-history and put it, as it were, 'on the map.'

His second invasion one year later and the expedition made by Claudius in 43 AD consolidated not only Roman power in Britain, but also a situation which was to last for a further 323 years from Claudius's journey, with significant consequences for the world, although they were not to become apparent until the sixteenth century and were certainly not appreciated at the time.

As they had done to other provinces, the Romans brought civilization to Britain. They brought their system of government, of law, of building, their

art, their Greek medicine, all that contributed to establishing within the
territories that they ruled a gentler society than they found, and a more
settled one.

They built posts, forts, roads, camps, towns, baths, villas and palaces;
they established agriculture, medicine, architecture and discipline.

They endeavoured to create that 'Pax Romana' which, centuries later,
the British Empire was to convert for its possessions into 'Pax Britannica';
they gave their citizenship in the same way as British nationality was later
extended to all races in the Queen's dominions.

Above all, they came with a firm belief in their own ability to mould
history, in their nobility of spirit and of caste and in their outstanding military
techniques and dicipline.

It is interesting to note that when Britain found itself in a position to
establish an empire of its own, it claimed and indeed displayed all the
virtues which the Romans had brought with them many centuries before.
As I shall observe later on, in the political sense there is no doubt whatsoever
that Britain was the successor of Rome.

The Italians (or Romans, if you prefer) who filtered over to Britain in the
three-and-a-half centuries that it remained a province of the Roman Empire
were not only those in overall command. As well as consuls, or pro-consuls,
there were army officers, soldiers, auxiliaries, farmers, technicians, doctors,
road builders: they permeated all classes of British society.

The extant records make it impossible to decide now what the effect
was in quantitative terms but, qualitatively speaking, it cannot have been
negligible.

I wonder how many English people carry Roman blood. Nor should this
be at all surprising, given the inevitable intermarriages; and it is hardly a
coincidence that a psychological Roman heritage exists, given the fact that
Britain was able to prove that it did by establishing a fairly close equivalent
of the Roman Empire.

One is reluctant to call the British Empire an atavistic regression to the
time of the Britons' emancipation from primitive life; but the pride of
Macaulay in his ancestors may have had justifications that went beyond
the purely historical and that were of a more physical/psychological nature.
Who knows?

In 1269 Henry III entrusted to an Italian ('Petrus Romanus') the task of
building the new shrine of Edward the Confessor in Westminster Abbey
and 200 years later Henry VII did likewise for his own tomb and for the
sculptures that decorate the New Lady Chapel there.

As is common knowledge, most of the English country houses are
indebted to Palladio, and Christopher Wren could certainly not have been
in a position to design St Paul's had it not been for his knowledge of Italian
architecture, and the influence that it had on him.

The Reading Room in the British Museum is the work of an Italian. Many
more instances will follow of circumstances where the Italian effect on
things English has been quite noticeable.

Let me be a little more specific.

Take poetry for example. One can talk of 'Italian currents in English poetry ' (Lytton Sells, *The Italian influence in English Poetry*) but I am not aware of any reverse influences. Great though the English poets have been, their influence on Italian poetry is slight, if non-existent. It is true that Eugenio Montale, during one of his stays in England, was inspired to write a poem about Eastbourne on a wet day with the band playing 'God Save the King'. But it is his view of that seaside resort that was embodied in the poem and his style was totally unaffected; he could just as easily have written a poem about Hong Kong and his poetry would have been exactly the same. One wonders, on the other hand, how different the poetry and style of Byron and Shelley would have been if they had never set foot in Italy. There, they were alerted to a new feeling for style and for life which intoxicated them.

Chaucer was in Italy in 1368, 1372 and 1378. (A man of some versatility, Chaucer, for in 1372 he went to Genoa to negotiate a naval treaty; he was a lawyer of the Inner Temple.) He 'took much from the Italians' (Dr Johnson - 9 April 1778.)

There is ample evidence (Op. Cit., pages 19 to 67) that Chaucer got ideas there from the three great Italians of that period, namely Dante, who died in 1321, Petrarca and Boccaccio, both of whom were still alive when Chaucer was in Italy - ideas as to subject-matter, style and rhyming techniques. The reader who wants to know the details upon which the foregoing statements are made is referred to Lytton Sells as quoted above, but it is common knowledge that his *Canterbury Tales* are derived from the stories in Boccaccio's *Decameron* and his *Troilus* from Boccaccio's *Filostrato*. And many other English works were inspired by Boccaccio: there are numerous instances where knowledge of his writings is apparent in both Byron's 'Childe Harold's Pilgrimage' and 'Don Juan.'

Shelley enthusiastically translated some of Dante's work and is well known for displaying the same spiritual approach to woman as that of the noble Florentine.

English writers of the period equally appreciated Italian romantic poetry such as is to be found in Boiardo, Ariosto, Tassoni and Pulci. In particular, Ariosto had a very marked and direct influence on Sir Walter Scott, his 'Ivanhoe' being a successor, in feats and in style, of Ariosto's Paladin Knights.

Thomas Wyatt and Henry Howard learnt from the Italian love poetry of Dell'Aquila, Aretino, Alemanni, Trissino, as well as, of course, from Petrarca (Op. Cit., pages 68 to 81).

John Cheke, William Thomas, and Thomas Hoby profited from their contacts with Italy: and Sir Philip Sydney could not have had the influence he exercised throughout his life unless he had been steeped in classical and Italian culture.

When it comes to Spenser, however, the ties become much closer. As Lytton Sells has pointed out (Op. Cit., pages 152, 156 to 159, 160, 166, 167, 171 and 175) he borrowed extensively from Machiavelli, Castiglione,

Petrarca, Boiardo, Trissino, Tasso, Ariosto and Sannazaro. His *Faerie Queen* echoes Ariosto's *Orlando Furioso*.

The influence of Italy on Shakespeare the poet is perhaps less noticeable than that on Shakespeare the comedy/tragedy writer; according to Lytton Sells it still exists.

When it comes to Shakespeare's language, any student will know the extent to which he relies on the kind of structure which originated in Latin and which Norman-French and Italian preserved.

But many words he uses are borrowed directly from Italian, for example:

Argosy from Ragusa; Bergomask, from the peasants of the Bergamasco, the area around Bergamo in Lombardy; Bezonian, from the Italian adjective 'bisognoso' (needy); Bona-roba; Canzonet, from canzonetta (a short song); Capocchia; Fardel (a bundle), from Fardello; Gaberdine, from gavardina; Hay, from hai; Monarcho; Traject, from Traghetto.

Quite apart from the linguistic aspect, the influence of Italian culture on Shakespeare the writer is very great. He was himself thoroughly versed in the classics, of course, and it was thanks to the Italian humanists that the studies of the classics had been revived. Shakespeare was no small humanist himself and he is in a sense the next link in the chain that started with Petrarca and continued with Boccaccio and Castiglione. Furthermore, it has been suggested (Frances Yates, *Giordano Bruno and the Hermetic Tradition*), that Shakespeare was extensively influenced by Bruno.

Principally, however, it can be said that Shakespeare was essentially concerned with human character, problems and emotions, as Italian writers had been before him. He was very much an individualist and a realist, both obvious Italian traits.

His 18 or more plays set in Italy or with Italian themes show him at his most charming and graceful. Ultimately, this is the debt that Shakespeare owes Italy, namely that its culture focused his imagination and awareness and gave it charm.

I have left the other major English poet prior to the eighteenth century, namely Milton, until last. If I believe Norman Douglas (*Old Calabria*, 1962 ed., pages 173 to 185) then Milton's *Paradise Lost* is a copy of a sacred tragedy by the title of *Adamo Caduto* written in 1647 by Serafino della Salandra. The reader who wants to know the details is referred to *Old Calabria*. It seems that without Salandra's *Adamo*, *Paradise Lost* as we know it would not be in existence inasmuch as Milton copied not only the layout and the idea, but actually the precise words. It is conceivable, of course, that Norman Douglas is wrong, or perhaps is not in earnest: I have not indulged in the kind of research that would enable me to say with any conviction what the truth is, assuming it to be capable of verification. Nor do I quote the above in any critical sense of Milton; quite the reverse. It is highly flattering for an Italian that Milton should have done what Norman Douglas alleges he did. Fashions change, of course, and nobody except students, who are forced to do so, now bothers to read Milton any more than they read Salandra; but it is all part of the general picture that I am painting that Milton should be so greatly indebted to Italy.

Whether Milton did or did not copy Salandra, it is a fact, ·as Joseph Addison has remarked, that Milton could never have described the garden of Eden without having seen the gardens of Italy.

By the end of the sixteenth century it had become fashionable for English noblemen to harbour Continental refugees, including scores of Italians, who were especially welcome. Queen Elizabeth I liked them and she is known to have been very fond of the Italian language, which she often spoke in public.

Amongst these Italian refugees was Petruccio Ubaldini, a Florentine, who first came here in 1545 but did not finally settle in England until 1562. He is remembered for his account, in Italian, of the victory over the Armada, published within a few months of the event. He was liked by Elizabeth, who gave him a pension. He always wrote in Italian, a fact that was readily accepted at the time. Apart from his writings, he was a skilled illuminator and some of his manuscripts have survived.

The seventeenth and eighteenth centuries were not marked by any great literary influence of Italy upon England; Italian literature at this period was hardly known in England and remained so until the middle of the eighteenth century when Dr Johnson's friend, Giuseppe Baretti, began championing the Italian literary cause in England (more about him later).

I don't think I have any need to mention Byron, the two Brownings (the lovers of Italy 'par excellence'), Coleridge, Keats, Hunt, Hazlitt, W. S. Landor, Macaulay, Meredith, Rogers, Shelley, Southwell, Swinburne, Tennyson and Wordsworth, all of whom had their own favourite Italian concepts, haunts and style. Keats is buried in Rome, in the Protestant Cemetery that also has the ashes of Shelley.

Most of them, if not all, wrote about Italy. Byron exalted it in *Childe Harold's Pilgrimage* (see for example the Canto no. 4) and his passionate 'Italia! Oh Italia! thou hast the fatal gift of beauty which became a funeral dower of present woes and past' - which recalls, strangely enough, our own Filicaia who, writing in the seventeenth century, had addressed his country by saying 'O fossi tu men bella o almen piu forte' (Would that you were either less beautiful or at least stronger) as well as his *Ode to Venice*. His *Don Juan* owes much to Italy. Italian history occupied Byron's mind in *Marin Faliero* and *I due Foscari*, and to a lesser extent in *Beppo*.

Robert Browning wrote *Old Pictures in Florence* and *Sordello*, Elizabeth, his wife, *Casa Guidi*, and many others, Meredith wrote *Mazzini's Doctrines* and *Italy Shall Be Free*, W. S. Landor *On The Slaughter of the Brothers Bandiera*, *Ode to Sicily* and *Milton in Italy* and Samuel Roger composed the ode *Italy*. Shelley is well known for his *Ode to Naples*, *The Cenci*, and *Lines Written Among the Euganean Hills* and Swinburne for writing *Halt before Rome*, *Songs before Sunrise* and *To Aurelio Saffi*, Landor for his Trilogy of plays on Joanna of Naples and Bulwer Lytton for *Rienzi*.

Nor should we ignore their contacts, physical or spiritual, with Italian women. Such contacts in themselves, whenever they occurred, must have had perhaps a greater impact on them than even the landscapes. After all, it is a fact that a man only knows another country, if at all, through contacts with women of that country; for in knowing the woman he knows her man: her wants are his deficiencies, her desires his failings, her passions his weaknesses. By knowing her we understand him; and vice versa. Contacts with persons of the same sex are not, in my view, quite so instructive; but perhaps I am looking at the matter purely from a heterosexual point of view.

When it comes to general knowledge of Italy, it is a matter of record that during the seventeenth and eighteenth centuries, but particularly during the Victorian era, the Grand Tour was part of the English gentleman's education.

One of the first Englishmen who crossed the Alps into Italy as part of the process of discovery to which somewhat later the label of Grand Tour was pinned, was John Dennis: he looked upon Italy as 'a garden protected by the Alps'. Quite a few Englishmen crossed the channel into Italy as early as the seventeenth century. Sir Thomas Isham and the Earl of Exeter were probably the most prominent as collectors of antiquities and works of art, but there were many others: and most of them liked what they saw. Bishop Burnet, for example, after having seen the 'Isole Borromeo' on Lake Maggiore in 1685, wrote that they were 'the loveliest spot of ground in the world' (G. Burnet, *Some Letters*).

By the end of the seventeenth century, the Grand Tour had become an established part of education for the English gentleman, whether he took it to study the country or its life, paintings, architecture, ruins or prints. The well-known names who followed this particular itinerary are legion: Gray, Walpole, Manby, Lassels, Bromley, Addison, Lord Shaftesbury, Richardson, Bishop Berkeley, Kent, Burlington, the Earls of Leicester and Warwick, Smollett, John Ealing, John Brown and John Wilkes, the Ladies Hartford and Miller, and Boswell. Indeed, the only Englishman of any significance at this time who does not appear to have set foot in Italy is Dr Johnson, which is probably just as well, or he would certainly have found something to complain about. He had, however, been to France, and as a result (Wednesday, 13 May 1778 in Boswell's *Life*) he wrote that 'the French are a gross, ill-bred, untaught people; a lady there will spit on the floor and rub it with her foot. What I gained by being in France was, learning to be better satisfied with my own country.' Which, I suppose, sums up the real purpose of foreign travel: to appreciate one's own home all the more!

The tradition of travelling on the Continent and especially into Italy continued in the eighteenth century and into the nineteenth and was interrupted only by the Napoleonic wars. Soon after Waterloo, however, the English swarmed into Italy; it is as though, having been deprived of it by the wars with France, they needed the culture and the sun almost like a drug.

The avowed object of the Grand Tour was to broaden the mind by contact with the civilisation of the Continent ('Home-staying youths have ever homely wits'). It is difficult to determine whether in its inception the Tour was an acknowledgement that the educational system in England was deficient (I think it was a a Frenchman, Alexis de Tocqueville, who had remarked that the English public school system strengthened the mind without broadening it) or whether it was an exercise in showing off, in its inception at any rate, a form of keeping up with the Joneses, by the wealthier English gentry. In a sense, the modern equivalent would be to fly off to exotic or distant holiday haunts instead of staying in Europe.

There were, however, some who stayed away from time to time (Byron was one of them) on the ground that Italy was too full of Englishmen, just as some of us avoid going to the Costa del Sol nowadays. Nothing ever changes.

The motives for travel to the Continent and especially to Italy were quite varied.

We all know Dr Johnson's dictum: 'The man who has not been to Italy is always conscious of an inferiority, for his not having seen what it is expected a man should see. The grand object of travelling is to see the shores of the Mediterranean.' (Thursday 11 April 1776.)

Culture was certainly the primary reason, at any rate the declared primary reason. But the slant was different over the three centuries. In the seventeenth and eighteenth centuries there is no doubt that the Englishman (and woman) who went to Italy acknowledged that the Renaissance was the fount of all Classicism; in the nineteenth century, however, the Victorians may have looked upon it differently. It is conceivable that many went because they felt that they had to commune with Roman civilization on the basis that the English were the successors of the Romans. Those animated by Protestant religious fervour may have gone to see for themselves the negative sides of the Catholic church, or if historically-minded maybe even to see the collection of Henry VIII's letters to Anne Boleyn housed in the Vatican Library.

Many went to improve their health. More than once it was said that the rheumatisms and the consumption brought about by the English weather could be cured in the Mediterranean, where one could avoid the English winter 'ending in July to recommence in August' (Byron, *Don Juan* - Canto XIII stanza XLII). Even here, however, the position is not entirely clear because in the southern Mediterranean the traveller was subject to the risk of cholera, malaria and typhoid: bilious attacks and diarrhoea were common. Many died in Italy and a few were even buried there.

Some went on the Tour for business purposes, like Sir Henry Wootton; some for botanical purpose or to improve their classical reputation or knowledge or to study politics or to improve their techniques if they were artists or possibly even to add to their already established fame. Scientists were there: Davy, Babbage and Faraday, as well as politicians: Brougham, Liverpool, Peel and Russell.

Others went to improve their manners. Writing to George Augustus Selwyn, for example, the fifth Earl of Carlisle considered that foreign travel - he had just crossed the Alps - could serve to improve the manners of some of his friends.

Many went because of the fatal allure of the siren, Italy. They went to the land of gaiety and sensuality where they believed that their behaviour would be less criticised than at home. This certainly applied to those English eccentrics who, coming from a wealthy background, could afford freely to indulge their whims in Italy; but it applies equally to those English homosexuals who were escaping from the somewhat stringent laws then prevailing in England.

It is, however, questionable to what extent the search for a totally different environment and culture was the result of a penchant for knowledge rather than the satisfaction of a craving for new experiences, an attempt to shrug off one's own background and way of living which were felt as unduly restrictive, or boring, or even hypocritical.

As a result, when books were written about Italian travel, facts were somewhat twisted and Italy (and its inhabitants) were shown as the visitor intended to find them rather than as they really were: a balanced view seldom emerged.

Accordingly, one finds writers being either too critical of the locals, or too eulogistic of what, under a different sky and breathing the air of the Mediterranean, appeared to be virtues when compared to some of the traits of the people that had been left at home.

Nevertheless, it is a fact that as a result of the popularity of the Tour, Italian literature revived, as did the language. To have an Italian master in the house of nobility was a mark of distinction and good taste. Indeed, as Professor Vincent has so stylishly observed, with Palladian influence extending to the stonework, Canaletto's paintings on the walls, Canova's statues in the halls and the Italian opera in the Haymarket, it can fairly be said that no other country exerted greater cultural influence on the England of the nineteenth century than Italy.

The nineteenth century was a particularly important period for the Italian influence upon England, which ranged from paintings to gardens. The fashion for Italy is also manifested during this period in the use of Italian words which became more and more prominent, especially in the artistic field. The Dilettanti Club was formed in 1734 by a number of English literary 'virtuosi' and 'cognoscenti', Sir Francis Dashwood being their prime mover (the paintings of the first members of the Dilettanti Club still hang in the drawing-room and elsewhere in the building of Brooke's Club in St James's): all members of the Dilettanti Club had been to Italy.

In fact, having travelled to Italy was the qualification for membership. However, Horace Walpole said that whilst having been to Italy was the nominal qualification for membership of 'Brooks's', the real one was that of being drunk. Is this true? According to Bernard Darwin (*British Clubs* in the series 'Britain in Pictures', Collins, 1943), it is certainly not true. He explains away Walpole's cutting remarks on the basis that members of the Dilettanti Club were 'a hilarious group, inclined to friendly foolery'. The reader will form his own view anyhow.

Of course, the Englishman who could afford to go on the Grand Tour was educated and had plenty of money: he would hire either a 'vettura' in which he could travel in comfort, or a tutor or a guide (cicerone) or a combination of the three. It was certainly not the lower class Englishman who could bear the kind of expenditure involved, which was not negligible.

Depending on the Englishman's background, tendencies, and finances the Grand Tour either stopped in Germany and Switzerland or continued into the Mediterranean through Italy. Italy was a staging post, so to say, for Greece, Turkey, Cyprus, the Middle East and Egypt. The further away one travelled, the richer one had to be. Richer not only as far as money was concerned but also in time, because journeys of this nature, at least initially (until the Saint Gothard Pass was opened towards the middle of the nineteenth century and until either railways or steamers came into their own towards the middle and end of the nineteenth century) took a long time indeed. For example, John Evelyn left England for his Continental Tour in 1643 and was away nearly four years, mainly in France and Italy.

It was therefore only the nobility who travelled to the Mediterranean, the nobility of title and the nobility of education, with servants.

The scenery changed in more ways than one as soon as the Alps were crossed. The novelty in the weather and in the landscape seemed to bring about a change in the pattern of behaviour of the travellers. They suddenly became more extrovert, they felt that since the people with whom they were mixing were so completely different in every respect (tradition, culture, appearance, eating habits, social customs and so on) they need no longer maintain the strict standards of thought and behaviour imposed by the society that they were leaving, albeit temporarily. In other words, they suddenly felt free. All Northerners do, as soon as they cross the Alps: it's as though they are escaping from the cage in which their society keeps them and they are at last free to behave in accordance with their instincts.

This freedom provokes firstly a change in outlook; but it has further consequences. The change in outlook is a concomitant of a variation in behaviour which is manifested initially by an increase in noise level. The pitch of voice rises and this is accompanied by a general disregard for others. Such manifestations are common to northern people generally. Whether they be Swedes, Germans, Belgians or British, as soon as they cross the Alps or the Pyrenees, they display features which, whilst interesting to observe, are extremely irritating. One might think that it is the novelty of being in a different country; but not so. The very same people act in keeping with the patterns of behaviour that they have established in their own countries whilst travelling through Scandinavia, Germany, France, Austria or Switzerland. But as soon as they cross the Alps or the Pyrenees they appear to be almost compelled to raise their voices, make more noise generally, be utterly unmindful of the well-being and the peace and quiet of the inhabitants of those countries where they are but guests. It is as though on the one hand they feel that they have to adapt to local habits - but few people make noise in Italy, Spain or Greece during the 'siesta' hours except the foreign visitors - and, on the other, that their stronger foreign currency provides them with certain rights of 'seigneurity' which are absent in their own countries. It is an interesting phenomenon which knows barriers neither of nationality nor of age: if they are from the north, this is the way they behave in the south.

I had initially thought that such a change in behaviour was due to alcohol. By this I mean that the general availability of cheap drink so interferes with established patterns of action and discipline that the urge to make noise and to be assertive becomes irresistible. I have now reached the conclusion that my initial assessment was wrong: alcohol does not figure in the psychology of the exercise, although it is a very potent factor in the practical problems that occur. The same people who are paragons of propriety in the suburbs of Dusseldorf or London, feel compelled to let themselves go when they find themselves in Italy, Spain or Greece. True, they have drunk too much because it was so cheap to drink so much: but the problem is primarily a psychological one and only secondarily a practical one provoked by alcohol.

It is the Mediterranean air, mood, mentality, tradition, impact, strength, and all pervasive aura. The Alps and the Pyrenees - Italy and Spain and, to a lesser degree, Greece - represent the geographical and cultural division between north and south and it is at that point that psychological barriers break down.

But what about France, you may be wondering? In my view the same does not happen there. France is not so markedly a Mediterranean country as either Spain or Italy.

The northerner who goes to France feels he's in a different country, but does not make so much noise, does not consider deep down that he can let himself go quite so completely as he does, undoubtedly, as soon as he crosses the high peaks of Europe. Whether it is because there is an element of contempt for Spaniards, Italians and Greeks which does not apply quite so strongly to the French, or whether it is because the northerner considers that he will be allowed greater freedom and sympathy in these three countries, is a little difficult to determine.

The net result, however, is the same: today, the northerner in the Mediterranean is, on the whole, a noisy, ill-behaved person, who has little regard for the locals and whose appreciation of what is available there is a function of the rate of exchange. It is sad. However, let us not dwell too much on the present but return to the Englishmen on their Grand Tour.

It was a long journey, at times difficult, at times worrying; in those days, the travellers were not really concerned with the dangers of the journey; indeed, those very dangers added to the excitement.

The sermonising of those who maintained that by mixing with the natives the visitors would be weakened did not seem to have much effect. True, there was a view in some quarters that by mixing with these instinctive, sensual and sometimes even slightly effeminate southerners, the aristocracy of England would be corrupted. But there seems to be no real evidence to support the theory that corruption affected those who did not wish to be corrupted.

Those who travelled to the south wanted to experience sensations that were denied to them in northern climes, they wanted to be light-hearted, when at home they had to be stern: they wanted to have fun, when at home they were miserable; they wanted to give free rein to their eccentricity, which at home had to be restrained; they tried to belong to the places they visited, so that Dickens may have preferred Genoa and Ruskin Verona; they wanted to have the heightened experience of the senses that only Mediterranean sunlight and life provide. As they crossed the Alps they left behind them all social and psychological constraint; the bright light, I suppose, was the first major impression, and then the sounds, and the people.

Their attitude to the people, however, varied. Some thought that the Italians were charming and polite; others felt that they were dark and mischievous and that there were bandits and crooks everywhere. Byron liked them, Landor disliked them.

Some thought that the Italians were childish and simple; others that they were vicious and corrupt. Some loved all they found; others complained of barbaric habits and customs. Even Byron, a great lover of Italy, objects to the custom of fasting in Lent. In his *Beppo* (stanzas VII and VIII) he complains about having to live for 40 days on 'ill-drest fishes' and recommends to those who intend to visit Italy that they should stock-up on 'Ketchup, Soy, Chili-vinegar and Harvey.'

But whatever view was taken, the northerner felt a great sense of liberation as soon as he got to Italy: he almost ceased to think and began to feel. If he was a nobleman who had been accustomed to strict hierarchies, he found that in Italy, and indeed throughout the Mediterranean, the structures of society were not so well defined; if he felt the so-called innate superiority of the Teutonic race, he began to realise that some of it would have to be left behind because, at least in the artistic field, that superiority meant very little in Italy and Greece; if he felt that the Church of Rome was corrupt, he was like Abraham the Jew in Boccaccio's second novel on day one: struck by the fact that the corrupt Church survived and attracted converts, despite the extensive superstition that was found particularly in the Italian hinterland; if he remembered the Inquisition, he was still bound to acknowledge the almost symbiotic life of Italian art with the Roman Church; if he felt that the Italians were degenerate, he still must have wondered whether their degeneracy did not have something to commend it. If one day the traveller felt like complaining about the natives' rudeness, dirt and uncivil behaviour, the next he would be surprised by their unexpected urbanity and restraint; after all if, having stayed a while, he thought he knew what the Italians felt, he must have wondered how their ability to make themselves agreeable could be reconciled with their apparent inscrutability of thought.

All in all, he must have felt as though he was on a see-saw, enjoying the sun one moment and malaria the next.

Apart from the different weather, manners, customs, eating habits, superstitions and so on, one of the features of the country that the northerner must have found quite unsettling was the comparative lack of social differences. This is not to say that social distinctions did not exist in the Italy of the time. Indeed, the number of titled heads all over the country, and especially in the south, was very substantial.

But the great divide between the classes that may have existed in England, Germany or Sweden was not so marked in Italy: Italy was not then, any more than it is now, a class-conscious country. People knew, of course, that there were distinctions between the classes, that there was a nobility of blood as there now is a nobility of money; but the bond of common humanity could not easily be dislodged and whatever else Bonapartism may not have achieved, it did achieve, particularly in Italy, a certain levelling upwards, at least in the basic aspirations of the common people.

In addition, I find that where the sun shines strongly, people seem to be reminded more of their common humanity. Deep processes of thought are not so easy to maintain; even the amount of clothes to be worn is reduced; and living in the proximity of antiquity, art and history serves as a reminder of one's comparative insignificance. This insignificance is universal and is not limited to those who may not have a title or be penniless.

This kind of natural religion has a levelling effect and it must have been unsettling, to say the least, for those coming from the north to find that a number of the strictures imposed upon them by their own upbringing and class structure had no meaning whatsoever in the southern Mediterranean. As a result, the visitor to Italy learnt not only about antiquities but also about life; he broadened his horizons extensively, despite his complaints.

One feature, however, about which there never was any complaint or any argument was the Italian garden.

The Italian landscaped garden seems to have been particularly prominent at this period and the English landed gentry and patrons of the arts vied with one another in providing new ideas in gardening based on what they saw in Italy, some going even so far as to incorporate Roman arches or ruins. Others introduced terraces, grottoes, fountains, waterworks, statuary, descending stairways, separate courtyards, mazes, mounds, orangeries, loggias, stone terraces, arcades, parterres, follies, sunken pools and little islands in lakes.

The Duke of Devonshire laid out at Chatsworth the waters of the Derbyshire Peak District in imitation of Tivoli.

Fountains Abbey was added to the local garden to give it character as part of a campaign to glamourise local ruins in the same way as the ruins of ancient Rome were used in Italy. In fact, such was the determination to follow the Italian pattern, that where there were no remains to incorporate into the new landscape, they would actually be created. This occurred, for example, at Scotney Castle which was partly pulled down to make it more like a ruin when the owner went to live nearby in order to give effect to his scheme. The operation was clearly artificial, but the search for what was natural was certainly genuine and heartfelt.

James I was himself very keen on the Italian type of garden and he increased the interest that was already growing.

As John Dickson Hunt has already stated so eloquently (*Gardens and Groves*, Dent, London 1986) all this was the result of Italian imagination: 'Italian gardens provided the imagery, the structures and the ideas for all northern gardens whether French, Dutch or English... there was indeed nowhere else whence such inspiration could derive.'

All this followed from the fact that the visitor to Italy saw many new types of garden on his tour, which he admired for the variety and the fullness of the design. Above all, he began to appreciate that they represented a world all of their own, self-contained as they were; and they were almost a theatre. Indeed, the owners of the gardens were the actors on that stage and many plays and operas were in fact set in the Italian gardens of the time. Niches, grottoes, pools, and other features were also added as if scenes from the theatre.

Just as the painters who went to Italy brought back their own vision of the country, so the visiting nobility who were impressed by Italian nature returned home with a particular idolisation of the natural world in the garden. They even went so far as to imagine that the 'genius' of the place inhabited their restructured English garden.

Alexander Pope held the traditional form of garden up to ridicule: nature came into its own in the English garden.

Gradually, however, the fashion faded. People began to feel that the Italian garden was too informal and that, as master of the universe, man should control nature in his gardens as well. Capability Brown then became famous, as the English type of garden took over with the claim that nature had been 'educated' in the garden.

This approach to gardening was exported from England to France with a similar impact on nature there, since the French were prevailed upon to change their mistrust of nature which had been the hallmark of their approach to gardening in the seventeenth century.

*   *   *

Right through the eighteenth and nineteenth centuries Italy continued to be 'invaded' and plundered. At this time, of course, the invaders were more civilised and the plunder occurred not through force of arms but by the use of money, market forces and stealth. One example, which I consider a classic, will suffice. Please note that the authority for what follows is to be found in Hutton's *History of Derby* published in 1791. (pp. 195-208).

At about that time, only the Italians had developed the technology for silk-throwing and consequently enjoyed an absolute command of the lucrative international trade.

During this period the wearing of silks was considered high fashion and British merchants were obliged to meet the Italian merchants' exorbitant prices for silk.

It transpires that a local Derby man, one Crotchet, thought he would make a fortune by throwing silk himself and started a mill; but he soon found that he needed the Italian machines and went bankrupt.

Next onto the scene stepped John Lombe, 'A man of spirit, a good draughtsman and an excellent mechanic'. He travelled to Italy 'with a view of penetrating the secret'. There he corrupted two servants of the manufacturer of the machines, copied the details and learnt how they were assembled.

Lombe was discovered but managed to flee back to England with two of his Italian accomplices. In 1717, he settled in Derby where labour and water were plentiful. There he did a deal with the city corporation for the buildings and water supply and he continued profitably for some three or four years selling silk at a lower price than the Italians.

Predictably, Lombe's operation began to undermine the Italian trade to the extent that the Italian merchants decided on revenge. They sent over to England a woman who found employment at Lombe's mill and then got together with one of the two Italians who had originally come over with Lombe. In 1718 John Lombe might have had the commercial foresight to apply for a patent, but he certainly did not appear to have the wit to realise that the Italians would surely have their revenge, which they may well have done - he was poisoned two years later and died in agony.

The Italian woman was questioned but was not charged. John Lombe was only 29 when he died but he was apparently already such an important local figure that he was given one of the most magnificent funerals ever held in Derby. Lombe, as it happened, died a bachelor, so his estate went to his brother William who, being of 'a melancholy turn' shot himself shortly after.

However, the mill prospered and 300 people were employed there.

When John Lombe's patent expired in 1732 his cousin, Sir Thomas Lombe, successfully petitioned Parliament for its renewal. The Government decided the technology was a good investment for Britain and made available £14,000 (an enormous sum in those days) to develop it. Further mills were opened in Stockport and Nathaniel Gartrevalli, the second of the two Italians who had initially assisted Lombe, worked there. Gartrevalli, however, died in poverty, Hutton remarking that such was 'the frequent reward of the man who ventures his life on a base cause or betrays his country'. But the business prospered; indeed, it has continued to do so until recently. Silks for the mills came from Persia, Canton and Piedmont in Italy (pages 278, 279).

Italy is quite accustomed to having things stolen from it. All its invaders obviously plundered it. This is part of the history of all empire builders and colonisers, and the traditional right of conquest in war. It is exactly what the Romans did with Greece. The difference, however, is that Italy was plundered when it was at peace, except for the German actions in 1943.

Ultimately, all conquerors have for those they have defeated a feeling more of superiority and contempt than of understanding and sympathy. The basis on which they can take what they want, is that they feel greater than the vanquished. The vanquished in turn are an object of contempt. They may look upon their antiquities with neglect and not care for them and leave them abandoned amidst ruins, lichens, moss and capers.

The conquerors' attitude is that they will take them and care for them by putting them in museums and galleries, on the basis that they know best. They do not look upon it as theft, but rather as a good deed. This is exactly the attitude of Britain towards the Elgin Marbles. The argument is that they are being preserved for humanity and posterity.

It must be admitted that there is some truth in this approach which, however, only stems from cultural conceit and not from true artistic sensitivity or appreciation. It is arguable that leaving works of art amidst ruins is more in keeping with history than to remove them to museums, just as leaving animals in their natural habitat is more consistent with nature than keeping them in zoos.

In the final analysis, this attitude is the outcome of a desperate psychological need. It is the result of extreme scarcity in the particular commodity which it is said should be preserved for posterity. It starts out as a whim of those people with money who, on the one hand, might have cared, and on the other were able to gratify their whims and their fancies as such. This renders the exercise laudable and to some extent more forgiveable.

With the passage of time, however, it becomes more difficult to justify this attitude, as the retention of the Elgin Marbles shows.

If all had to be returned to Italy which was taken from it, most major museums and private collections of the world would be denuded and some would actually cease to exist.

It also has to be said that the present constant copying of things Italian by the 'outside world' is truly a disgrace. It is within my own knowledge that a number of people throughout the world actually take great trouble to go, say, to the Milan Fair in April to see exactly what new ideas emerge from Italy. Of course this is the nature of commercial life today and, in a sense, is highly flattering.

The copying of the machinery for silk throwing resulted in the establishment in England of the textile industry in the Midlands. History repeated itself in the case of Meucci for the telephone and Pacinotti for the dynamo and it is my own direct professional knowledge that there have been 'thefts' of design or know-how in respect of industrial machinery (cutters, staplers, etc.), furniture, perpetual calendars, and a lot more. Dishonesty, like fraud, is infinite and I have to accept the fact that Italy is by no means the only country to have had its ideas pinched.

On the other hand, it is not always easy to copy successfully. For example, the Victorians tried to copy Majolica and they produced nothing like the original. Nor could they: the artistic spirit was not there.

Even when the supreme styling of Italian cars has been copied either directly or, as is more common, indirectly in the sense that the lines are not reproduced as such but the overall concept is adopted, the results are hybrid and they do not have the clean cut of the original.

It is inevitable, because line is influenced by an overall view of style and of life which cannot be transplanted. One may certainly copy the practical features of any machine or motor car; but you need style to copy Italian styling and, if you had the style in the first place, you would have no need to copy.

In turn, the Italians were also quite expert at fraud. Many a fake painting or sculpture must have been sold to foreign visitors. On the other hand, I wonder how many masterpieces left Italy either without any payment or in consideration of a pittance. One need only think of Joseph Smith or Sir William Hamilton. 'The Italian Collections were stripped' says Scott-Fox (Op. Cit., page 52). Nothing unusual in that.

In 1851, A. W. Franks reported to the trustees of the British Museum that 'the whole of Italy has been so ransacked by foreign dealers that it is useless to expect any number of specimens to be discovered in that country' (Wilson, Op. Cit.). He was referring to Majolica, but the same thoughts could be expressed about other artefacts. The unfortunate reality is that the Italians have always been careless about their artistic heritage. The reason is simple: people attach no value to what they have in abundance; we had then, to use modern terminology, a masterpiece lake or mountain and all those who could, helped themselves to it. More recently, the Italian Government has tried to tighten up the export of art from Italy, but, as in the case of currency exportation, it has acted too late and all it has done is to shut the stable door after the horses have bolted; and how many horses; and what horses!

(Nor should we be any more grateful to the Germans who, with the excuse that Italy had in 1943 become an enemy country, tried to smuggle out as many antiques and works of art as they could. Some have been recovered, but not all. That was unkind, because the Germans did not really deserve to have them; in a sense, much better that they should go to the English or to the Americans who at least, throughout our history have, on the whole, befriended us.)

One can go further and say that the modern appreciation of antiques and works of art is prompted more by venal than aesthetic consideration. It is the rarity of the item that provokes the desire to possess it in the first place; the rarity adds to the value and the combination of the scarcity/profit factor overrides all other considerations.

Those who have little of a particular (artistic) commodity are in my view the least well equipped to appreciate the true nature of the intrinsic value, as distinct from the market value, of the work of art or the chattel or whatever. It is a misconception to assume that because one is a collector of rare items, one understands their true value and their real nature. I find that the contrary is true, namely that it is the people who are surrounded by things of a particular kind or of a particular style, who, although superficially contemptuous of them because they have them in abundance and therefore attach no significance to them, are in reality the very people who have a deeper psychological inner understanding of what it is they are surrounded by.

In other words, I do not believe that because a northerner had the means of travelling through Italy and collecting rare items of art or beauty he, for that reason alone, had a better appreciation of what he was collecting than those from whom it was taken away. It is obvious that the uneducated locals who allowed the abstraction of what was of such apparent value to others had little understanding of its market value. But it does not follow that they had no appreciation of the intrinsic nature of what they were giving away. That nature was part of their make-up, psychological certainly and probably also physical; and that could never be taken away.

Be that as it may, the greatest impact of Italy on England occurred through architecture. The debt England owes Palladio is very great indeed.

*   *   *

Palladio was easy to imitate. His four books on architecture were easy to read, digest and follow since they proceeded from the premise that so much could be achieved by modular construction.

The English were quick to seize on this concept which produced immediate, impressive results without any need to strain a deficient imagination and the results can be seen in their thousands all over England. However, if anyone needs a reminder of the keenness of the English to follow the modular type of construction, the four telephone kiosks at the rear of the Law Courts in Carey Street, London, show that even to this day the modular, lego-type approach has continued.

Furthermore, Palladio's buildings, though derived from Rome, had certain static, almost severe effects that were eminently suited to a cold climate. London is to this day full of Palladian ideas: his solidity appealed to the British much more than the decadent, ornate Baroque style. But mainly, I suppose, his exteriors made allowances for the weaker northern light and enabled the features of a building to stand out even under a cloudy sky. In England, Palladio is still king, and English architects had to go to Rome and Vicenza to learn about his style, as well as architecture generally. Sir John Soane would not have designed the 'new Law Courts' or the Bank of England if he had not studied Palladio's work; Nash's Langham Place comes from the same source; and George Basevi's buildings on the Grosvenor Estate in Belgravia owe an even more obvious debt to Italy.

Nor should I omit to mention the bands of Italian travelling craftsmen such as stone masons, painters, intaglio experts, wood carvers and cabinet makers. They used to come over for specific jobs, stay the time it took -

sometimes years - to complete their task, and then move on. As England had had its itinerant judges, so Italy had its itinerant craftsmen. Indeed, it still has them, as anyone who is conversant with the construction of major building works or petrochemical plants in developing countries well knows. (See 'Pottery' for the influence that Italian master craftsmen had on the English delftware industry.)

Italian influence on English painting is not so great for the simple reason that England has not produced any truly great painters. Or is it the other way round? Could it be that there are no great painters in England because Italian influence was slight? Possibly, I am not sure; perhaps there is something in the make-up of the English people that prevents them from attaining true greatness in the artistic field.

As I have shown, Hogarth adapted the caricature for his own ends. But even though Sir Joshua Reynolds knew Italy and its art, it is difficult to see where the Italian influence in him really occurs. True, Gainsborough was inspired by Italian landscapes and Turner studied Titian very carefully indeed. To a layman like me, however, Turner's Italian passion for light is offset by his disregard for line. In that, he certainly is not Italian and I think that he was influenced by the Mediterranean sun more than by Mediterranean art: but I am no expert on this point. Still, it is rather odd to see in one of his paintings Mount Snowdon against the background of the Roman 'campagna'.

Other than in their name I personally see nothing Italian about the pre-Raphaelites either; but, here again, I am ignorant. The influence of the Roman and Neapolitan countryside upon the English water-colourists of the eighteenth and nineteenth centuries, of course, is indisputable.

Turning to prose, the English-speaking lovers of Italy who were all influenced by her are numerous. In alphabetical order they are: Butler, Compton McKenzie, Norman Douglas, Dickens, Disraeli, T. S. Eliot, George Eliot, E. M. Forster, Gissing, Augustus Hare, Hazlitt, E. Hutton, James Joyce, Macaulay, Ouida, Ezra Pound, F. Rolfe, John Ruskin, Scott, J. A. Symonds, the Sitwells, Swinburne, Thackeray and the Trollopes.

Each of them found something different in Italy. What is it, I wonder, that draws the Englishmen to Italy almost irresistibly like mosquitos to the light?

I am not thinking of the English tourist who flocks to the Italian beaches to enjoy the sun, some pasta and vino. I have in mind, when I say the Englishman, northern races generally. Basically, what I say about the English also applies to, say, the Germans or the Scandinavians.

It is too easy to say that it is the sun or the music or the art or the ruins or the museums or the Vatican. All these are of course important but, apart from the Vatican, they can all be found in differing degrees in other countries. The attraction of Italy for the English lies in something totally different, namely in the fact that there the Englishman can afford to be himself, because on the whole that is exactly what the natives are doing, namely being themselves. It is also true that, generally speaking, the Italians are probably the most hospitable people in Europe; they are certainly friendly and extrovert and they believe in making guests, whoever they may be, feel at home. Indeed, sometimes that hospitality can be overpowering for those spirits who are incapable of opening up to warmth. But overall, nobody can accuse Italians of xenophobia.

We make people feel comfortable and we pander to their desires; we take them as they are, no matter who they are and we have found it very easy to do so because, until recently, our experience of foreigners has always been an exceptionally good one. Take the English, for example; the Englishman who came to Italy on his Grand Tour whether in the seventeenth, eighteenth or nineteenth century, or to study, was the better class of Englishman with plenty of money. There is no more enjoyable country to be in, when you have money, than Italy. I am not sure, however, what view Italians have of some of today's visitors.

Nevertheless, when he gets to Italy the northerner suddenly feels free. It may be that the sun forces him to be himself and the effect of the diet. It may be a combination of factors. But he is a different person and after a long stay he sometimes ends up by thinking the way Italians do; which may not necessarily be to his advantage: but that is another story...

It is this effect which ultimately produces the contrast in the hearts and the minds of the English and affects their judgement of the Italians. The English, as it were, cannot help loving us, because we, the Italians, are inherently lovable; and yet the English resent the love they are experiencing because they find that they are appreciating something which deep down is alien to their nature.

Their reaction to that is a form of dislike which sometimes turns to hatred and which always results in attributing to the Italians faults which are associated in historical terms with Italy but which are not always present nowadays and, very often, in ascribing to the Italians their own English vices, but acclimatized to Italy.

Hence the marked contrast between the views held by Ascham (see 'Manners') and John Ruskin (discussed later) on the one hand, and the enthusiasm of Robert Browning on the other when he said, 'Open my heart and you will see, graved inside of it, "Italy".'

Nowhere is this ambivalent attitude of the English more noticeable than when it is experienced by women. (I am taking the Englishman as distinct from the Englishwoman because I have never found that the Italians present problems for English women. They may not understand us; but they have no real, fundamental dislike for us. As a matter of fact, they quite often like us for what I may call 'technical' reasons.)

In the case of the Englishman, however, things are different, basically for two reasons:

The first reason is that the Englishman learns as part of his everyday language an Italian word which represents all that he, as an Englishman, is incapable of being; that is to say, he knows what Casanova was and did and represented. I believe that the Casanova myth is one of the greatest exercises in public relations that the Italians ever indulged in. I cannot believe that a Venetian could be as good as Casanova makes himself out to be in his memoirs; nor do I accept that his indefatigability was a fact. Decency, however, prevents me from going into detail over this and, in any event, it is not an important point.

The fact remains that whatever my beliefs are about Casanova, the Englishman is brought up to believe that, generally speaking, the Italian male scores pretty highly on the 'Casanova' scale. Nothing could be further from the truth.

But herein lies the problem. This belief is one of the sources of tension in the relationship between the two nationalities. It arises from the fact that the Englishman has what I would call a complex in sexual and amorous behaviour where he feels that the Italian is more at ease. He is bothered by our easy way with women, by the apparent facility with which we flatter all and sundry, by our spontaneity and our apparent brilliance. He would like to imitate us and be more demonstrative but on the one hand he does not think he should and on the other he feels that he would do it without conviction; and therefore, not quite so well. Hence this constant tug-of-war in feelings and emotions to which I have already referred.

You will have noticed that when I consider 'womanising' I refer exclusively to Casanova and not to Don Juan. There are two reasons for this. Firstly, I am concerned only with Italians and not with Spaniards. Secondly, I find that there is a difference between the two types of lovers. Casanova is Mediterranean, Don Juan is affectively northern; Casanova is truly erotic, Don Juan is only intellectually sensual; the former has always seemed to me more human, the latter is a devil and as such he is portrayed by Mozart; Don Juan seems to enjoy the thought of possessing a woman whereas Casanova appreciates the actual possession; and is considerate and friendly to those he has relations with.

There are libertines both in Mediterranean and in northern countries, but their motivation is different: for the northerner, the ravishing of a woman is a manifestation more of pride than of love. In my opinion, Casanova had on the whole more tender feelings than Don Juan, and, because of this fact, had probably a greater understanding of women.

Such fundamental difference between the two renowned seducers is reflected in the duality of approach which I am considering, and underlines it. According to his servant, Don Juan had had at least 1,003 women in Spain alone; it is a pity that one cannot ask them what they felt after the event.

The second reason is historical. If one reads the poems of Macaulay one cannot help feeling that his admiration for ancient Rome is so indiscriminate that it amounts almost to veneration. He, like Kipling, correctly believed that all the virtues which he attributes to the Romans (strength, discipline, respect for authority, patriotism, etc.) were the very same that made the Victorians great. It was obvious to him and many others that the English were, in political terms, the successors of the Romans.

The English had in fact created an empire which could compare with that of Rome; they had extended their citizenship, as Rome had done, to all those who lived under the British flag and they had created respect for that citizenship.

All this is perfectly true. To that extent, the English are the true political successors of ancient Rome. Or rather, were; and just as Rome fell through the corruption of its body politic, so the British Empire crumbled away when Britain had fulfilled its historical function.

If then a proud Englishman looked to Italy, he found that those who should have been the natural successors of the Romans were in a sorry state indeed because, after the fall of the Roman Empire, they had failed conspicuously to reassert themselves. The people seemed incapable of national unity, the country itself was more like a cemetery. Looking at Italy through the rose-tinted spectacles of Romanticism, one saw a lot of art, of course; but mainly ruins. Ruins everywhere; ruins punctuated by trees. But in the arid south or the Roman 'campagna' or throughout Tuscany, so much favoured by the English, what was the principal tree? The Cypress, the tree of the dead. The tree of the dead in the land of the dead. Byron started the idea, Ruskin repeated it; they meant it kindly, of course. Lamartine, however, meant it most unkindly; whether through a misunderstanding of the real position or because of the gentle antipathy that has always existed between the Italians and the French, I cannot say.

But there seemed no doubt at the time that the country was in a sorry state and that the Italians were not up to much. They were quite incapable of formulating any coherent policy for their own nation and this state of affairs could be said to have continued right up to the twentieth century.

The Italians, therefore, cannot be the successors to the Romans, for they display none of the civic qualities that made Rome great. So the English think, forgetting that England has been a united country since 1066 and a democracy since 1688 whereas Italy has been a united country, basically, since 1918 and a democracy only since 1948. And it is easy enough to ignore the fact that throughout the whole of our post-Roman history we have been slaves; that we had to suffer over two centuries of Spanish domination; that we have never known until recently what it means to be masters in our own home. In fact, all in all, considering our history, we could have been a lot worse and much more incapable.

Nevertheless, in political terms, this assessment is perfectly correct. In historical terms it is inevitable. In economic terms it is irrelevant. But in cultural and psychological terms it is totally untrue. And it is the Roman culture in which Italy was and still is steeped and the Roman heritage, factual and psychological, that has provided some of the redeeming features of the Italian nation. The Italians are of course the cultural successors of the Romans. These contradictory features of history have always appeared mystifying to the English and have been a constant source of irritation to them. They have always failed to understand how one can be motivated by culture and not by political ambition or efficiency: Italian reactions and traits have always been a mystery.

The English have criticised us, correctly, for our lack of civic sense, but they have ignored the fact that our feeling for beauty is virtually unique. They have smiled, understandably, at our lack of stable Government, but have not considered that our cultural heritage is rock solid. They have caricatured, with justification, the number and proliferation of political parties in Italy but have taken no note of the significant fact that at least 90 per cent of those entitled to vote in general and local elections in Italy actually take the trouble of going to the polls.

It is a fact that apparently we have no self-discipline; but if necessary, we can fight for our families as well as the next man, if not better.

There may have been little historical merit, and even less ability, in conquering Abyssinia; but great strides have been made in overcoming poverty and illiteracy.

It may be taking us a long time to eradicate centuries-old evils like the 'Mafia', but the fact that police chiefs and judges are killed from time to time in the fight against organized crime, and yet are replaced, shows ultimately the strength of a system where the investigating magistrates ('pretori') emerge as the storm troops of justice.

And so it goes on.

Generalisations are born of misunderstandings.

On this subject of generalisations I beg your indulgence in making one further digression.

Earlier on I mentioned that I would come back to one of the many commonplaces amongst the English that concern the Italian male, namely bottom-pinching.

As I have already said, I do not believe this sterotype to be true. Some generalisations obviously have an element of truth in them, but I think this one is no more correct than many general beliefs that the Italians hold about the British.

For example, did you know that until, say, the early 1950s, when the Italians started to take a keener interest in Britain as a holiday country - and indeed, they have continued to do so in ever increasing numbers, sometimes hordes, to this day - Italians believed that the English had five meals a day? This rumour was set about by the Mussolini regime, in the days when that regime had to justify its invasion of Ethiopia, to explain to the poor Italian peasant that he should support a cause that provoked the British, since the British were doing so well when he, the poor peasant in southern Italy, was not; so well that they were having five meals a day when that peasant struggled to have one. Italy had to have its own back over perfidious Albion. It might have been true of the eighteenth-century English aristocracy but is a nonsense today. In fact, by Italian standards, the modern Englishman is thoroughly underfed and it is a matter of doubt whether he has two proper meals a day.

Did you also know, for example, that until recently the Italians had always believed that English cities and London in particular were perpetually shrouded in fog, the kind of fog described by Edgar Wallace in his thrillers; that numerous Jack-the-Ripper-type criminals roamed the streets of London;

and that Englishmen on the whole went about molesting very young girls?

All dreadful stereotypes.

It is exactly the same with the Italian bottom-pinching stereotype. I have a theory that this is a rumour which is spread by both northern men and women. It is a kind of conduct which northerners think is in keeping with the picture they have of southerners, as it corresponds to what they would expect southerners to do; and it is a regrettable fact of life that people are more inclined to believe that others would behave in the manner in which they expect them to behave, than otherwise, regardless of factual evidence.

May I also say that I have never met any northern woman - and I have met many, in some form or other - who, when the subject was mentioned, could answer affirmatively to my question as to whether she had ever experienced bottom pinching. It was always someone else who had. I think what happens is that some Italian men do take advantage of what they believe to be the willingness of the northern woman, to caress her bottom. Caress, not pinch; I am very keen to put the record straight. The former may elicit a slap, a giggle or an upset look; the latter elicits contempt. Let us not confuse the two.

*   *   *

Coming on to the fields of general culture and manners, we start really with Henry VIII who was a great patron of the arts and encouraged Italian culture. Indeed, we are told that he spoke Italian well and that he appreciated the then famous Castiglione and Virgilio, as well as ensuring that his daughter Elizabeth should learn Italian.

Earlier, I discussed the impact of Italy upon Shakespeare. Look at the names in his plays: Othello, Antonio, Prospero, Romeo, Bassanio etc., as well as Desdemona, Portia, Juliet and so on. How many of his plays are set in Italy? And has it not occurred to you that those which are so set are really the most cheerful ones? You do not believe that *A Midsummer Night's Dream* is really set in Athens, do you?

Throughout the Renaissance, Italians were employed at the English Court as secretaries, riding and fencing masters, and as musicians; they were particularly well established as physicians.

The influence of Italy declined dramatically in the seventeenth century; amongst other reasons, the association with Popery was too much for the Puritans. It is hardly surprising that Addison did not like the Italians at all.

Things changed in the eighteenth century. Baretti arrived in 1751 and by the end of the 1790s Italy was fashionable again.

Furthermore, English taste in the eighteenth century was quite Italianized by Paolo Antonio Rolli, a Roman who, as master to the English Royal household for nearly 30 years, had quite an influence both on it and on England. In the same century, many Italian perfumiers were to be found working and living in the Haymarket and in Pall Mall; and the odd 'castrato' was always to be found in London at about the same time.

The list of Italians who spent time in England being appreciated here and contributing to English culture is very long indeed. Some of the more prominent were John Florio, Francesco Algarotti, Alessandro Verri, Vittorio Alfieri, Ugo Foscolo, and then the painters and the sculptors (right up to the present day Paolozzi and Annigoni), the architects, the musicians, the singers. To mention them all would be well outside the scope of this short summary. But certainly anyone who has visited Westminster Abbey knows the impact of Torrigiani, the sculptor; and the statue of Richard the Lionheart opposite the House of Lords is by another Italian, Carlo Marocchetti.

At the same time, the practice of speaking Italian amongst the upper classes was revived and became widespread. Lord John Russell, Charles Fox and Lord Holland all wrote and corresponded in Italian. According to G. M. Trevelyan, Gladstone's knowledge of Italian was 'An essential part of his soul'.

Another Italian who had an impact on England was Giordano Bruno from Nola near Naples. But his influence was of a totally different kind. He came to England in 1583 and spent two years here. He went to Oxford and took part in disputations there but did not get on at all well despite being befriended by Gwynne and John Florio as well as Greville, in whose house he spent some time. They disliked him in Oxford, whether because of his religious views or his neoplatonism or his animistic view of the world, does not seem too clear. Certainly, his outspokenness as to the barbarity of the London populace and his criticism of the amenities of London which he describes as being full of mud and puddles, with no lighting, or the table manners of both the more humble folk and the nobility, as well as his having compared the mentality of certain English doctors with that of a ploughman, were not made to endear him to his hosts.

It is, however, difficult to blame Bruno when one considers certain practices prevailing in England at the time which were (for an educated Italian) quite objectionable. For example, after dinner when the ladies had left, it was customary for the men to get out the chamber pots stored in the sideboards, and relieve themselves in them. But Bruno's criticisms went beyond this display of grossness in personal habits. More particularly, his ridiculing of Petrarca ran counter to the admiration that the learned English people of the period had for our greatest lyric poet. Still, he was an admirer of Elizabeth I, whom he called the 'diva Elisabetta'; and this admiration cost him dearly, for such praise for a 'heretic prince' was thrown at him by the Venetian inquisitors when he went on trial at a later date.

Bruno was able brilliantly to expose the new astronomical views of Copernicus and his criticisms of Aristotle and of orthodox theology anticipated the modern mind. Kant and Schelling followed in his footsteps.

According to one writer, 'In the course of his demonstrations and deductions Bruno anticipated Descartes's position of the identity of mind and being; he supplied Spinoza with the substance of his reasoned pantheism; and Leibniz with his theory of monadism and pre-established harmony. He laid down Hegel's doctrine of contraries and perceived that thought was a dialectic process. The modern theory of evolution was enunciated by him in pretty plain terms, thus anticipating Darwin. He had grasped the physical law of the conservation of energy. He solved the problem of evil by defining it to be a relative condition of imperfect development.' This is a much shortened version from John Addington Symonds. Bruno appears in Italian textbooks as one of our three major philosophers of the sixteenth century. The English, except for John Florio (but was he an Englishman?), did not take to him, and in his *History of Western Philosophy* Bertrand Russell does not even mention him. Oversight or policy? The latter, I suppose; he was being quite English and the English did not, and still do not, like Giordano Bruno. And yet, as has been said, Bruno's reflections on infinity were not in vain: they represent one of the most important beginnings of modern consciousness (C. G. Jung, *The Structure and Dynamics of the Psyche* in Volume 8 of his *Complete Works*).

Perhaps Bertrand Russell did overlook him...; on the other hand, Coleridge was very keen on Bruno whom he compared, I believe, to Milton.

A special mention should be made at this stage of Giuseppe Baretti, who spent a great deal of his life in England. A friend of Dr Johnson, he was a sensible, temperate man and as such he appears in the portrait of him by Sir Joshua Reynolds which still hangs in Holland House, painted in 1774.

He was a great Anglophile and wrote much about the Italians for the English public. He was also a keen observer of the English scene.

He wrote, for example, that London in his time contained over 10,000 prostitutes (I wonder how he managed to calculate that figure) and was 'the centre of all virtue and all vice'. He repeatedly compared his compatriots to the English and, generally, the Italians came out of it worse. According to Baretti, the Italians were superior to the English in only four things: painting, sculpture, architecture and music. In every other respect, the English were better and all Italians ought to strive to emulate them. Hurrah for Baretti!

But let us carry on.

The nineteenth century was the time when most Italian patriots and political exiles came to England.

The list is long and some of the names are well-known.

The poet Ugo Foscolo arrived in 1816. He is the best known of the Italian exiles and had been preceded by his fame.

His was a long stay in England. He died, in poverty, at Turnham Green on the 10 September 1827 and was buried in the churchyard of Chiswick Parish Church according to his wishes. His remains were transferred in 1867 to the Church of Santa Croce in Florence.

Foscolo was extremely popular with the ladies and, surprisingly, also with their husbands. He was a regular frequenter of the centres of Whig influence - Holland House and Lansdowne House. Indeed, Lord and Lady Holland had just returned from Italy when Foscolo first set foot on English soil.

He loved England. He did not really miss the sun of Italy very much and, in common with other exiles who followed him, he took the view that the sun that shone in England was the freedom of the country and not that big frying-pan that lights up the sky, as an earlier Italian poet had put it.

Indeed, on occasions, he seemed not to care very much about Italy nor, as he proved, about his Italian nationality. In his writings, he complained bitterly about all Italians, arguing, with some justification, that their factious nature would for ever prevent their liberation. He did not even approve of the revolutionary movements and in a letter of March 1820 he used terminology that, 150 years or more later, strikes us as odd. He said: 'Italy is a corpse with no hope of resurrection.'

In 1820 he was not sufficiently ill that one could forgive him for a faulty judgement. It seems to me that he was most probably swayed by what he saw in England. If he compared the magnificence and the power of England with the divisions that tore Italy aside at that time, he must have found it very comforting to be in a country where he was revered and welcomed wherever he went - which is more than would have happened to him in his own country - and where everyone was free to express his view. In addition, he mingled with the nobility who, recovering from the Napoleonic Wars, were enjoying a reasonably pleasant and financially secure time.

This view of the country that gave him hospitality, fame, and freedom, through rose-tinted glasses, is shared by the other patriots and exiles who followed in his footsteps. Guglielmo Pepe, fresh from the revolutionary attempts in Naples, arrived 1821; Santorre di Santarosa in 1822; Gabriele Rossetti in 1824; Giuseppe Pecchio, escaping an Austrian charge of high treason, in 1833. Shortly thereafter, Giovanni Berchet and Ferdinando dal Pozzo also settled in England, as did Beolchi and Mossotti.

Mazzini was here, after he was expelled from Switzerland to which he had retreated when things became a little too hot for him in Austrian Italy; and at later dates, Cavour, the father of the Italian state, and Garibaldi, possibly better known in England for his biscuits than for his contribution to Italian unity. Canova came, as did Gino Capponi and Count Confalonieri.

I suspect that the impact on England of these Italian intellectuals was not very great - except perhaps, for Garibaldi, who made an impression on the masses; the others moved in the rarefied circles of literature, poetry, good taste, nobility and politics. It is true that they kept alive the flame of Italian independence; but I should be surprised to find that the man in the street had any knowledge about most of them.

There is, however, one Italian who came to England in 1823. He is also almost totally unknown to the general public but his contribution to English cultural life is very substanial; his name is Antonio Panizzi.

Panizzi was an exile from the Grand Duchy of Modena which also took a dim view of early nineteenth century patriotic fervour. At first he earned a living by teaching Italian but soon got to know the lawyer Henry Brougham, who was to become Lord Chancellor seven years later. Through him he was appointed to the first Chair of Italian Language and Literature in the newly opened University of London in 1826 and then, as a naturalised British subject in 1832, he joined the staff of the British Museum where he distinguished himself for his zeal and administrative abilities. He introduced the card-index system for cataloguing and was instrumental in strengthening the copyright law which requires that a copy of every book published in England is deposited with the Museum (today, the British Library).

Although a private Act of Parliament made him a British citizen, he remained closely associated with Italy and its slow progress towards emancipation. He is said to have contributed to Gladstone's enthusiasm for Italy.

It is to him that we owe the Reading Room at the British Museum, which he designed himself, and which was opened in 1857, above the doorway to which sits his bust. When he died in 1879, having been made a Baronet by Queen Victoria, the British Museum had completely catalogued more than a million books.

I wonder how many people who use the Reading Room at the British Museum today are aware that they owe it to an Italian. *Britannica* records his efforts on page 864 of Volume R.X., but the reader who is interested in discovering more about this period of Italian exiles should read Margaret Wicks' study, *The Italian Exiles in London 1816 - 1848*, Manchester University Press, 1937.

The other examples of the impact that Italy has had on England are on the whole of a much more modern and less cultural nature. They can be summarised very briefly in the 'Dolce Vita', the Mediterranean diet, the open air enjoyment of food and wine, and the impressive post-war record of Italy in matters of style: cars, clothes, furniture, shoes, fashion, domestic appliances, etc.

There is a whole aura about things Italian which is seized upon by advertisers and marketers even to the extent of inventing Italian-sounding names for motor cars and other consumer goods. It is a revival which reminds one of what happened in England in the early part of the nineteenth century, especially after the defeat of Napoleon, when the constant decline since the seventeenth century in the fashion and study of things Italian, was halted. The Victorians in particular were wont to use Italian words and phrases in their conversation and letters, as a mark of distinction and taste, in the same manner in which English authors took to quoting from Dante, Boccaccio or Metastasio.

After about 1850, however, Italy and things Italian gave way to an interest in France and Germany until about the 1950s.

Over the past few years, I have even detected a form of snobbery in the revived use of Italian words of greeting, for example, or in other contexts. I do not consider it a cultural development by any means; it is more what I might call an environmental reaction which follows from the ever increasing tendency of the English to take holidays abroad, especially in the Mediterranean, and a form of wishful thinking.

I cannot leave this section without returning to one aspect of Italian influence on Britain which is so often overlooked, namely - the film industry. Indeed, it has been so much forgotten that when a review of the British film industry spanning more than four decades was recently shown on television, the person with whom I shall be dealing shortly was hardly mentioned; he certainly did not receive the prominence he deserves - summarised in the words of Laurence Olivier who said of him: 'I know of no-one else in British films so kind, generous, imaginative and courageous.' The person he was referring to was Filippo Del Giudice.

Olivier had good cause to be thankful to Del Giudice because it was through him and the filming of *Henry V* that Sir Laurence won his first Oscar. The following passage, borrowed from *The Oliviers* (Felix Barker, Hamish Hamilton, London, 1953) shows how conscious Olivier was of Del Giudice's contribution:

'For Olivier, who was given his first "Oscar", the award of the Academy of Motion Picture Arts and Sciences, it was an artistic triumph, and for Del Giudice, who had fought so many battles on behalf of his ideal, its success was particularly sweet. Conscious of all the Italian producer had done to make the film possible, Olivier went to visit him at Sheepcote, his home on Wooburn Common, one day in 1947 just after he had received the Oscar from Hollywood. When he arrived, Del Giudice noticed he was carrying a parcel, but had no idea what it contained or why Olivier took it into the study on the first floor; not until he joined Olivier a little later did he find out the answer. Standing on his desk was the golden statuette. "I wish you'd have it, Del," Olivier said to him. "Henry V would never have been made without you, dear fellow." It was a gesture which, coming at a time when Oscars were not so profuse as they are now in the Olivier household, Del Giudice has never forgotten.'

Del Giudice kept Olivier's Oscar until he died. After his death, Sir Laurence asked the Executors for its return, and they agreed.

This particular character, for a character he undoubtedly was, who became known in his time in the cinema world as 'Mr Del', was a refugee from Fascist Italy, who first came to London in 1932 as a penniless lawyer, aged 40. When war broke out he was interned as an enemy alien, but released after about three months, probably through the intervention of Mrs Churchill and her daughter Sarah. He then drifted almost by accident into films and rose to be managing director of Two Cities Films Limited.

In 1941, with England at a low ebb and with the English film industry practically non-existent and swamped by the prestige and the money of Hollywood, Mr Del decided to set about reviving the ailing local cinematograph business. He had great imagination and great flair, but no experience of films whatsoever. His first film, *Unpublished Story* was released in 1941. It was not particularly distinguished. But soon after, with the assistance of the Ministry of Information and the intervention of Noel Coward, he produced *In Which We serve*, described by Alan Wood in *A Study of J. Arthur Rank and British Films*, (Hodder & Stoughton, London, 1952) as 'one of the crucial films of the British cinema and the starting point of many careers.' Quite so. The then unknown actors John Mills, Richard Attenborough, Bernard Miles, Celia Johnson, and the director, David Lean, made their first appearance. *In Which We Serve* was followed very quickly and successfully by *French Without Tears*, *The Gentle Sex*, *This Happy Breed*, *The Way Ahead*, *Blithe Spirit*, *The Way To The Stars*, *Odd Man Out*, *Henry V* and *Hamlet*, all the work of Del Giudice who, over a period of only four or five years, was able to bring together scriptwriters like Noel Coward, Eric Ambler, Peter Ustinov and Terence Rattigan, as well as actors like David Niven and Trevor Howard and director Carol Reed. Del Giudice was the first to bring Shakespeare to the screen: the forerunner of the screening of the literary masterpieces, and of opera.

Del Giudice's greatest contribution, in my view, however, lay in his ability to determine at an early stage that what British films needed was more money spent on them. He was good at overcoming obstacles and brilliant in succeeding where others had failed or had failed to try; but his greatest ability was in raising finance. By the time *Henry V* had been completed, nearly half a million pounds had been spent on making a single film. England had never seen anything like that before and, in context, half a million pounds in those days was a very substantial sum of money indeed.

The British film industry owes him a debt that can not easily be forgotten. And yet, the entry that refers to him in one of the major books of reference, Leslie Halliwell's *The Filmgoers Companion*, dismisses him in two lines as 'Italian Producer who settled in England and became the Managing Director of Two Cities Films Limited.' But then, England has always been the country of the understatement.

Opinions on Mr Del vary. Some consider Del Giudice as one of the founding fathers of the British film industry; others dismiss him as an adventurer.

I find the notion of Del Giudice as an adventurer an amusing one. Indeed, it is my experience that the word 'adventurer' is applied almost indiscrimately by English-speaking people to those whose abilities and success they cannot understand.

I suppose both Drake and Raleigh were adventurers of sorts. No doubt Clive of India was as well. It is an interesting label to apply and it is the result, in my opinion, of on the one hand a complete inability to understand the motivation of the person to whom the label is appended and, on the other, of a sense of inadequacy and failure.

The fact that he succeeded where others had failed, and possibly his exuberant nature and flamboyant style caused quite a few raised eyebrows.

Mr Del had his share of problems with the J. Arthur Rank Organisation and to all intents and purposes withdrew from the film industry in 1947, retiring to the Italian Riviera. He ended his life in a monastery. Even so, a larger-than-life character, overtaken by people like Arthur Rank, Alexander Korda and John Davis, but certainly not outshone by them.

OUR CHILDREN

I NOSTRI FIGLI

Attenta ai brutti incontri, Cappuccetto Rosso.

Sta tranquilla mamma, ho la pillola.

"Beware of nasty encounters, Little Red Riding Hood."
"Don't worry, mummy, I'll be all right — I've got the pill."

2.

Who Are the Italians?

A very brief look at Italy and its history is a necessary starting point for the analysis that follows, both in this and in the next chapter.

The Italian peninsula is long and narrow, running from north-west to south-east for a length of about 800 miles. Its land boundary is about 1200 miles; the remainder is coastline. Its coastline extends to about 2600 miles (5300 if one includes the Italian islands).

It hangs in the Mediterranean Sea almost like a reversed appendix from the intestine: its usual description is a boot. Its northern part is clearly attached to central Europe, but its southernmost tip of Sicily is almost contiguous to Africa (it was once joined to the African continent). To the west, it is a long way removed from Spain, whereas to the east it is much closer to the Balkans. Its northern regions of Lombardia and Piedmonte are fertilized by the River Po - one of the longest rivers in Europe, which intersects an almost rectangular plain well cultivated and irrigated, with good centres of activities and excellent communications with the rest of the world. Indeed, it is interesting to note that, despite the Alps, communications between northern Italy and Europe have always been good, even before the building of the more recent Alpine tunnels. Nevertheless, the Italian side of the Alps is much steeper than the outside accesses and one of the consequences is that it is easier to travel into Italy from the north than out of Italy from the south: a well-established geographical fact which has had great historical repercussions.

The rest of the peninsula is so long, so lacking in centres of activity and so clearly cut into two by the Apennines, that the inevitable result was the isolation of certain parts of Italy. In the old days, as now, the rivers there were of no significance because they were mainly torrents, and, until the advent of the motorway network, which is fairly extensive now in Italy, certain parts of the south remained inaccessible and totally isolated. Italy is largely a mountainous country (plains cover only 23 per cent of its total land mass), with about 1500 lakes, a wide range of soils and varying climatic conditions. Even some parts of the south can be bitterly cold, as the Eighth Army found to its cost in 1943/44.

This is Italy's geography, in a nutshell. Now for a similar thumbnail sketch of history.

The Indo-European inhabitants of the Italian peninsula were firstly affected by the Greek colonisation of Sicily towards the eighth century BC. Around the sixth century BC, this colonisation spread northwards up the south-east tip of Italy and into Naples and the surrounding areas.

About the same time, the Phoenicians hopped over from Malta and the Carthaginians occupied the western coast of Sicily whilst the Venetians occupied Sardinia.

Some time around 600 BC, northern Italy was occupied by the Ligurians and the Venetians, south of the Po was the domain of the Umbrians, further south the Etruscans, and, close to the Tiber, the Sabines and the Latins. West of them were the Samnites and in Apulia the Iapigians.

The two principal civilisations of Italy at this time were the Etruscans and the Greeks.

All these different populations were ultimately consolidated into what became the Roman Empire which lasted for about nine centuries. But when that Empire collapsed, the pressure of the barbarians along its boundaries ultimately became impossible to resist.

The Goths, led by Alaric, were the first, sacking Rome in the year 410 AD: they were followed by the Huns led by Attila, and then Jenseric's Vandals who in 455 AD took possession of Rome again. They came from Africa and it was easy for them to occupy both Sicily and Sardinia as well as to rule the Mediterranean. As pirates, they met with no resistance.

But hardly a century had elapsed before the first German invasion occurred. These were the Lombards, so called because of their long beards, who had previously settled along the Danube. They created quite an impression. Their king, Alboin, entered Italy by the north-east in the Spring of 568, and moved south-west.

About two centuries later the Lombards managed to come to terms with the Catholic Church but in turn were defeated by the Franks roundabout the year 750. In the subsequent conquest of Italy by the Franks, Charlemagne exercised considerable influence over the country - now that it was once again part of a major empire; it ceased to be, therefore, the centre of gravity of the western world as it had been basically since the time of the Romans. The Frankish occupation obviously made it very difficult for Italy to have any kind of autonomy.

The result was an Italy split into the north held by the Franks, the centre held by the Popes, and the south still controlled by Byzantium.

The only benefit was that roundabout the year 850 some of the Italian sea ports began to acquire a certain amount of independence. Naples and Amalfi, in particular, started to develop their fleets. Not a minute too soon because the Arabs from Tunisia began attacking Italy, taking possession of Sicily and pushing as far north as Rome.

This situation continued for 200 years or thereabouts, that is to say until the next lot of invaders, the Normans, turned up. By the year 1030 the Normans were settled in Naples and started attracting their brethren from the mists of Normandy to the sun of the south.

The next group to 'invade' Italy were the Crusaders. This was not a war-like invasion and it resulted in a great exchange of business, information and culture between east and west. Italy hardly took any part in the Crusades in the sense that it sent very few of its men to fight. It did, however, deal with the transport and provisioning of the Crusaders and in this way it strengthened its importance as a business centre as well as allowing its maritime powers (Venice, Genoa, Pisa, as well as Naples and Amalfi) to prosper.

The greatest contribution to the Crusades came from the French knights. They established certain concepts of chivalry which had no impact whatsoever on the Italians, save possibly in Sicily as a backcloth for the Mafia that was to develop later.

In 1194 Henry of Swabia was crowned Emperor in Palermo, concluding his campaign of control of Italy. The Germans were back.

In 1266 Charles of Anjou was crowned King of Sicily. The French were back in southern Italy, but their occupation was not such a success. They had great problems with the locals and in 1282 the so-called War of the Vespers (which gave Rossini the idea for his 'Sicilian Vespers' opera) broke out.

When Charles of Anjou died, as a result of various dynastic complications Sicily and the south of Italy passed to the Spaniards. In 1494 Charles VIII of Spain took over. From this very moment Italy ceases to have any significance in European history.

We have to wait until the war of Spanish succession for the next change. Effectively, as a result of the Treaties of Utrecht and Rastadt, the Austrians replaced the Spaniards. This may have been very useful from the administrative point of view because the Austrians were more efficient. But we were replacing one master who was inefficient with another one who was not quite so bad; we were still slaves and thus we remained, except for the short interlude that occurred from Napoleon's entry into Italy through the Great St Bernard Pass in May 1800 to his final defeat in 1815 when the Congress of Vienna consolidated the position of Italy, divided into a number of little states, as an appendage of Austria.

Indeed, it is true to say that the Congress of Vienna, which aimed at restoring the old order, seems to have been particularly keen to restore it for Italy; at any rate in the sense that the whole of the Austro-Hungarian empire over northern Italy was considerably strengthened. Effectively, the most promising region of Italy had its development blocked. This prompted

the French writer Lamartine to say that Italy was 'the land of the dead' and
Prince Metternich to call it a 'geographic expression'. That Italy was not
dead was proved shortly after by the first revolutionary attempts of 1820.
Whether Metternich was right or wrong to call Italy a geographic expression
must remain to this day a matter about which there can be difference of
opinion; but would not most readers agree it is a rather beautiful geographic
expression?

There were further revolutionary movements in 1831 and, as is common
knowledge, the first Italian war of independence started in 1848, continued
as the second war in 1859 and resulted in a glorious end to that decade,
for in 1860 Garibaldi conquered southern Italy for the Italian Royal House
of Savoy.

The third war of independence took place in 1870 and it resulted in the
fall of Rome (held until then by the Popes) on the 20 September of that year.

To all intents and purposes, therefore, the first Italian State was constituted
in 1861 and completed between that year and 1870.

Other than by the Germans and the Allies during the Second World
War, there were no further military invasions of Italy.

I must apologise to those readers who are 'historians' for the somewhat
cavalier manner in which I have condensed nearly two thousand years of
Italian history into a few paragraphs. The point is, I wish to remind the
reader of a very simple fact, namely, that the make-up of the Italian people
has been influenced by all those who ruled over the peninsula. The
intermingling of blood ('native', barbaric, Muslim, Norman, French, German,
Austrian, Spanish) by invasion is greater than has occurred in any other
country of the world that I know. This is the primary consideration to bear
very clearly in mind when we look at the causes, as I see them, of Italian
successes and failures.

But before we consider them, let us look at who the Italians are.

WHO ARE THE ITALIANS?

It would of course be too trite to say that the Italians are the inhabitants of
Italy, a country, as we have seen, which in the opinion of Lamartine was
dead and in that of Prince Metternich was not a political entity.

But according to one of our own, Vincenzo Gioberti, the Italians do not
even exist. Writing in the nineteenth century, he went so far as to say that
the Italian people were not a fact but an ambition, a hypothesis rather than
a reality. They were so divided in terms of government, laws, institutions,
speech, customs, tendencies and habits, that they could not be dignified
by the term 'people'.

He was not being unkind. He was trying to awaken the national
conscience. But in so doing he was reminding us of the very unusual political
nature of the Italians. He was recalling how varied their nature is and how
marked the regional differences. He was, in essence, being an Italian
himself; but of the better kind.

This is hardly surprising, because there is no such thing as a typical Italian; there are a number of Italians diversified according to the part of Italy from which they come and the social class to which they belong. And in any event, it is usually easier for a foreigner to paint his own picture of a people. But such pictures are invariably stereotypes; also because foreigners are so difficult to please.

In 1902 Edward Hutton (*Italy and The Italians*, Blackmore) wrote: 'The Italians! It was easier to find them 20 years ago than it is today. Today there are Romans, Florentines, Neopolitans, Venetians...' Who was right, I wonder: Gioberti or Hutton?

These stereotypes are fairly well established. For instance, according to R. Brown, in *Social Psychology* (New York, 1965) when students at Princeton University are invited to describe Italians, they say that they are 'artistic, impulsive and passionate.'

Other foreigners ascribe to the Italians certain characteristics which they feel are typical, namely that they are kind-hearted, intuitive, lazy and undisciplined, hard working, sceptical, womanisers, and so on.

Italians are always described as paragons of Machiavellism and duplicity. Indeed, according to Ann Radcliffe who wrote *The Italians or the Confessional of the Black Penitents* in 1786, the typical Italian is 'a creature with arms and legs of enormous size, who always dresses in black with a large hat that covers his half-open eyes prone to betrayal.'

Some fifty years later, around 1820-24, Paganini was to be seen always dressed in black and often wearing dark spectacles. Radcliffe, therefore, could hardly have invented her stereotype. Furthermore, Italians, she states, are Machiavellian courtesans and papists worthy of the Spanish Inquisition. That an educated English lady could claim to define an Italian in these terms some 200 years ago is clearly absurd. Stendhal thought that she simply did not know what she was talking about. She certainly displayed the (by then) well-established xenophobic tendencies of the British.

In the early nineteenth century a Swiss writer by the name of Bonstetten in his work *L'Homme du midi et l'Homme du nord* commented that the Italian was basically a happy-go-lucky, cheerful and improvident peasant, the light-hearted fly that lives from day to day, and contrasted him with the man from the north who, having to spend most of his time indoors because of his country's inclement weather, had more time to plan his future and was in effect the wise virgin of the Gospel.

The descriptions are never-ending but it seems to me that what we may call the character or nature of the Italians changes according to the time and place of the analysis and, above all, it changes according to the point of view of the observer.

I believe that it is almost impossible to define the character of a people. The only way one can do it is negatively, by referring to their history. That is useful as a canon of construction of the people as a whole, but no guide whatsoever to the character of the individual. There is no relation, in my view, between the two.

Take, for example, the fact that Britain created a great empire. Is it to be believed that it succeeded in doing so because of its innate ethnic or racial superiority? It seems to me that the reverse is more likely to be true, namely that because it had established an empire, it was able to develop a kind of ethnic and racial superiority mentality which was perhaps latent and which would never have come to the fore but for the historical accident of the empire.

The same considerations apply to all peoples. We are what we pretend to be or, alternatively, what others believe us to be, or, in the last resort, what history has made us.

In our case, those who have purported to analyse, describe or classify Italians have been foreigners who may have travelled through the country, historians purporting to identify a particular type of artistic or political behaviour or philosophers trying to make a synthesis of certain presumed common traits; they might also have been detractors, who found them inferior.

I have already referred to the view that Roger Ascham thought he was able to form after only nine days in Italy. About three centuries later, John Ruskin, who after the initial shock of his first visit to Italy became a devotee of Italian art, was only slightly less unflattering of the Italians. Upset by the apparent neglect of their antiquities and artistic treasures which he considered part of the patrimony of humanity as a whole, he wrote: 'Take them all in all, I detest these Italians beyond measure...: they are Yorick's skull with the worms in it, nothing of humanity left but the smell' (John Ruskin, *Works*, Volume XXXVI, page 48), But he went even further: he looked upon the Italians generally as corrupt and decadent; he considered the ordinary Italian to be idle and totally unconcerned about his heritage. Elsewhere, he wrote that the ordinary Italian was 'lazy, lousy, scurrilous, cheating, lying, thieving, hypocritical, brutal, blasphemous, obscene, cowardly, earthly, sensual, devilish' (Letters to his Parents, 23 October 1845).

Italian postillions, douaniers and country people 'appear knaves of the first and most rapacious water' (*Ruskin in Italy*, ed. Shapiro, Clarendon Press, 1972, p. 50); Italian people 'seem bad enough for anything' (ibid, p. 51). Beggars, mosquitos, customs officers, priests even, were a great nuisance, evil, smelling, and vile (ibid, pp. 86 & 160). Compared to the Swiss, Italians grumbled and swore: they were 'very barbarous', uncaring about art and about anything that was good (ibid, p. 114).

But that is not quite sufficient for Ruskin. He also finds the opportunity to say in very much the same vein: 'If I were the devil, I wouldn't buy these Italians to roast at a farthing a pound - they smell so abominably already' (ibid, p. 154); elsewhere: 'I am quite sick of Italy - the people are too much for me - it is like travelling among a nation of malignant idiots, with just brains enough to make them responsible for their vices - they have taken the whole feeling of the country away from me' (ibid, p. 194).

You may feel at this stage that Ruskin was going too far: not so; here is another sample: 'Now, if I could put these Italians in a waterbutt with the top on, or roast them in sulphur a little, or wash them in steepdown gulfs of liquid fire, or in any other way convey to them a delicate expression of opinion, it would do my heart good, but as it is I am so sick that I believe I shall have to give up art altogether' (Letters to his Parents, 7.9.1845).

One hears echoes, in these unkind qualifications, of his complaisant Protestantism which came under pressure from Catholic art as soon as he set foot in Italy, one sees a reaction to his strict Chapel upbringing and one realises how great the impact must have been on a northerner (arguably almost a Scot) - who had led a secluded life until about the age of 20 - of places bursting with beauty like the Alps, with history and art like Venice and with power and sensuality like Naples.

I wonder why, if he disliked the Italians so much, he felt he had to return to Italy from time to time throughout his life. It surely was not just for the cheap food.... On one of his many stops on the road, he dined on 'macaroni soup, an excellent beef steak, a dish of fresh-cut asparagus, cheese, a bottle of lemonade, and wine of course, ad libitum' all for 2½ 'Paoli', about 13 pence. Not bad, I suppose, even though all he could see around him was 'ugliness, meanness, vice, folly, idleness, infidelity, filth, misery, desecration, dissipated youth, wicked manhood and withered, sickly, hopeless age' (*Ruskin in Italy*, op. cit., p. 51). To be fair to him, he did give the Italians credit for their music. Comparing them to the French, (*Ruskin in Italy*, op. cit., p. 242) he states that 'the music in the Italian churches beats them hollow. I used to think music was an art, but I am sure now it is nothing but an instinct, since those brutes of Italians have it in what God has given them as a substitute for souls.' Perhaps he should have remained in England; but no, he went abroad repeatedly. He enjoyed both France and Switzerland but, despite everything, Italy above all. His first trip to Italy dates from 1833-1834 but he returned there in 1840-1841, 1843-1845, 1846-1848, 1849-1850 and 1851-1852. In 1845 he went for the first time on his own, with a servant.

Up to this date, although he had been once to Rome and Naples, he had spent most of his time up north, especially in Venice.

Ruskin was greatly attracted to the Alps. Perhaps in the majesty and whiteness of the scenery he saw a reflection of himself, 'everything pure and bright.'

He wrote in his diary for the 23 November 1840: 'How often, in the monotony of the English scenery, I shall remember that panorama of snow and marble, with a wild, sick yearning - the desire of the moth for the star, of the night for the morrow.'

But there is probably a less romantic explanation. Ruskin suffered from consumption; the pure air of the Alps would have certainly proved more congenial to him than that of other parts of Italy.

The impact of the south, however, was of a different kind. It did not seem to be too immediate but it has been said that his first visit to Naples 'started trains of thought which did not take clear course till 40 years afterwards.' (*The Wider Sea - A life of John Ruskin*, John Dickson Hunt, G. M. Dent &

Son, London, 1982.)

In 1854-1856 he went back to northern Italy again, much taken by Turin. In 1860 he returned to Milan to copy the frescoes of Bernardino Luini. In 1869 he was back in Verona and Venice and he returned to Venice in 1870, the year in which he also revisited Florence, Pisa and Siena.

In 1871 and 1874 he made two more visits to Pisa. Also in 1874 he was in Rome and Naples and he travelled as far south as Sicily which he was seeing for the first time. In 1876-1877 he was again in Venice and in 1882 he visited Pisa, Florence and Lucca once more.

In 1888 he made his last trip abroad and visited Venice. But this was to be the last time. He died on 20 January 1900.

Unless I have got it wrong, he visited Italy 15 times, on occasions for stays greater than two years.

I wonder how he reconciled his view of the Italians with his love for Italy and for Italian art. I am not being unkind to him, for he rendered Italy a great service by publicising its deficiencies in caring for its artistic heritage; and he was a lover of the country, and as such worthy of the utmost respect. He also rendered enormous service to the English by imparting to them a true knowledge of Italian art in all its forms.

For present purposes, however, I am mainly interested not in his artistic leanings but in his judgement of the Italians and I find that it is suspect, since it was too obviously influenced by the deficiencies in his own personality and make-up: it lacks objectivity, it is too rhetorical. After all - and one does not need to be an iconoclast to make the observation - what was he if not an imitator and commentator, a teacher, and an interpreter? But he created nothing, either in the artistic or in the physical sense. He was a restless soul, he could never stay put in one place, except Italy, for longer than about six months; but his was the restlessness of impotence, not of creativity.

Are these the right qualifications for passing a thoroughly negative and highly critical judgement on a whole people? Did he perhaps consider that Luini, Carpaccio, Tintoretto, Veronese and Tiziano, to choose at random, were not Italian or, maybe, ought not to have been born such?

How Ruskin must have suffered, I have no doubt, when he thought that it was these pale, effeminate, lazy, cheating, animal-eyed, listless, sulky, filthy, unhappy, sensual creatures who had been able to find that balance between beauty and everyday life which meant so much to him, who were able to live amidst the ruins of antiquity apparently entirely uninfluenced by and uninterested in them; and yet, who were the creators of the very art and beauty for which he longed, but which he could not either in his mind or in his body ever attain. (All the adjectives I have used above are taken from Ruskin's Letters to his Parents as applied to the Italians, especially of central and southern Italy. He was not so aggressive about northerners.)

As I have already observed, these hasty criticisms stem on the one hand from arrogance and on the other from an impacted psyche: the northerner's intellectual pseudo-superiority finds itself under pressure in the Mediterranean. It is hardly surprising that Ruskin should have concentrated on the brutality, obscenity, earthiness and sensuality of the Italians when he himself was impotent; his six-year-old marriage was annulled because of his incapacity to consummate it by reason of incurable impotence. The decree of nullity of his marriage weighed on him all his life and I am not aware that, even though he claimed it was wrong, he was ever able to prove otherwise.

It is entirely possible, of course, that some of the adjectives Ruskin used to describe the Italians in his time, could be true even today of *some* Italians. Incidentally, I wonder whether Ruskin would himself have obtained any notoriety whatsoever if he had not had the opportunity of studying and living in proximity to the works of those very Italians he failed utterly to understand.

If I have spent an undue amount of time considering Ruskin's petulant observations it is because I believe that they represented the view that, on the whole, the Victorians formed about the Italians. Put differently, Ruskin offset the great service he rendered Italian art by his assessment of what the Italian people were like. The caricatures he published permeated educated English society for the whole of the nineteenth and for part of the twentieth centuries. Indeed, it can be said that Ruskin's views retained their authority in England until the early 1950s. It was only then that with the advent of mass tourism the English were able to see for themselves what Italy and the Italians were really like and began to appreciate that, despite her defeat in World War Two, Italy was anything but dead. The vitality of Italy is a feature that strikes most visitors today: it is as though Italy were coming into its own, after centuries of slavery and comparative decay. But that is anticipating somewhat the conclusions that I shall be reaching: Let us first return to the nineteenth century for a few further observations.

About 70 years separate Ruskin's pronouncements from the escape to Italy of D. H. Lawrence, accompanied by Frieda Richthofen. If one reads Lawrence, the Italians have altered so dramatically that it is impossible to believe that they had changed in that period.

Lawrence viewed Italy from an entirely different angle to Ruskin's: more working class, less inclined to rationalisation, more reliant upon his instinct for common humanity and much influenced by his own sexuality.

There are a number of permutations to be considered here in order to explain the substantial difference between the judgements formulated by Ruskin and D. H. Lawrence. In the first place, it is possible that the Italians themselves had changed in the intervening 70 years. This, as I have said, is almost impossible to believe because the change is too dramatic and could not have been achieved over such a comparatively short span.

One must therefore consider whether either Ruskin or D. H. Lawrence saw the wrong picture. A decision on this is dictated by whether one prefers the view of the impotent to that of the dynamic, the assessment of a critic steeped in artistic beliefs to that of a man ready to be affected more or less objectively by the images he saw.

Lawrence was in Italy in the company of a woman and not on his own with a manservant, like Ruskin. He got on well in Italy. He still thought that the locals had a dark soul and he was perhaps too insistent upon what he called the 'phallic divinity' which he claimed marks the Italians' way of thinking. But he liked the common people and he understood the spirit of the country.

He was a keen student of things Etruscan and correctly identified the influence that those articulate, sensuous, pleasure-seeking, 'modern' people had exerted on the Italian spirit. He ascribed greater impact to Etruscan influences on Italy than to Roman; and he was instinctively in the right about this.

In a sense, however, he may have laid undue stress (*Twilight in Italy*, William Heinemann, London, 1956) on the all-pervasiveness of sexuality. From that outlook upon Italian life (op. cit., pp. 35, 45 & 137), he drew the conclusion that it was an absolute dedication to matters sensual rather than spiritual that was sapping the energies of the Italians, whereas the same was not happening in northern countries. This is a typical northern judgement of southern races generally and is one which I cannot share, since it stems from a psychological northern obsession with matters sexual that fails to find a satisfactory physical outlet.

It seems to me that the sexual appetite, in so far as it represents primarily a physical need and only secondarily a psychological one, is satiated by its satisfaction in the same manner as the pains of hunger are assuaged by the intake of food. It is only those who battle with sexuality who perforce have it constantly before their eyes.

Furthermore, I doubt that it is correct to overrate sensuality or at any rate to assume that powerful sensuality reduces strength of mind and purpose. I find this a common misconception: whether it arises from a failure to understand to what extent one can separate physical from mental activity or whether it is the main plank in the argument that, in certain intellectual respects, the northern races are superior, I have yet to determine.

For these reasons I am not too sure how correct an analysis even D. H. Lawrence makes of the Italians. The distinction between sensuality and rationality, between the mind and the body, art and ugliness, beauty and technology, is as marked in Italy as the distinction between the sacred and the profane: they all co-exist. It is a mistake to suppose that because conduct is capable of being classed as profane according to certain standards, one is therefore incapable of appreciating and attaining the sacred: St Augustine is the best example.

There is here a dichotomy that northerners who come to Italy because of their artistic leanings find somewhat difficult to explain. They are so enthralled by its art and beauty that they are reluctant to accept, as concomitants, poverty and ugliness, darkness and neglect. Such reluctance arises because they start off on the wrong foot, almost divorced from feelings of common humanity: their enthusiasm for art is too great.

There is a certain type of foreigner, of which Ruskin is a classic example, whose avowed love or appreciation of Italy is no more than a reaction to a desperate need to commune with the country that has always been capable of communicating the message of its history and civilisation to those who sought it in order to transmit it to their own country.

This search for the spirit of civilisations past is the outcome of a basic deficiency. Hence the anger and annoyance at the apparent neglect by the locals for their art.

The trouble is that when you grow up amidst art and antiquities, they become part of yourself and no longer have any extraordinary meaning. To the extent that they are absorbed by the intellect and the eye, they blend so intimately with everyday life and the landscape that they cease to have any especial significance. In a somewhat similar context, it is the converts to any religion who feel more strongly about it than those who were baptized or initiated into it at a very early age.

By this token, any judgement of the Italians made by those whose sole purpose in visiting Italy is to remedy their own cultural deficiencies rather than to comprehend its true spirit is, in my view, not worth very much at all. And it is extreme conceit on the part of such persons even to attempt to express an opinion. Consider Roger Ascham again; he must have had a truly superhuman intuition if after only nine days in Italy he could express himself with such conviction about the Italians.

Fortunately, not all Englishmen are like Ascham or Ruskin. Edward Hutton seemed somewhat more enthusiastic when he said: 'Without Italy I am beggared. Though God saw fit to make me an Englishman, it was in Italy I caught my first glimpse of heaven.'

And in its Italian supplement for 21 March 1934 the *Times Literary Supplement* said: 'The world's debt to Italy is infinite: for these last two thousand years and more the influence of Italy, ancient, medieval and modern, has shaped the history of civilisation and set the course of its achievements.' This comment is almost paraphrasing G. M. Trevelyan when he said that the cultural gain that England made at the expense of Italy represents 'a debt that England can never repay.')

Goethe was equally flattering. In his *Italian Journey* - 22 September 1786 - he remarks that the Italians 'consider themselves the finest people in the world, an opinion which, thanks to certain excellent qualities which they undeniably possess, they can hold with impunity'. How nice of him. He was less flattering on his second trip to Italy, perhaps because he saw things a little more clearly.

These totally opposed and contradictory judgements of the Italians highlight the difficulty in reconciling some of the features that they display, which are so multifarious as to defy classification and analysis.

The Italians themselves have not bothered to make a synthesis, historical or psychological, of these contradictions and it seems to be a fact that all the people who have put pen to paper to describe the Italians have in the main been foreigners. There is no doubt that only very rarely have they been Italian.

In the Introduction I have already referred to the lack of writing by Italians about Italians. In 1768 one of the Italians who spent a considerable time in England, Giuseppe Baretti, wrote his *Account of the Manners and Customs in Italy*. But his was an apologia of the Italians in comparison with the English. He was really trying to say that we were at fault because we were not more like the English. The other Italian writers who covered the same subject matter (Beccaria, Verri, Filangieri, Sismondi) were more concerned with the failings of our political institutions. For his part, Alfieri was in turn berating us because we were not more like the Romans; so, to that extent, his feelings were almost English, and perhaps that is why Byron admired him so much.

In 1828, Leopardi was quite scathing about the Italians. He found them both divided and divisive, unworthy of being a nation.

It strikes me that all these Italian writers were highly critical of their fellow countrymen, and understandably so. But none of them, as far as I know, except for Sismondi, ever embarked on any analysis of the good that we had done. Take for example, the Italian republics of the Middle Ages, starting with the tenth century and ending with the defeat of Venice. Naples, Amalfi, Pisa, Genoa and Venice were the pillars of the then civilised world. In business terms they were what today Japan and the United States might be. No-one gives Italy credit for them, especially not for little Amalfi.

I suppose it is true to say that most people know that Venice was once the Queen of the Adriatic, a major centre of business and a great political power.

Venetian sea-power and efficient government are too well known to require restatement by me. In terms of civic amenities, Venice was well ahead of its times: the first dogal ordinance to prescribe compulsory street lighting at night goes back to 1128. In pursuit of an ever more efficient navy, the Venetians thought up the idea of mounting cannons on ships and, anticipating Henry Ford by many centuries, devised also a form of assembly line in order that they might build galleys in a hurry.

Everybody knows Pisa because of its leaning tower. Equally, most people will have heard of Genoa for one reason or another; and if they are opera lovers, Simon Boccanegra reminds them of the conflicts within the Fieschi family. Genoese sailors and merchants have left their mark throughout the Mediterranean, from Mallorca and the Costa Brava, to Constantinople, Algeria and Tunisia. And of course, everybody knows of Naples.

But I am confident it never occurs to the average tourist sunning himself on the beach of Amalfi that when in his own country his ancestors were eking out a meagre existence either as serfs or in any event as poor, uncouth peasants digging potatoes, the Republic of Amalfi was, as far back as the ninth, tenth and eleventh centuries, a major centre of civilisation and culture.

I have already mentioned its rules of the sea under the heading 'Law' and the discovery or at least extensive use of the compass by one of its inhabitants. But in any event, as early as the twelfth century, business was thriving at Amalfi, Praiano, Positano and Ravello. The whole of the coastline from Naples to Salerno was punctuated by small towns and villages inhabited by rich merchants and sailors who lived in houses surrounded by gardens and fountains (see Boccaccio's *Decameron* Day 2, Novel 4). Indeed, so great was the enterprise of the people of Amalfi that in the tenth century it had already established itself as one of the major commercial centres of the world, competing with Venice, even though it had no port, its ships being roped on to the beach by the people.

Nor should it be forgotten that to Amalfi we owe the Order of the Knights of Malta, formerly the Knights of Rhodes. In the year 1020 merchants from Amalfi obtained the right to establish a hospital and a church near the Holy Sepulchre. That was the origin of the Order which stretched its influence over the Mediterranean basin for many centuries.

Amalfi itself was a thriving town. Guglielmo Appulo wrote that during the eleventh century no town in the world was richer than Amalfi in gold, silver and cloth; it was a busy centre of trade and was frequented by Arabs, Sicilians, Africans and Indians.

Leaving history aside, it is meaningless to try and ask oneself who the Italians are and attempt to consider a people in isolation. It was Sir James Hudson who, in about 1864, is quoted as saying that the English were thoroughly well informed about Italy but in the most hopeless ignorance as to the Italians (cited in *The Golden Ring* by Giuliana Artom Treves, Longmans Green & Co., London, 1956). Such ignorance still prevails today.

Of course, we all know who the Italians are. Obviously, the failed successors of the Romans, the allies of the Germans in World War II and the founders of the Mafia. That may give us some information about the history of Italy, but I believe it tells us nothing at all about the Italian male or female. In my view, any attempt to determine national character is doomed to failure unless it is related to the national character and culture of other peoples. It is only in this way, which is a somewhat negative way of looking at it, that we may be able to say that the Italian art of cooking is better than the English but the English have greater civic sense than the Italians. Having said this, I am not quite sure exactly what is proved, save that the Italians are different from the English.

Historically, Italians are an amalgam of different races and different needs. But, surprising though this may sound they are a cohesive amalgam. Though the political bond may be tenuous, cultural ties are solid.

Our Roman tradition governs us much more than we are prepared to admit. The fact that Italy has a civilisation which antedates that of any other people in Europe makes it slightly anomalous. Indeed, as Curzio Malaparte has pointed out, in Europe we represent 'A live element of opposition to the triumphant spirit of the nations of the north; we are duty bound to defend an ancient civilisation which derives its strength from the values of the spirit against a new heretic and false outlook which relies upon physical, material and mechanical values...; to assimilate this modernity would lead us to irreparable decadence.' What pride, what conviction. And yet, he was only half Italian: his father was German, his mother from Lombardy. Malaparte was baptized Kurt Erich Suckert.

This reluctance to assimilate modernity, this ability to remain almost entirely unaffected by technological change - and indeed, by that most frequent of events in Italian history, namely political change - has resulted in a certain constancy of pattern of behaviour in the Italians who, on the whole, appear to have changed throughout the ages less than most other peoples.

Overall, Italians tend to emerge as quite conservative, in thought as well as in behaviour and, to some extent, also in attire. This conservatism is a feature which foreign observers usually fail to identify; and when they do, consider very puzzling indeed.

3.

The Causes of Italian Failures and Successes

FAILURES

If you couple the discoveries made by the Italians with their contributions to knowledge, science and art generally, it is a record that is very difficult to match. Indeed, there is no field of human knowledge or endeavour where the Italians have not left their mark - except in the fields of symphonic music and theatre: so far, the Italians have not been able to produce either a Beethoven or a Shakespeare.

This is to me a cause of considerable regret. If one could claim Shakespeare and Beethoven as Italians, then I have no hesitation in saying that the cultural and scientific primacy of Italy would be incontestable. As it is, that primacy is still there, but the absence of a major contributor in these two fields does allow those who do not like Italians to dispute it. But then, I am not sure who can be substituted for the Italians. Can the French match the Italian record? Can the Germans or the British?

Fortunately for the reader, I shall not indulge in any analysis of the French or German contribution nor indeed of that of any other culture because the purpose of this section of the book is to attempt to consider the reasons why the Italians are as they are, and not to determine whether they are the best.

Take for example the question why the Italians have been unable to produce either a Beethoven or a Shakespeare. It is an interesting one and it does lead us on to causation quite directly.

First, music. Everyone knows that the Italians are musical. Indeed, it has been said repeatedly that they are the most musical people in the world. I believe that statement to be perfectly true, but the reasons for it are not simple. It cannot just be to do with the Mediterranean climate or the sun, because the Welsh, too, are said to be a musical people, yet the rainfall in Wales is quite high.

FREEDOM OF INFORMATION

LIBERTÀ D'INFORMAZIONE

Non c'è scritto "Il direttore",
ma "Il diretto".
E non è un errore di stampa.

"No, it doesn't say 'the Editor,' it says 'the edited'
and it's no misprint."

It is also a commonly-held view that the Italian language is the most musical language in the world. That statement is equally true but there are good scientific reasons for it. For example, the seven Italian vowel sounds are basic and they occur quite freely and abundantly. Indeed, there is an Italian word — 'aiuole' (it means flowerbeds) - which consists of all five principal vowel sounds and only one consonant. (There are, in fact, five vowels, but two have two sounds.)

Furthermore, the Italian language has no harsh notes. All the consonants are pronounced simply and there is an abundance of soft doubled consonants such as l, m, and n, which produce some perfectly natural, flowing and easy sounds like 'palla', 'mamma', 'nonna', etc.

And finally, in order to speak Italian properly, you have to open your mouth in the shape of an O. It is a natural movement, but less exaggerated than the one you make when you go to the dentist or the doctor. You do not have to twist your mouth, or smack your tongue against the palate or the teeth, or move your lips in an awkward direction, either as if you were grimacing or as if you had swallowed a hot potato, as indeed you have to do if, for example, you are speaking French, German or Russian.

And I am not the only one to make this observation. In his *Beppo*, stanza XLIV, Byron has this to say about Italian:

'I love the language, that soft bastard Latin, which melts like kisses from a female mouth, and sounds as if it should be writ on satin, with syllables which breathe of the sweet South, and gentle liquids gliding all so pat in, that not a single accent seems uncouth, like our harsh northern whistling, grunting guttural which we are obliged to hiss, and spit, and sputter all.'

So it is clear that there are technical reasons why Italian is a musical language.

When it comes to music, however, all we can say is that the Italian approach to it is what I call a purely melodic one. Music for an Italian does not exist unless there is a melody, preferably but not necessarily an easy melody, that he can sing, hum or whistle. Indeed, there are some people, of whom I am one, who maintain that you cannot call anything music if in fact you cannot whistle it, sing it or hum it.

It was Arturo Toscanini who used to keep telling his orchestra that, when they were playing, they had to sing. All the time, they should be doing nothing else but singing; not with their voices but with their instruments. Indeed, he is recorded as saying that 'Music, unless you sing, is nothing.' (see Bernard Shaw, *The Orchestra Speaks*; the same concept is re-stated in Howard Taubman's *Toscanini*.)

Italians therefore only appreciate music if it is pleasant to listen to or is simple in outline. When we listen to a melody we do not wish to listen to anything else, for we are being transported into a world of fantasy where we can forget the more sordid features of everyday life. We are moved by the music, which strikes the hidden chords of our psyche.

Ours is an emotional reaction and not an intellectual one, as the melody is associated with sound and the sound is associated with the person who utters it. That is why the Italians have been so successful with their operas because sounds have been coupled to persons and to characters, to their passions, to their laughter and, essentially, to their humanity. There are no demi-gods or gods in Italian opera; there are only human beings, heroes or villains, but always human beings. Sound divorced from the human voice and the human theme has no particular meaning or significance for an Italian.

That is for me the principal reason why we have been quite incapable of providing a Beethoven.

There are of course other reasons, namely the lack of patriotic enthusiasm, of religious concern or of spiritual excitement. These are not on the whole national traits; and we are deficient in them.

What there has always been, however, is great feeling, great sensuousness and, all the time, melody, even in passionate situations.

But passions have never been allowed to become too great and even where they have not been kept under control (like Othello's jealousy or Manrico's heroism) they have never reached peaks of Teutonic perseverance. This is ultimately due to the fact that Italians are quite incapable of taking most things too seriously, as I have already remarked more than once, except their culture and their families.

As John Addington Symonds has pointed out, we are a smiling people. We can boast of a smile all our own - 'Il sorriso Italiano'; it is part of our charm and it does not detract from what we do.

We can be quite engrossed in something important, or serious, in which we are wholeheartedly involved; and then, a moment later, we can stand aside from it and smile at our seriousness.

It comes naturally to us to do it; a northerner, for example, cannot, unless perhaps, he is in Italy, or has had too much to drink.

It is an asset, of course, since life is not worth taking too seriously. After all, one of our greatest men, Verdi, could end his last opera *Falstaff*, composed when he was 80 years old, with the fugue 'Tutto nel mondo e' burla' - 'Everything in the world is a joke.' (The common translation of it as 'All the world is a stage' is not only semantically incorrect, but it fails to render the true Italian spirit of the words. Pace Harold Rosenthal and John Warrack in the Concise Oxford Dictionary of Opera, 1973 Edition, page 126.)

It must be admitted, however, that fewer people nowadays smile in Italy than used to be the case. Italians are becoming a less happy people. In a strange sense, they are slightly more introverted and much less friendly. This is inevitable, because Italian cultural traditions are under constant attack, principally from America. It may be just a phase. It is really too soon to tell.

Furthermore, it is a cause for regret that we are not always able to smile inwardly. On the whole, I do not think we find it so easy to laugh at ourselves since it is so much easier to laugh at others.

We have a tendency to take ourselves much too seriously and there is a certain innate susceptibility in us that causes us to fail totally to appreciate the jokes that others make at our expense. We do take ourselves much too seriously at times.

Nevertheless, our smile is an asset; but it is an asset that has not helped us much in remedying our second failing.

When it comes to our failure to produce great drama, the national characteristics are equally to blame. The obvious first Italian contribution to writing is the 'Novella'. A number of great contributors exist here, as you will no doubt recall: Boccaccio, Straparola, Giraldi Cinzio, Machiavelli.

They all wrote interesting and entertaining stories, or comedies, but they attained no great heights. Nor could they. There was no real centre of learning from which these writers could operate. There was no capital city, no large city like either Athens, Paris or Elizabethan London to hear them, apart from Florence. The greater part of the Italian public lived in the country, and could hardly read or write, so that only the scholars and the members of the various courts in the individual towns had any knowledge of their language. The general public was ignorant. There were no leaders, no sense of power, no feeling for history other than in the sense that the Romans were our predecessors, and no political enthusiasm of any kind. We were, and still are, far too sceptical; we were, and still are, not too religious nor too profound.

It is not that the material was not there. Ample material was available to Boccaccio and others; so much so that if there had been anyone of sufficiently great intellectual calibre, he could have turned to excellent advantage the very features that militated against Italy developing drama as England did. The disunity of the people, their suffering, the Naples plague, their extreme ignorance and poverty, the very sinister religious revivals which resulted in the growth of Italy being stunted by the Catholic Church in the second half of the sixteenth century (if you have read Italian history you will recall that Carnesecchi, Paleario and Bruno were burnt alive in Rome in 1567, 1570 and 1600 respectively; Vanini was burnt at the stake in Toulouse; Gentile was executed by Calvinists in Berne; Campanella was kept in prison for nearly 30 years in Naples in the Castel Dell'Ovo; Galileo was forced to recant; and Sarpi was knifed, although he survived that).

All these facts, tragic in themselves, could have elicited a tragic response; but they did not because, as already noted, the Italians have never taken life too seriously. After all, as Symonds reminds us, the nation had witnessed the slaughters of the Viscontis, the cruelty of the Sforzas and the poisonings of the Borgias: these were all Italian tragedies which in their own way gave the English great enjoyment. Marlowe, Webster and Shakespeare thrived on Italian themes, whether happy or villainous. Indeed, as we have seen, no less than nineteen of Shakespeare's works are set in Italy or are inspired by it. But the Italians were not moved.

There is a further reason, which has nothing to do with history but with personality. The Italian is constantly being both himself and playing a part. He plays a part in his love life and in his job and he has learnt at an early age to be an actor. He is, as Barzini has observed, a small showman; and that is why for 22 years he appreciated Mussolini, who was a big showman. Because, no matter what else you may hear, the Italians did approve of Mussolini. There were some independent spirits who decided they could not put up with a dictatorship and went abroad: Toscanini is the first example that springs to mind but there were many others, less well known. Many came to England; others emigrated to the USA and to South America.

But the majority of the people were pleased with what they had. If you speak to those in their seventies who were around at the time, they will disclaim any love or even acceptance of Fascism. But their disclaimers sound somewhat hollow.

The Italians at the time appreciated what Mussolini was doing; he was restoring the glory of Rome, he was, they thought, making Italy great. They felt that he was giving them back dignity in international affairs and they accepted him in the same way in which the Austrians and the Germans accepted Hitler. They accepted him because he was strong, and Italians will always admire and respect power in preference to goodness or justice; and because he was one of them, in the sense that he displayed, to a very marked degree, all the virtues and, even more, the faults of the Italian people. If this judgement seems harsh, consider for a moment the following facts. Mussolini proclaimed himself a dictator, suppressed freedom and constitutional rights, condoned the killing of Matteotti and wantonly attacked Abyssinia: he withdrew political rights from the Jews and declared war on England. The Italians applauded these deeds which were all contrary to their own tolerant nature. Why? Because he made them feel good.

In other fields, Mussolini was conceited, as most Italians are; he loved the sound of his own voice, as all Italians do; he proclaimed himself a believer in God but that did not prevent him from sinning, a normal feature of Catholic Italy; his bark was worse than his bite, and that is not too unusual in Italy either; he was a good father and probably also a family man, but he had no compunction about keeping mistresses: indeed, he died effectively in the arms of one. No, do not believe those who say that Mussolini was not wanted by the Italians. If it be an historical fact that people get the government they deserve, then the Italians at the time thoroughly deserved Mussolini.

Returning to the point, however, I should say that the Italian's feelings are not, on the whole, repressed; therefore, he feels no need for any extra, greater theatricality on stage. That is the reason why, generally speaking, Italians do not make great tragic actors, although they have provided one of the greatest comic actors of all times, Eduardo De Filippo.

Great acting and great tragic works belong to the English, or to other northern people, who repress their personality in everyday life and who therefore enjoy acting out on stage, or in choral societies, all the feelings that they have so repressed, whether they are sincerely felt or not. In exactly the same way the English love to dress up or play a part, whether in the Territorial Army, the school play or in amateur theatrical groups. Anything in order not to be themselves. (I should add that this is a common feature of northern peoples in any event and is not only confined to the English.)

The ultimate reason is that in Italy life has always been something of a tragedy and no-one ever felt the need to glorify its tragic features in writing. On the contrary, starting with Boccaccio, Italian writers have enjoyed underlining its funnier sides.

This almost carefree approach of the writers reflects the attitude of the people as a whole. They have no wish to be serious for too long: they want to feel, not to think. It is almost as though one were afraid that thinking might cause the brow to furrow, that it might produce premature ageing. There probably is something in this approach: if you think too much or too hard, you grow old more quickly. One should remain a child at heart, I suppose.

The same attitude emerges if one considers the discoveries made by the Italians. Once made, interest is lost in them and the scientist, artist or whatever he might have been classified as, went on to something else. This lack of perseverance and continuity, this perpetual search for something novel or different, this desperate attempt to escape from the boredom of routine and repetitiousness is another facet of the tendency of the Italians not to be serious for too long. Foreigners call it levity or flippancy: I prefer the adjective 'fickle'. Perhaps neither description is accurate; the answer may be that if at heart you are a cynic and yet love life, the only way to survival and to psychological salvation is not to take things too seriously.

Historically, Italian tragedy went into realistic painting, as anyone will appreciate who has looked at the Sistine Chapel ceiling. It is only in his Rondanini Pieta that Michelangelo gets close to abstraction in a desperate attempt to express the inexpressible. I suppose it is ultimately true that, if one is surrounded by tragedy, one does not wish to read about it.

It is a pity, of course; just imagine how exciting an Italian Shakespeare or an Italian Beethoven might have been. Or perhaps not; perhaps the fascination that the south holds for all northerners is not something that can be turned upside down.

And so, regrettably, here are our two cultural failings. The reasons for them are to be found in ourselves, in our history and in our make-up.

SUCCESSES

One can really divide the history of Italy into several parts: pre-history, the Greek phase, the Roman phase, the Middle Ages; after that, taking as a starting date the year 1000 AD, there is a further sub-division up to about the year 1500. Thereafter we have the period of the Renaissance and then a further period from, say, the beginning of the eighteenth century to the end of the nineteenth (I am ignoring more modern history).

They are historically convenient periods since they highlight some of the principal phases of Italy's development as a country but the three last periods are particularly relevant to the development of Italy as a nation.

The first of these last three periods includes such events as the travels of Marco Polo and the initial contributions by Italians to science and knowledge. Before we deal with this period we must try and visualize what had happened from the fall of the Roman Empire up to its beginning. Italy, as has already been established, was invaded by all and sundry. Let me repeat the list of invaders, for it is long: Arabs, Goths, Vandals, Lombards, Franks, Huns, Normans, Spaniards, Swiss mercenaries, French, Germans. The world was aghast when Rome was sacked by Alaric in the year 410: but that was only the beginning.

The first thing that the Italians had to learn, therefore, was survival. Each town or area developed its own techniques.

They had to learn when to make way for the invaders and retreat to the hills or to the mountains with their families and their cattle, and when to stay and fight or negotiate with them.

One finds signs of fortifications all over Italy. There are castles and defensive walls in all the major cities. The Sforzesco Castle in Milan is a classic example, but there are many others; from the tip of Italy (Castel del Monte in Puglia) to Naples (Mastio Angioino) through to Rome (Castel Santangelo), Florence and Bologna.

With the passage of time, the fortifications became in themselves a means of expressing the personality of the inhabitants and style was applied to them; but they started out as purely functional means of defence.

Even in Venice one finds a form of fortification, as the inhabitants retreated onto the island from the mainland, thus escaping the invader.

All these defensive needs developed what I would call a siege mentality. People who retreated within the walls of the city in the face of the invader, often resisting sieges lasting for weeks or months, and sometimes years, had to learn two essential virtues which have been an Italian fundamental characteristic ever since; resourcefulness and improvisation. (Incidentally, have you noticed how this same mentality is reflected in the Italian style of soccer playing? The players retreat almost to a quadrangle, which is very difficult to penetrate and where they show all their defensive skills and resourcefulness. Thence they make sorties, at speed, to score. Having scored, they retreat to defence again. It is a classic example of the mentality that I am describing.)

Gradually, each city found an activity that was useful for its survival in exactly the same way as Venice found that it had to retreat to the islands, or the Jews to control money which in turn can buy those who wish to harm them.

It is of course true that, at about the same time, cities started fighting one another. This in-fighting obviously brought about one of the classic faults of the Italian, namely the constant bickering between one another. This has in turn developed into something of an antipathy towards his fellow human beings which is not always too successfully disguised by his easy manner and his gregariousness.

On the other hand, one has to be a little careful not to exaggerate the extent of this internecine fighting. It was frequent rather than occasional but the frequency was not proportionate to the intensity. Fights went on for years between one city and the next; take Florence and Pisa, who fought each other for decades; or Venice and Genoa, who did so for centuries. But there were more prisoners than casualties, for the particular reason that they were used for ransom.

In a sense, the in-fighting between the various factions in the individual cities (Florence is a particularly good example) was much more bitter, as fights between neighbours usually are. But peace was made as often as war and even in these local internecine battles the numbers killed were not so great: each faction being able to run for shelter to its own 'palazzo'. Indeed, we must remember this was the period when Italian cities were at their most prosperous - demographically, artistically and economically.

At the same time, this very in-fighting was also one of the sources of improvement for those individual characteristics of resourcefulness and inventiveness which have served the Italians in good stead. After all, hostility stimulates imagination and there is nothing like the need to survive to excite mental ability. In any part of the world the need to survive sharpens the intellect. In England, that old saying 'necessity is the mother of invention' sums it up nicely.

The constant invasions also explain the great love the Italians have for their homes. Every time an invader dislodged them or destroyed their villages, these were rebuilt with stubborness and determination, almost as though the home represented survival against future perils.

By concentrating on his own ability to survive and to rebuild what was destroyed, the Italian also developed, at a very early date, two characteristics which, in modern times, would represent probably his principal social and political drawbacks, namely his contempt for the state and his utter disregard for authority. The reasons are not far to seek: since the state, or whatever was the equivalent at the time of constituted authority, had been unable to prevent his territory being invaded and his home destroyed or his family molested, it could not obviously be worth very much. The individual, on the other hand, derived great strength from the fact that despite the destruction that occurred around him, he found himself quite capable of surviving. Hence, the natural sequence of the individual considering himself better than the state; and in Sicily, the Mafia.

On the positive side, this concentrated, dogged resolve to rebuild and regenerate, led to the development of a technical and aesthetic sense that blossomed into the full flower of domestic, religious and public architecture, both during and after the Renaissance.

Since one could find some sort of protection from greater numbers, the houses were rebuilt each time in greater densities - hence the rapid early development of Italian cities.

These desperate, instinctive needs and ability to survive account for many contradictory and at times humiliating features of Italian history. They explain how one can revere a dictator for 22 years and then, having shot him and his mistress in tawdry circumstances, allow his body to hang in Piazzale Loreto for the benefit of the mob. (Here one almost hears faint echoes of what happened to Cromwell and to Cola di Rienzo.) They explain the almost inconceivably ruthless reaction of Italians in circumstances where their own survival instinct is paramount.

The average Italian, single or married, is constantly on the lookout for changes, whether in his job or surroundings, which might result in betterment to himself or his family. He lives like a pointer, his nose up in the air, sniffing the wind. Whether it be the more or less gentle wind of change or a real gale, it is always an ill-wind against which he must seek protection. It brings no good news and therefore he must remain on the alert.

This hypersensitivity to change and to surrounding circumstances raises survival ability to a fine art, but it also has drawbacks for him. It causes him to throw overboard without too much compunction those whom he believes will only prove to be ballast, or whose usefulness is becoming less noticeable - and, in so doing, often results in his backing, metaphorically, the wrong horse - as well as to behave in a manner which, if it were not essentially fickle, could be said to be cruel and short-sighted. He adopts a policy of 'shoot first and ask questions later': such a policy, in peace as in war, may be understandable when it is a matter of survival but it is not too efficient at guaranteeing that one does not shoot down the best people, or at any rate those who might ultimately be better for one's future than others who it is believed may be taking over from them. Hence the Italian's apparent disregard for people: 'When the Pope dies we elect a new one.'

In personal terms this attitude to life (and death) often makes for short-lived friendships since the relationships themselves appear to be based on the notion of usefulness rather than conviction or commitment: in political terms, it makes for short-term solutions, as we have already seen, and in moral terms it is machiavellism refined: the end always justifying the means.

This same attitude explains how a separate peace could be made with the Allies leaving the Germans to fight on. It is true, of course, that the alliance with Germany was ill-matched; one cannot conceive of more diametrically opposed characters and temperaments than those of the Germans and the Italians. But the welcome given to the conquering Allied Armies, though undoubtedly genuine, was totally disproportionate in circumstances where, until a few months previously, the same Allies were the declared enemies of Italy.

I was in Rome at the time and speak from personal recollection. I suppose the hosannas to the British and American tanks were a reaction to many months of terror by the Germans. I suppose, too, that people who have been without food will kiss the hand that at long last feeds them and be quite unable to appreciate that with corn and sweet potatoes came not only 'K.' rations (meat and vegetable stew in a tin is excellent stuff when you have been starving, I promise you) but also cigarettes. One of the consequences was that the starving bodies were filled up at the same time as an addiction was encouraged which would kill many by lung cancer. All this was done, it is true, in the name of democracy and well-being. But the reality is that the power in marketing and advertising terms of the Americans never allowed any other voice to be heard such as would have been the case in truly democratic circumstances.

Italians sold their souls and prostituted their bodies for cigarettes. The same situation has recurred in the poorer countries of the world like Greece, Turkey, the Philippines, Thailand and South Korea, where youngsters were set to copy American filmstars. Cigarettes became their stance and Coca Cola their habit.

*   *   *

If one goes back to Roman history one is reminded of the fact that Hannibal, that great warrior who had the ingenuity and resourcefulness to bring his elephants across the Alps, was ultimately conquered when he got to Capua near Naples, not by any army, but by sloth. There, he found that the more genial weather and the local sensuousness caused him to slow down and relax and unwind. Unfortunately for him, he stayed long enough to allow the Romans to re-group, with the result that he was ultimately defeated on the other side of the Peninsula at Cannae. One wonders whether the course of history in Italy might not have been different if the Carthaginians had managed to conquer Rome. I suppose it can be said that one of the minor contributions of the south of Italy to Italian history was indeed to conquer Hannibal by means of its pleasure-loving techniques.

Nor was Hannibal the only one to be so affected by Naples and its district. Lord Acton and Lord Nelson, each in their own way, felt the extraordinary fascination of the area, although in the case of Lord Nelson it was insufficient to enable him to behave as a gentleman either in the personal sense or in the political one. In the personal sense because, as is well known, he caused great scandal by his open affair with Emma Lyon; and in the political sense because, in restoring the Bourbon dynasty to Naples, he arranged the court-martial and hanging of Admiral Caracciolo, a brilliant Neapolitan who, apart from being a patriot, had also served under him.

It may be worth reminding ourselves of what happened. The Neapolitans, inspired by the French, had revolted against their Bourbon king. Caracciolo, who was an admiral in the Bourbon navy and as such had also served under Nelson when the two navies had joined forces earlier, decided that he would go over to the revolutionary side. In a sense, he was in the wrong in doing so because he had sworn allegiance to the Bourbon king; even assuming that his sympathies lay with the revolution, he should not have taken up arms against his previous ruler. But then, regrettably, Italian history displays many instances of this kind where a complete 'volte-face' takes place. Having said this for the sake of historical accuracy, Caracciolo certainly did not deserve his end; after all, if the revolution had succeeded, he would have been a hero.

Nelson's attitude to the revolutionaries, according to his historians and biographers, was ambiguous. He wavered, which was unusual for him: first he decided to destroy them, then he granted an armistice which forbade reprisals; he then went back on his word, and hastily hanged Caracciolo in addition to hundreds of other Neapolitans.

English historians are clearly in a difficulty here. On the one hand, there is the fact that Nelson is a national hero, was a great sailor, the victor of Aboukir, the Nile, and Trafalgar; a legend in his own lifetime. On the other, he had given his word that the terms of the armistice which forbade reprisals would be honoured. Many Neapolitans fleeing Naples, took Nelson's word as his bond. A major contradiction here which no-one, as far as I know, has succeeded in explaining away.

It is the consensus of historical opinion that Nelson was influenced by his mistress. She was, after all, quite close to Queen Caroline, who had been deposed and was being restored to power thanks to the British navy. Perhaps she even felt that what she was doing on behalf of the queen would have been appreciated by her and by the British government. Perhaps there was in Emma a streak of cruelty. It must be remembered that she had had what one can only call, if we wish to use a euphemism, a somewhat chequered past. She had been one of the girls of Mrs Charlotte Kelly, the well-known procuress, whose establishments in Arlington Row and Duke Street, St James's, in late eighteenth century London were much frequented by the wealthy and the nobility. Much easier, I suppose, to blame a woman, particularly one with Emma's past, than besmirch the character of a national hero.

It has also been suggested that Nelson may have been jealous of Caracciolo's seamanship. This seems less likely, although nobody can tell: it is more likely that the reverse is true.

In a recent biography of the admiral (Tom Pocock, *Horatio Nelson*, The Bodley Head, London, 1987) there is a suggestion that Nelson may not have fully appreciated what he was doing since he was still recovering from the head injuries he had suffered at the battle of the Nile. This is also quite possible since there appears no real evidence of cruelty by Nelson until the Naples incident.

I personally do not hold it against Nelson that he hanged Caracciolo because strange things happen in politics and in war and, as I have remarked, from a technical point of view, Caracciolo could be said to be a traitor. However, whilst Caracciolo was being hanged in full public view on one of the ships in the British Fleet (the *Minerva*) the Admiral was having dinner on board his new flagship, the *Foudroyant*, with the Hamiltons and other friends. Whether this is an example of phlegm or callousness none of us will ever know. I can only assume that when the British government encouraged the first patriotic movement in nineteenth-century Italy, then occupied by the Austrians, they were to some extent atoning for Nelson's behaviour at Naples.

Not too far away, the people of Nola - better known as the birthplace of Giordano Bruno and of the brigand Pascalone - had for centuries indulged in orgies that were well known to the locality, especially at harvest time, and compared to which we are told the phallus-carrying processions of the Greeks pale into insignificance (interesting accounts of Nola and its varied celebrations can be found in Thomas Ashby's *Some Italian Festivals* - London, 1929). Sensuousness surrounds one in Naples.

Goethe could not deal with it either. On 16 March 1787 he wrote (*Italian Journey*): 'Naples is a paradise: everyone lives in a state of intoxicated forgetfulness, myself included. I seem to be a completely different person whom I hardly recognise. Yesterday I thought to myself: either you were mad before, or you are mad now.' Goethe was not alone. Thomas Nugent thought Naples was the most pleasant Italian town, struck as he was by the gaiety and exuberance of the locals.

But to return to the point, it is often said that Italy civilised its conquerors. This is certainly true if one means by the statement that Italy taught them manners and appreciation of the finer things in life. But the national genius that was born as a result of the constant tug-of-war between the cities and their constant fights with invaders also brought in its turn something to Italy, namely the virtues and vices of the invaders themselves. After all, most of the invading people must have had characteristics that encouraged and ensured their success. The Normans who went to Sicily had a very long way to travel, as had the hordes of Huns and Goths: they were all strong, cruel people; their individual genius matched the local ones. Italian genes embody all theirs, Italian psychological heritage is partly theirs.

The trouble with Italy's national genius, however, is that the clash between civic duties on the one hand, and private and family business on the other, is too great; individualism causes the pendulum between the two to swing too far in a particular way, always in favour of the 'particulare'. That is the reason why individuality does not lead to national unity: indeed, the situation is quite the reverse.

Each coin, as usual, has its two sides. The strength of the English people has lain in the willingness of the Englishman to sacrifice his individuality to the well-being of the community as a whole. For example, there is no way in which a disc-jockey could be successful in Italy, as the immediate reaction of an Italian would be to consider that no-one had any right to impose his choice of records on others.

On the other hand, the English have always accepted that ability can often result in eccentricity or failure to conform and have indeed encouraged such forms of eccentricity. It is not too far from the truth to say that in the days when English eccentrics were an acceptable part of the English establishment, England had an empire; it no longer has an empire now that we frown upon anything which results in deviation even in the

THE CRUSADES

LE CROCIATE

Per Nostro Signore,
Dio di misericordia, tieni.

"In the name of the Lord God of Mercy, take that!"

slightest degree from the norm. The power of compliance and uniformity has become so all-embracing nowadays that it is hardly surprising that individuals have lost their sense of direction.

Italians often say, quite mistakenly, that they like the Englishman as a person but dislike England and its history. This is a highly superficial assessment. It seems to me that the Englishman as an individual is not necessarily any more or less worthwhile than any other individual of a different nationality. It is Great Britain as a whole, as a nation, that is a great historical fact, the greatest nation that has ever existed after Rome. It is a nation that conquered the world and brought its language and its civilisation to distant lands. A nation worthy of respect as none of its individual components could ever be. A nation with pride and conviction, until post-Second World War times, when it lost its sense of history.

It is not for nothing that the saying 'My country right or wrong' has become established in Britain. It is interesting that there is no such equivalent of any description in the Italian language. If one had to be coined, it would read 'Right or wrong, my culture': our culture and our way of life are our patriotism. An Italian would never say 'my country right or wrong,' but he might say to his neighbour 'I am right and you are wrong'. And herein lies the difference between the two nations. The revival of learning which occurred in the sixteenth century put Italy at the forefront in the western world because it had already developed a language and a culture that, although never consolidated into any form of political unity, represented continuity with the Roman tradition. And although there was no national unity at the time, there was political freedom combined with considerable academic freedom. There was also a great amount of commercial prosperity at a time when other nations were still semi-barbarous; so, if one can put it differently, the second phase of Italian development, the Renaissance, was almost predictable.

The revival of learning was also encouraged by some of the movements of the people and the establishment of the great Italian families that gradually replaced the communes. Nevertheless, it is odd to consider that the first democratic movements known to the western world, after those of ancient Greece, occurred in the Milan Commune. In 1037, for the first time, the people there decided to be represented in a local sort of parliament by what you might call members of parliament known as consuls. From there were selected the members of the Gran Consiglio (if you like, a sort of Inner Cabinet) and from those members a 'Credenza', a sort of Privy Council. All were more or less supervised by the Bishop; but even so, it was a democratic process of sorts.

There were other examples. In 1212, in the village of Abbadia San Salvatore in Tuscany, the inhabitants complained about the rule of their feudal lord who lived in the local castle. They were granted certain rights to be represented, such as the right to elect consuls or the right of succession through direct lineal descendants rather than forfeiture to the local Vassal or the local Abbot, and the right to make a money payment in place of feudal labour. This, as Edward Hutton (*In unknown Tuscany*, Methuen, London, 1909) reminds us, was three years before Magna Carta.

One does not wish to belabour these early stirrings, these seedlings of democracy because, in effect, they did not amount to very much. The system did not work. And that was to be expected: the Italian virtues all have their corresponding faults and these faults are, on the whole, incompatible with democracy.

Gradually, therefore, the more capable families in each city took over and established their own form of government. Dictatorships, in the political sense; but very paternalistic dictatorships as far as the arts and learning were concerned.

As the great families took over from the old communes they also made war upon one another and that in turn resulted in constant changes in government. Such constant changes taught men to fend for themselves, thus sharpening their ingenuity and their intelligence. At a time when moral considerations were not relevant, the versatility thus acquired was all-embracing. It led to the ruthlessness of the leaders and the ruthlessly political thought of Machiavelli, but it contributed above all to the formation of an original character and many-sided intellects in greater profusion than in any other nation in Europe.

Furthermore, there was not then, any more than there is now, any great hierarchy of classes in Italy: those who came to the fore were people of merit and they were all individuals. This is very well evidenced by each town having its own expertise. Genoa, Venice, Pisa, Amalfi were all great maritime powers; Florence went into banking; Milan developed state techniques; Naples was well known for the appreciation of the finer things in life and for its comforts (it was, after all, the city that inspired Boccaccio, even though Boccaccio was born in Paris of a French mother): the great intellectual freedom of the Renaissance stirred the imagination.

If there is one thing that the Italians have in greater abundance than any other people I know of, it is imagination. It has, of course, in the past led them to great crimes. One is only too well aware of the sophisticated poisoning techniques of the Borgias. More recently, say over the last two hundred years, it has also led them to sophisticated forms of criminal association and vindictiveness (the Mafia and the Camorra are classic examples.) But when applied to practical life, it has allowed them to be at the forefront of most human activities. Love, hatred, lust and business are all feelings and activities where Italians display a great deal of imagination.

It is interesting to note that this exercise of imagination has not led Italians to any exciting writing. The Italian is not romantic enough to be introverted nor morbid enough to turn to melancholy. Boccaccio is possibly the best example of this, practical and open as he is; his novels are bawdy, but sound in commonsense; he is witty but never gross. (Thank God they did not allow him to burn his manuscripts, as he intended to do in his old age.)

Nor has it made Italians go and search for new political solutions; we are not revolutionaries. It took us 22 years and a defeat in World War II to get rid of Fascism. Partly because of our cynicism, we are inclined to accept the existing order on the basis of the French saying that 'plus ca change, plus c'est la meme chose'.

It is true that in Boccaccio's day adultery and unnatural passions were somewhat commonplace; but this was the price that had to be paid when the spirit was given an unbridled rein and it is a fact that people of great culture and considerable aesthetic temperament develop a sort of high intellectual approach to their vices, when they indulge in them.

On the other hand, this intellectual quality of the Italians has its redeeming features. For example, Italians enjoy drinking; but drunkenness is not a problem amongst us. The reasons are firstly that we adopt too Epicurean an approach to food and drink and, secondly, that in psychological terms we have no need either to forget what we are doing or to project a different image of ourselves. Indeed, the Italian approach is always practical and we like to be in possession of our faculties in order to enjoy the pleasures of our senses to the full.

Again, the northerners went to the crusades in the Middle Ages because they were religiously enthusiastic about them; the Italians, particularly the Venetians, made money out of the crusades as contractors and as merchants. In the Middle Ages the northern races were poor and barbaric and they lived for the most part in villages; Italy on the other hand had a wealth of experience behind it and developed its own civilisation in towns and cities which were centres of learning and a high quality of life. In a strange sense, its political disunion encouraged and stimulated intellectual growth because each town competed with its neighbour. Each despotic family wanted to show the leaders of other cities that it was better, that it entertained more interesting artists, that it spent more money, that it was more powerful because it had better armies or better mercenaries. The leaders at this time were all people with very marked personalities.

The world has reason to be grateful that Italy did not at that time develop as a nation for, because of this failure, it was able to give the world its culture. It was a very humanistic culture that replaced patriotism at every level. It was also an outward-looking culture. It had to be, because of its multifarious origins. In the south, the Arabs and Islam; throughout the north, Venice and Genoa through their maritime contacts brought news of different civilisations. In particular, Venice maintained close relations with Turkey, as Shakespeare confirms in Othello. In the centre, the business interests of Florence and Pisa.

At this particular moment in its history, Italy also reached its trading peak. It was at the centre of all European trade because it stood in the centre of the Mediterranean. At this time, Italian fleets (whether from Genoa, Venice, Pisa or Amalfi) controlled that sea; it was in the true sense of the word 'mare nostrum', for Italian sailors had taken over from the Arabs and the Muslims and also exercised a kind of policing function to weed out the pirates. Textiles, spices, corn and salt were practically a Venetian monopoly. Genoa and Pisa did very well on the commercial side, too, the former holding Corsica and the latter Sardinia. Despite the fact that they made war upon each other, they still developed their trading interests. Indeed, Venice ended up by controlling all the Ionian Islands, some of the ports in the Peloponnese, the greater part of the Aegean Islands, Crete and even a part of Constantinople, which enabled it to trade with Bulgarians and Hungarians. By the beginning of the thirteenth century it had extended its trading activities to the Asian Muslims as well as Africa.

It had taken the Italian maritime cities time to reach their hegemony. They had to fight the Saracens and the Africans. (Pisa led a victorious expedition to Africa in 1088; the Genoese dealt with the Cypriots, obtaining trading posts there.) Ultimately, Genoa beat Pisa and then fought it out with Venice.

All this resulted in the Italians developing a great knowledge of the peoples with whom they came into contact. The Italians also had great familiarity with the mixed races of Spain, including the Jews there; they traded with all northern nations.

A different type of people, I suppose, from those today. Or perhaps not. Perhaps it is a misconception to consider the Italians temperamental; perhaps we are more cold and calculating than we are normally given credit for.

I have already referred to one description of our characteristics as a people, as being artistic, impulsive and passionate. I am not sure that this is the picture that emerges from what I have been saying. The archetypal Italian in my view defies analysis, and, for this very same reason, so does the Italian nation. Nevertheless, the picture that emerges is of a concrete, practical people, with no romantic quirks and no great mysticism, proud of its Roman heritage, its great civility and its great knowledge. A people that, as has been said, was born old and as such was incapable of illusion and thrived on cynicism. In a strange sense, a solid people that ought to have been much more successful than it has as a nation when it ultimately became one. A people with two feet firmly planted on the ground and much peasant good sense. (Incidentally, it is interesting that one of the Italian proverbs, 'contadino, scarpe grosse cervello fino' equates a fine mind with the peasant.)

The language itself owes much to peasant jargon. This is by no means unusual: even in the twentieth century most languages retain expressions derived from an era when there were no rockets to the moon, and no television. In English as in Italian, we go looking for needles in haystacks long after the stacks themselves have disappeared and have been replaced by silage pits; stables are no longer so common as they used to be, but we still shut the stable door after the horse has bolted; we still fall from the frying pan into the fire; and so on.

In Italian, these recollections of times past are even more marked than in English. For example, Italians still use idiomatic expressions that describe handwriting similar to hens' legs ('zampe di gallina') or the sleeping hours of hens ('andare a letto con le galline'), all the verbs defining either aggression or masculinity which are derived from the cockerel ('fare il gallo,' 'ringalluzzire,' ('to get cocky') 'alzare la cresta'), the trapping of pigeons with broad beans ('cogliere due piccioni con una fava') or the terminology taken from the movements and habits of cats or dogs ('sgattaiolare,' ('to sneak off') 'scimmiottare,' ('to ape') 'scodinzolare,' ('to wag one's tail') 'fare la gatta morta,' ('pretending to be dead') 'menare il can per l'aia'.) Even the poplar has been prayed in aid by the Italian language ('appioppare'.)

All these are matters for those who study etymology and semantics but there are very marked examples that identify a culture which is tied to the land. As I have already observed, not for nothing even in the twentieth century, Italian parents say to their male children 'moglie e buoi dei paesi tuoi,' i.e., choose your wife in the same place where you buy your oxen.

During the Renaissance, toleration and compromise prevailed. This resulted in the extinction of any kind of moral conscience. Ultimately it represented a culmination of twenty-five centuries of history in Italy.

In the Renaissance, Italy reached its peak. And what a performance. It was, however, accompanied by immorality and corruption, but, strangely enough, the Italians seemed to thrive on it and the circumstances surrounding them ultimately stimulated their artistic impulse. In everything that they do there appears to be something different and individual. As one of our best poets, Torquato Tasso, put it, there is 'Un non so che,' something one cannot quite describe.

And so we come to the third phase of Italian development, which really started in the second half of the sixteenth century when Italy's growth gradually became stunted. Whether the fault for this temporary atrophy is to be attributed to the Church, or to nearly three centuries of Spanish domination, or to the fact that the effort had been so great that Italy had exhausted itself, or to the increasing modernization and progress of other European countries, or to something completely different, is a question about which historians, particularly social historians, have written volumes. Whichever way one looks at it, however, one has to wait until at least the nineteenth century before one can detect any signs of a revival in Italy. The revival came to the fore with the Risorgimento, reached a patriotic peak in the First World War and to all intents and purposes appeared to end with the arrival of Fascism and the Second World War.

SOIL, SUN AND DIET

Whether sun and soil go hand-in-hand, or not, their effect is joint and considerable. It is easier to make a general statement of this nature than to explain it away. It certainly cannot be explained away in terms of a grading of the soil according to the Ministry of Agriculture classification, or of an analysis of its acidity. It is not the pH of the soil of Italy that I have in mind, but its intrinsic physical/philosophical nature.

Think of the countless people who have trodden it, whose bodies are buried there, whose blood has fertilized it. Visualize a powerful Mediterranean sun baking the soil and actually sealing-in all the energy and vibrations of millions of people over thousands of years.

And it is a different sun that shines in Italy. The air is different from any other part of the world, as is the light. If we ignore modern pollution, it is the same light that can be found in certain parts of Greece and on the Spanish Plateau. In Greece, however, the temperament of the people is totally different. The Spanish Plateau, on the other hand, is a long way from the sea; it is a harsh part of the world, unsoftened by sea breezes; and harsh are its inhabitants.

On the contrary, every part of Italy, except for the Alps, is close to the sea, because of the very shape of the Italian peninsula jutting out into the Mediterranean. You may counter that by saying that England is surrounded by the sea and the sea breezes are on the whole not too far away. Regrettably for those of us who live in England, the same sun does not shine there. As a Neapolitan (the Marquis Caracciolo) once said: 'There's more warmth in the moon of Naples than in the sun of London.'

I do not for a moment believe that the statement that sun, soil and sea have influenced our development can be supported in scientific terms. I am not aware of any instrument that can measure the amount of energy or of blood baked into any soil, or its energy-giving qualities. If we are looking for scientific, demonstrable facts supported by any kind of authority, then the foregoing statements can be considered as the ravings of a lunatic.

And yet, there *is* something about the soil of different countries (not just the soil of Italy) about the way things grow in it, how plants develop, the flavour that the soil, combined with the sun and the air, imparts to fruits (and wine), vegetables, herbs and human beings. Yes, even human beings have a flavour. This is demonstrably so, in physical as well as in psychological terms. Its demonstration in scientific terms is a little more difficult.

Let me give you a small example. In recent years the English have learnt to grow basil. It is a herb which is now a well-established part of English cuisine and it forms part of a number of recipes which, as I have already indicated, have been 'borrowed' from Italy. You can buy the plant even in greengrocers' shops and garden centres everywhere.

But I assure you that the basil that is grown in England has a completely different taste from that which is grown in Italy, even when exactly the same seeds are used. Any good gardener or cook will be able to verify this simple statement. I can tell you with certainty that the leaves have a different colour, a different texture, a more pungent aroma, a different taste and, all in all, are dissimilar. The same can be said of other vegetables like courgettes, peppers and aubergines.

Whence does this difference arise? Some gardeners I have spoken to maintain that it is not derived from the soil but rather from the sun. I disagree; this is not to say that the sun is unimportant but even in the hottest summer

England has experienced in recent years (in 1976) the basil that I grew in my garden tasted very different from that which I sampled in Italy, even though the seeds were exactly the same.

Some of you may think that I have been imagining things: I am not so sure.

There is a feeling about certain places that can only be explained in terms of some physical or magnetic energy being present which we cannot identify in scientific terms, but which we can certainly feel. I am somewhat comforted in my view by the recent development of the science of geo-biology, whose aim is to identify points of cosmic energy.

Furthermore, science has not yet explained why the same vine transplanted to California or Australia produces wines with different taste. The wine-making techniques are the same as in France, Germany and Italy; the root-stock is the same; the age of the vine is often the same. But the continental shades of flavour cannot be matched. What else can it be if not the different quality of the soil?

Has it never occurred to you to meet someone and shake hands with them - to be, in other words, somewhat closer to them than you normally would - and suddenly feel for no apparent reason a flow of either dislike or coldness from them? Or even, to be in a place where there is no-one else and still feel the presence of someone there? If so, does this 'energy' come from the air, the person or the soil or a combination of the three? I myself do not know nor pretend to know and no-one that I have spoken to does either. But that is not to say that the feeling one experiences has no justification or no cause.

I am not sufficiently blinded by science to acknowledge that if something cannot be proved in scientific terms, it does not exist.

There is more in my theory about the soil that I can neither prove scientifically nor have the ability to convey. I believe it to be true, but leave you to formulate your own judgement. I am nevertheless comforted by the fact that other people have considered what I would call the mystery of the earth. Others, more informed than I, have found no paradox in the above concept. I am reminded that in America the skull and pelvis measurements of all the European races began to indianize themselves in the second generation of immigrants. That is the mystery of the American earth. The soil of every country holds some such mystery.

We have an unconscious reflection of this in the psyche: 'Just as there is a relationship of mind to body, so there is a relationship of body to earth.' (C. G. Jung, 'The Role of the Unconscious' in Volume 10 of his *Complete Works*, page 13.)

This would explain why no-one really conquers a foreign soil, as Italy has demonstrated throughout its history: it has always assimilated its conquerors.

If Jung is to be believed (ibidem, page 49) the ancestor spirits of the conquered reincarnate themselves in the newcomers. The Americans who invaded us in 1943 and 1944 are living proof of this: they went back to their home country carrying with them Italian leanings and habits which, particularly for the humbler folk amongst them, were to prove a reminder of better days.

In or about 1945 there was a popular jingle in Rome - I recall it exceptionally well to this day - which, to the tune of 'Yankee Doodle' captured both the same concept and the Romans' cynical appreciation of 'KP' rations and baked beans. In verse, it pictured Johnny's changed behaviour the moment he got back in the United States after his stay in Rome. He has acquired Roman habits (eating broad beans with 'pecorino' cheese, drinking wine and 'stuffing himself' with spaghetti), he looks back nostalgically to his dinners at the Grand Hotel, to his drunken bouts and to the dinner dances at Pighetti's. And as he lights a cigarette stub he has picked up from the gutter, he reflects sadly on the many packets of Chesterfields which he could buy freely and cheaply at the Tor di Nona black market.

The doggerel verses ended somewhat sadly by reminding us that, as he reverts to doing his job as a shoe-shine lad in New York, he remembers the Roman youngsters who were always hoping he would let them shine his boots for a pittance.

*   *   *

The fact that because of its geographical position Italy has throughout the centuries had the benefit of a temperate climate has in its own way contributed to some of the Italian characteristics.

One does not have to go as far as some of the ancient peoples who thought that the sun was God. It is easy to understand why they should have reached such a conclusion, in the absence of any revelation as to what the true religion might be.

But one can take it for granted that the sun has a beneficial effect not only on plant life and ecology generally, but particularly upon human beings. We are all affected by it, each in our own way.

The face of London, for example, changes completely on a sunny day. I suppose it is the same everywhere. People become more extrovert, more loquacious, more inclined to smile, they spend more time in the open. People actually become friendlier when they have the opportunity of living in the open. They see things in a better light, their shape is more marked, their line is more significant, the aesthetic value of things becomes more prominent and capable of better appreciation.

A blue sky has an extraordinary effect on most human beings. Some of Shelley's best poetry was written under the sky of Rome - *Prometheus Unbound* - 'the bright blue sky ... in that divinest climate,' as he puts it himself. I for one find the Roman climate enervating, and there is no doubt it has a similar impact on many foreigners.

A blue sky also slows down physical activity. The northerners' passion for work or at least for activity has to be moderated in a very hot climate. In moderating it, they provide for themselves more time to reflect and to philosophise; they begin to learn a few things about the meaning of life which had escaped them in the hustle and bustle of a rainy or cold or hectic environment. This is inevitable, for the northerner has to alter his reactions and go back to square one: he has to re-learn what life is.

In his own country, most of his time is dedicated to work. There is after all not much else to do in the cold and the rain. He becomes ever more industrious and his only solace lies in recourse to alcohol.

The southerner, on the other hand, even if poor can live like a king, for he needs less clothes, less housing, less work., This prompts the belief that southerners are lazy: not true. They merely work to live, and rather than live to work they live to enjoy themselves. It is a question of choice, but then choice is dictated by the weather. Sunshine and joy of life go hand in hand.

In a different sense from alcohol, the sun heightens one's aesthetic sense and reduces one's inhibitions. That is why the Italians are always intoxicated: it is not alcohol, it is the sun.

One of the direct consequences of this is the extraordinary sense of light and line that appears in and guides everything Italian. In a different sense, the sun gives realism. On a bright sunny day, the colours are exactly as they should be: white is white, black is black. If there is a grey, it has a life and tonality of its own and it does not occur simply because white or black cease to be perceived as such. This makes for realism, and Italians on the whole are realists. This allows things to be called by their proper names; and on the whole, Italians are capable of doing this.

This enables Italians to sin quite blissfully without confusing beliefs and thoughts with high-fangled doctrinaire or romantic notions. After all, it was Horace who put it quite bluntly: 'Video meliora proboque, deteriora sequor' (I see good things, and I approve of them; but I do worse things).

So, on a personal level, the sun enables one to provide a more constant pattern of personality. It is interesting that as far as the English are concerned, the Latins, and the Italians in particular, are said to be volatile and unpredictable. This is true as regards their mood but I am not too certain that it is correct as regards their character. More constant and reliable weather patterns result, in my view, in a more constant and reliable pattern of personality.

In a strange sense, I find the English much more unpredictable than the Italians; and I have reached the conclusion that this follows from the instability of the English weather.

The effect of the sun is quite clear on Italian buildings. They have line, style, are pleasing to the eye and are open. This is very marked in the original style of Palladio.

The sun obviously has a marked effect on food. First of all, one has more time to appreciate it and therefore one approaches it with more of a cultural outlook. The food itself is tastier because of the combination of sun and soil, as I have already pointed out. This in turn has an educational effect upon people, at any rate as far as their taste-buds are concerned.

In conclusion, therefore, it can fairly be said that the sun has affected the Italian temperament and character in a number of ways. It has enabled us to judge things more clearly, it has made us realists, and it has given us a taste for good things. The combination of these factors has also resulted in our being happier and kinder then most other peoples. The sun gives us that sublime appreciation of beauty that puts us in a tender mood and protects our hearts from the sorrows and the bitterness of life.

Fortunately, the next item, the Italian diet, is capable of scientific proof. The case is proved abundantly by all the recent publications on food allergy. It is a fact that a number of illnesses, or so-called illnesses, do not always originate in the mind even though for many years they were inexplicable. Food allergy is now established as a branch of medicine.

If, therefore, food can influence you negatively by causing you to become hyperactive or come out in spots or be sick or whatever, it must by definition be able to influence you positively. I do not need to labour this point too much: food is all important.

Obviously food is essential for survival. But surely how you survive is also relevant.

Under 'Gastronomy' I have already made my position clear. It is that you are what you eat. It is your diet that determines your reactions and influences your temperament; that provides mental and physical energy, and sexual drive. Put differently, can you imagine what drive of any description you would have if your diet consisted of nothing else but bread dipped in milk, as we say in Italy? I am sure you would survive; but how? Equally, a diet of stodgy foods and fats may give you some physical energy but I wonder how much intellectual strength is really provides.

We are now assailed from all angles by dieticians who tell us that our diet ought to be balanced. I believe that the Italian diet has been balanced for centuries; obviously the poorer people have not fared quite so well; but vegetables, fruit and olive oil have been available in abundance to all Italians.

This diet has created a certain type of physical make-up. I am not saying that this make-up is better then other people's because the diet of any people is obviously related to the climate in which they live. I am sure that an Italian diet, even assuming it to be available, would not be of too much use to an Eskimo; and vice versa. But it must be a fact that the dietary intake of your body affects your overall performance and your personality, as well as your outlook on life.

If I am right, the Italians are due for a change: a MacDonalds has recently been opened in Piazza di Spagna in Rome.

Also, it occurs to me that perhaps what we eat does ultimately affect how we think as well. After all, there is little doubt that there are major dietary differences between the north and the south of Italy. Is it diet that determines our destiny? Look, for instance, at the differences in output between different regions in Italy.

In this context you will recall that, in the facts section, I have recorded whenever possible the place of birth of the people whose names are listed. I have done so partly for my own benefit because, when I started out on this exercise, I was not too knowledgeable about the extent of the individual contributions of the various regions of Italy.

For the purposes of understanding this contribution, after I had collated the evidence, I proceeded to divide the country into three parts, namely, the north, that is to say the totality of the northern regions down to approximately Bologna; the centre, that is to say, all that part of Italy from Bologna southwards to Rome; and the south, that is the remainder of the country including the two major islands.

If we are thinking only in terms of numbers, the contribution made by the centre of Italy is double that of the south and that made by the north is double that of the centre. I am not considering quality; for example, Galileo comes from the centre of Italy, as does Leonardo; Marco Polo and Christopher Columbus come from the north; the south saw the Salerno School of Medicine, two Nobel Prize winners (Deledda and Pirandello) and Piria who discovered salicylic acid. It is difficult to draw firm conclusions from these findings save to this extent: the contribution of the south has been more of an historical, philosophical and literary nature, that of the centre more of a cultural, intellectual and aesthetic kind, and that of the north more of a positive, practical and scientific type.

The southerners, of whom I am one, may complain about my way of putting things. They may wish to remind us that when the north of Italy was still in a semi-barbarous state, then the central part of Italy knew the civilization of Etruria, and the south and Sicily that of the cities of Magna Graecia. Indeed, some towns in southern Italy and Sicily were centres of civilization when Rome was still a village; Pythagoras was born more than a hundred years before Plato, Archimedes came from Syracuse, and the Temples at Paestum, south of Salerno, antedate both the Parthenon and the Great Wall of China. Southerners may also wish to point out that in the seventeenth century Naples had over 300,000 inhabitants and despite a major eruption of Vesuvius in 1631, the Masaniello revolt of 1647 and the virulent plague of 1656 it was, after Paris, the most important city in Europe.

Southerners would say this, and there is no denying the facts as so stated. But those facts merely prove that the south had a very ancient civilization and not that the southerners' contribution to the discoveries that I have recorded previously is that substantial. Progress and civilization are not the same thing and there may be a reason for this comparative failing on the part of the southerners. It is possible that southern climes are conducive to theorizing and philosophizing more than to action and positive thought. Hence the common accusation levied against southerners, namely, that they are lazy. I do not believe this to be true. They are not. They are, however, indolent, because the sun makes them so. But when the southerner emigrates to the north of Italy, he proves that he can work quite hard.

It is interesting that within the framework of the general ambivalence that the English show towards the Italians, there is very marked ambivalence towards southerners.

Lord Nelson's family and heirs are still Dukes of Bronte, in Sicily, and Lord Acton enjoyed his stay in Naples. On the other hand, others have been scathing about Neapolitans; for example, hear what Hutton has to say: 'Less civilised than ourselves, perhaps, the Neapolitan is at least never vulgar in our fashion. He may be a villain, but he is a courteous one; he may be a thief, but he steals politely; he may murder you for less than a lira, but he does it with perfect grace. Even his curses seem magnificent. Altogether, he is not to be despised.'

Altogether, not an unfair assessment of some perception; but I cannot forgive him the 'perhaps'. Whether one likes Naples and its inhabitants or not, its civilization is the oldest in western Europe. But on second thoughts, I shall be magnanimous; I shall forgive him even the 'perhaps', because he was a lover of Italy. And what he says about the Neapolitans can, to some extent, be generalised to include many other Italians.

Still, the myth of laziness persists. Even such a knowledgeable and sympathetic writer as Constance Stocker Giglioli (*Naples in 1799* John Murray, London, 1903) makes the same point: 'the Neapolitans, lazy by nature, were born in manifold servitude, bred in darkest ignorance, inured to suffering and privation, devoid of ambition....'

Perhaps the circumstances described above explain away the laziness... but I retain my own view: not lazy, but indolent.

Nevertheless, that we are prone to theorizing and philosophizing in the south is well established. It can hardly be a coincidence that all Italian philosophers (Bruno, Telesio, Campanella and Croce) come from the south. Indeed, more famous Italian writers came from Sicily than probably from any other part of Italy (Pirandello, Verga, Capuana, Sciascia, Tomasi di Lampedusa, and many others.) Their 'verismo', simple tales of real life and descriptions of fate and injustice, are renowned the world over.

It is conceivable that those who are favoured by the kind of weather that will allow them to spend almost the totality of the year in the open air will be less inclined to sit at a desk or in a laboratory trying to unravel the secrets of life in the physical sense.

And yet, I wonder why this should be so, because if one has a scientific mind then it does not matter where he is to be found: science and the cold climate do not necessarily go hand in hand.

I am at a loss to explain this obvious imbalance between north and south for, to be objective, it must be recorded that northerners have achieved four times as much as southerners in the field of scientific discoveries.

The imbalance surely exists. It may be the diet, or it may be history: probably both.

Without going into too much detail, it is nevertheless understandable. The ancient civilizations of the south and of Sicily occurred at a time when there had been little opportunity of making great scientific progress. The first real kind of scientific progress was made by the Salerno School of Medicine.

But that School had no means of advertising its courses the way universities and colleges do nowadays. It must have taken decades for people to get to know of its existence and many weeks, if not months, of travel for those interested to reach it.

By the time we get to the Renaissance, and beyond, the south had remained fairly isolated. The isolation of Sicily is apparent from the fact that it is an island; the isolation of the rest of southern Italy is underlined by the Apennines that ultimately divide the country into two and also, to some extent, serve to separate the centre and the south of the country from the north.

Whereas the northern plains of Italy were open to all influences, especially trade and the general movement of goods and people, the south continued to live in a world of its own. If you add to that three centuries of Spanish domination or rather repression in the south of Italy, which only ceased in 1707 with the entry into Naples of the Austrian Army, coupled with the strictures imposed upon scientific research by the Catholic Church, the feudal organization of society and agriculture, the Neapolitan Camorra equivalent of the Mafia and the general apathy, in the political sense, of the southerners, who are all highly sceptical of authority and of the State, it becomes easy to realise that it was almost impossible for the south of Italy to make any true scientific contribution to its development.

Furthermore, the southerners were the last Italians to become emancipated politically. They clung to the monarchy as they had, maybe unwillingly, to their Spanish rulers. It is no coincidence that in the referendum on whether or not Italy should become a republic, held on 2 June 1946, the south voted in the majority for the monarchy and it was left to the north to provide the extra two million votes by which the House of Savoy was ousted from Italy. Politically, the south has been mainly for the Church party. When the first general election took place on 18 April 1948, the south made a great contribution to the victory of the Christian Democrats, who got 48.5 per cent of the vote against the Communists' 31 per cent. (I remember well how throughout Italy the respective slogans were displayed: a badge with the word 'Libertas' across it for the Christian Democrats, and a red star with an image of Garibaldi in its centre for the Communists.)

Similarly, it is hardly a coincidence that those who emerge best from my analysis are the northerners. That is to say, those inhabitants of that part of Italy which geographically has easy access to France, Switzerland, Austria, etc., and which is, despite the Alps, a plain where communications are easily sustained - as regards both road and river transportation. The River Po runs the whole length of northern Italy and has always provided an important communication link between one centre and the other. It is a fact that was already well known to Shakespeare, who refers to the Po valley as 'Fruitful Lombardy, the pleasant garden of great Italy' - (*The Taming of the Shrew* - Act 1 - scene 1 - line 4.)

If you add to that the fact that northern Italians have acquired some of the features of the Slavs, the Austrians and the Germans, overall you get a different type of personality in the north: a more disciplined one, and one which is stimulated by the pursuit of scientific research. This is not praise for its own sake of the northerner or criticism of the southerner. It is a fact of life or of history, whichever way one wishes to look at it.

Those from the centre of Italy partake of both the north and the south. But they need not feel in any sense at a disadvantage because of the ratio of the discoveries made by them vis-a-vis those of the north, for they can rely on Leonardo and Galileo; nor should they be too conceited towards their southern brethren, because the very culture which Florence was able to project to the whole of the civilized world during the Renaissance came from southern Italy.

THE CHURCH

I mean, of course, the Catholic Church. The effect the existence of the seat of the Catholic Church in Rome has had on the Italian nation has caused gallons of ink to flow. Between those who maintain that it was the Church that ultimately saved Italy as a nation and those who argue that Italy would have found its way much more quickly but for its existence, the shades of political and historical beliefs are so varied as to be almost incomprehensible.

In the Middle Ages, the Church was surely an asset. It preserved for us the Greek and Latin texts and the classical tradition and it represented a bulwark against the emperors. The association between the Church and Italian literature was marked in more ways than one. It cannot, for example, be mere coincidence that Dante had first admired Beatrice in church, Petrarca at the age of 23 fell desperately in love with Laura in church on Good Friday in 1327 and Boccaccio surrendered to the looks of Fiammetta again in church at Partenope when he, too, was aged 23, but nine years later than Petrarca. There is a clear association at this time between Church and Italian literature; the influence of the Church on architecture, sculpture and painting is equally great.

On the other hand, in the seventeenth and eighteenth centuries it stifled thought and development, thus undoing, as some have said, all the good it had done four or five centuries earlier. In the nineteenth century it interfered with the Italians' search for freedom and for a national identity. It is too soon to determine what use it has been in the present century, though its contribution to Italian post-war politics should not be under-estimated.

I mentioned, earlier on, that it was thanks to the rather compact southern vote that the Christian Democrats managed to beat the Communists when the first general elections were held in Italy in 1948. To that extent, the

Church performed a valuable historic function if we proceed from the premise that Communism in 1948 had to be defeated.

But these statements stem from an historical appraisal of the role of the Church in Italy and they have no significance whatsoever, in my view, when we have to deal with the psychological impact of the Church on the Italian character. In this context, what the critics of Rome say ceases to have any great significance. Let me explain. It is quite correct for those critics to say that as a result of the Church's criticism and banning of Galileo scientific progress was stultified in Italy for about two centuries. That criticism is borne out by the facts and is certainly well founded.

It is equally true to say that inasmuch as the Church is a state within a state in Italy, it has a vested interest in the Italian state never being too strong. Again, that seems to make sense.

But, to proceed from these rather easy and well-documented premises in order to criticize the Church's role in Italy in its totality, seems to me not only unwarranted but also unnecessary. It is, for example, far too easy to say that the social development of Italy has been impeded by the Catholic Church because, amongst other things, it opposes divorce. That, to me, is an irrelevancy. It is not the Church's present stance on divorce that has made any contribution of any kind whatsoever to what the Italians have or have not been able to achieve, but it is the very existence of the Church in Italy through the centuries that has left its mark on the Italians; well apart from the other consideration that the stance of the Church has not prevented a divorce law being passed in Italy in the same way that the stance of the Church in Ireland will not prevent a divorce law being passed sooner or later in Ireland.

It seems to me that there is a basic fallacy in certain of the criticisms of the Church which proceeds from the equation of divorce with progress: to me, there is no such connection whatsoever. If there has been no emancipation of the Italian woman over the past fifty years (and I do not accept that this is correct, because enormous strides have been made in that respect) it is not because there has not been a law of divorce but rather because the impact of the Church over the preceding 1,500 years has been such as to create a mentality and a psychological heritage which have delayed the emancipation of women. But to assume that progress and the emancipation of women are coincident is begging the question.

The influence of the Church has certainly ensured that woman in Italy has had a different role from that which more modern tendencies ascribe to her. But at the same time, it has had an impact on the role of the man as well. This influence has been substantial and it has in the main manifested itself in four forms.

The principal form in which the Church has affected Italians, of both sexes, has resulted from its great power. This power was used for both good and evil and this is not the place to review the history of the Catholic Church. But there is little doubt that, after ancient Rome, the Catholic Church was the principal champion of things Italian. And to that extent it has permeated Italian life in many ways, some obvious, as for example in the prohibition of divorce, and some much less obvious and more subtle. What the Church has in fact done in Italy is to create a kind of benevolent freemasonry or Mafia. I mean this statement in no way disrespectfully. The body that wields possibly the greatest power on earth has always exacted gratitude and loyalty from those who have entrusted themselves to it. In Italy, particularly in the smaller towns and villages, the priest is most important. A word from him may mean the difference between finding a job and remaining unemployed. It is not merely a question of the power that the priest has exercised over the souls of his parishioners but much more a matter of the real power that he has wielded over their ordinary lives.

To that extent, until very recently, the Italian has been placed in the position where his primary loyalty, after that which he owed to his family and his children, was to the Church more than to any other organization. For these reasons, the creation of a strong state in Italy has certainly been delayed, if not impeded.

But in psychological terms, the exercise of this power by the Church has deprived the average Italian of freedom of thought because he has been constantly reminded of the debt that he owed to the Church and, through it, to his Maker. This loss of freedom of thought has been compensated by a basic, elementary religious belief (I dare not say religious fervour, for we are considerably lacking in that) which, on the other hand, has led him to a tolerant and benevolent view of life which is always a distinguishing mark of the believer. I hasten to say that I am not attacking the unbeliever; nor am I making a religious point. But I think that purely on a probabilistic principle a person who believes in any god is more likely to endorse, in his daily behaviour, certain principles of tolerance and compassion than one who does not.

All this must be viewed over, say, at least a thousand years. The constant repetition of formulae and the maintenance of certain beliefs must inevitably have affected the psychological make-up of those subjected to it. The second way in which the Church has influenced the Italians has been by its constant, determined and sometimes stubborn upholding of the principles of the Catholic faith as it has propounded them. The enforcement, successful or otherwise, of a morality which has changed little over the centuries has had a great effect on the make-up of the Italian.

Probably the best example of this is the Church's approach to marriage. This has been consistent since the days of the catacombs. The Church has taken the view that a marriage is made in heaven. Since, so the argument runs, it is God that in reality has joined the parties in the sacrament of matrimony, it is obvious that only death can separate them. After all, the parties got married with the intent of remaining in that state 'until death us do part.' This is certainly a point of view. In simple language, it is argued that one gets married for better or for worse.

There is also the other argument. This is put forward by more liberal-minded or more progressive people (may I repeat at this stage that I subscribe to the view that progress and civilisation are not coincident) and it runs along the lines that marriage is no different from any other contract with the consequences that, as the parties enter into it, so they can get out of it at will, or indeed, at whim. I pause at this stage to remark that there is no other solution to the argument: in logic, a marriage is either indissoluble or capable of being terminated at any time by either party for whatever reason.

I find that the attitude of the Anglo-Saxon world, and the English world in particular, is highly hypocritical when it comes to marriage. Firstly, it was the Christian/Catholic approach that was adopted, namely that marriage was basically indissoluble. Then in the middle of the nineteenth century we established the concept of the matrimonial offence, to the great joy of divorce lawyers and private detectives. More recently, no doubt as a result of feminist pressures, in Britain we have adopted the concept of the breakdown of the marriage without having necessarily to attach too much significance any longer, save possibly when it comes to financial considerations, to the matrimonial offence.

The reluctance to go the whole way and be logically consistent, namely to say that once you accept that God has not joined two people in matrimony, they can get out of it at any time, I find very difficult to follow. It is almost as though there were an innate fear or shyness in the English in reaching the obvious, logical conclusion. Lest you should think that it is a poor, temperamental, misguided Latin talking who does not understand what it is all about, look at what Sir James Fitzjames Stephen has to say: 'If the parties to a contract of marriage are treated as equals, it is impossible to avoid the inference that marriage, like other partnerships, may be dissolved at pleasure. The advocates of women's rights are exceedingly shy of stating this plainly' (from *Liberty Equality Fraternity*, 1873.) Stephen was a well-known lawyer; but he certainly was not a feminist because he proceeds from the statement I have just quoted to argue that, in such a situation, woman would be the loser. In any event, Stephen was not saying anything new.

Divorce by mutual consent had long existed in China and among the Eskimos, the ancient Welsh and the ancient Germans. After Stephen wrote the above, the principle has become established in countries of such disparate cultures and traditions as Luxembourg, Switzerland, Rumania and Japan.

The logic of the argument was underlined centuries ago by Milton, and somewhat more recently by Shelley and by Montesquieu. In most other countries, Italy included, the puritanical or Catholic inheritance is causing people to sit on the fence and behave hypocritically. Leaving aside for a moment the Catholic Church, no-one has any longer the courage to say that we either believe in the 'mystical' nature of marriage, or, if we do not, we should accept that as we embark on it, so we should be allowed to disembark from it when it suits us.

However, the Church's logic on marriage is in my view unexceptionable.

Of the two solutions just mentioned it has adopted the former. It has said repeatedly that man is quite incapable of separating what God has joined, that the spouses become a single flesh and that accordingly the purpose of their coming together is the procreation of children and the establishment of a family. Such approach may be right or wrong and this is not the place to consider its merits or otherwise. But it has one major consequence which has resulted in the greatest possible impact by the Church on the Italians. The consequence is that it has strengthened the marriage bond and as a result the family as a unit. (This is not to say that Italian spouses have respected the integrity of their bond or have honoured their marriage vows in a way that other people have not. This is not the point at all. It is the principle that I am considering, not deviations from it.)

This concept of indissolubility has in turn created the kind of mentality whereby the mother has been glorified as the centre of the family, as indeed she is, and the father has accepted that his primary duties to the family prevailed over everything else, including any commitments he may have undertaken towards either the state or his mistresses. Consider how this is expressed in Italian art where woman reigns supreme. Look at all the Madonnas; the number of Italian artists who have painted them is great and the result is highly flattering to woman. Look at all the Holy Families; the glorification of the family as a unit is apparent there too. As woman reigns supreme in Italian art, I would suggest it is also a reflection of real life.

The supremacy of Italian woman has also manifested itself in the tendency of the Italians to express concepts in terms of woman. Under the heading 'Motor Car' I have already referred to the link that the Italian male makes between women and cars. This is interesting because it shows that woman is taken as a standard of either goodness or beauty or reliability or acceptability or whatever. She may be a good standard or she may be a bad standard: but she is the metre by which most things are measured. (In Tuscany, however, she may be an inferior standard, as witness the old Tuscan proverb 'Words are females, facts are males'.)

Nowhere does this emerge more clearly, in my view, than in a book written in 1625 by Cesare Ripa, under the title *Iconologia*. The book contains representations of women of different shades of colour, beauty, attire and animalistic features, which are supposed to represent different virtues, vices or situations. So you open the book and you see, for example, the title Virtue, underneath it there is represented a saintly-looking, rather coy woman and beneath that appear a few verses to explain what virtue is all about. The book is not merely about women: it is about concepts. But in the majority of cases, the concepts are represented by women. This is a part of the glorification of woman that I am dealing with.

A further result of the strengthening of the family unit has been a clear-cut distinction, for example, between the sacred and the profane which is one of the principal features of Italian art and society and which in itself is no more than a form of realism. It is in effect a recognition of instinct and of the basic necessities of life. It is the result of a practical approach to relationships, unaffected by romantic notions.

Ultimately, it is less hypocritical than in other parts of the world and, because of this, it provides inner strength. I have always subscribed to the view that the acknowledgment and recognition of one's instincts, while usually resulting in lack of conformity and often in formal deficiency or inadequacy, gives inner conviction. On the other hand, formal correctness and apparent strength acquired at the cost of sacrificing beliefs and instincts, though at first blush impressive, derives no great strength of inner feeling and character. To that extent, northern people, who seem outwardly composed and in possession of themselves, tend to emerge inwardly weak. As Jung put it, those who ignore their instincts end up being ambuscaded by them.

The third way in which the Church has affected the life and the psychology of all Italians, whether practising Catholics or not, has resulted from its position as a state within a state. It is a peculiar kind of state, the Vatican, because whilst it has to cater for the wellbeing of the Italian Catholics, it has an even greater duty to other Catholics from different nations. In practice, therefore, the Church has always come to terms with the Italian government, even to the detriment of its own faithful. In practice, too, as I have already remarked, the Church has never had any great interest in strengthening the Italian state and has never provided the slightest encouragement in giving to Caesar what is Caesar's but only in taking on behalf of God that which is said to be God's.

Furthermore, to avoid problems with the state, the Church has always encouraged the faithful to do their duty by the existing, established authority. Any attempt at new or revolutionary politics has always been frowned upon by the Church. The result of this has been that Italians have developed a split view of life. In a sense, it is slightly schizophrenic. They have had to steer a middle course between what the law has decreed or allowed, and that which the Church has recommended or condemned. Never was this more clearly underlined in the political context than in the 1948 fight between the Christian Democrats and the Communists. It may have been easy for others to sit back and chuckle about the event. It was not funny in 1948 when the Russians were represented by the Church as the devil at the door of Italy.

The Italians are gradually becoming more emancipated as far as the influence of the Church goes in matters of politics. Indeed, it is probably true to say that the present-day generation attaches increasingly less importance to what the local priest has to say about that subject.

There is another sphere where the Catholic Church has had an impact, perhaps even unwittingly. It has reminded us throughout of our equality before God. You may say that other churches do the same. But, for example, in England, the identification of the Church of England with the State, resulting from the fact that the titular head of the Church is the monarch, has not had quite the same result.

I am concerned here with class consciousness. I think that it can be said that inasmuch as the local parish priest has, in theory at any rate, related to both the nobleman and the peasant, on the basis of equality (before God), coupled with extensive contacts that the Italians had as a result of travelling, banking and merchant shipping, this has resulted in dilution of the concept of class consciousness in Italy. This has not happened in England, which is still a class-ridden society. On the other hand, Italians are not at all class conscious. There is no great divide between the classes in Italy solely because of social differences. Insofar as the Italian is a snob, he is, contrary to the English, a cultural rather than a social snob.

There are reasons for this, also apart from the impact of the Church. The first of these reasons is that the Italians are very much aware of what I should term our common humanity. For this reason, we are essentially a kind people, with a great deal of understanding, if not compassion, for human foibles and frailty. That is probably the reason why, like the Chinese, the Japanese and the Greeks, we are exceptionally fond of children whom, as parents, we spoil endlessly. Indeed, it has been correctly said that Italian parents spend their lives spoiling their children when they are young and trying to put that right as they grow up.

There is no doubt that Italians on the whole are also an exceptionally tolerant people. Because they themselves have so many weaknesses and so many faults, they attach no great significance to human foibles. After all, aren't we all God's creatures and very much alike? For this reason the Italian lacks, on the whole, the crusading spirit. It is better not to seek to convert anyone to a way of thinking nor to impose one's own views on others. If you believe (wrongly, I suspect) that the best way to enjoy life is to be drunk at the end of a party, fine, that is your choice: who am I to criticise? If you believe that your football team is the best in the world, just as fine: we shall see at the end of the championship whether you are right or wrong but, meanwhile, you are entitled to wallow in your dedication to your home town or whatever. If you believe that your party is the only one that will redeem the sins of the past and make the country great, still fine: after all, you may well be right, one political party is very much like another. Who am I to tell you that you are wrong?

But please, no airs; no arrogance; no thought, no matter how remote, that you may be better. The Italians believe that they know it all, have seen it all and have had experiences which are all embracing: no airs. If you behave, there will be no need to remind you of the fact that the Italians were there before you, a fact which is but an accident of history. I am addressing you, the reader, but I could be addressing the world at large. The approach is typical. Italians do not bother others as they have no wish to be bothered themselves. When they are, they often react disproportionately to the nature of the offence. It is almost as though the biblical saying 'Fear the wrath of the just', or whatever the correct equivalent is, takes possession of the average Italian when he is confronted with arrogance and forces him in one direction only, namely that of proving that he is better than the next man. It is quite an interesting development, for in normal circumstances the Italian does not feel any need to assert himself in an arrogant manner. True, when as usual he feels well dressed, he does have a tendency to strut about like a peacock, especially when there are women present. But it is a fairly harmless performance. Whether he is too busy enjoying his food and his women or whether he feels that by the average manifestations of a sexual nature, he has already sufficiently asserted his personality, I cannot tell: but it is true that an Italian will seldom if unprovoked go out of his way to score a point or prove himself; he will watch tolerantly as others do just that and he will not be unduly troubled. But please, no airs: we are all human beings. No airs: it is so unnecessary to put any on. No airs, or one might be tempted to cut you down to size. These reactions are especially true of southern Italians, although those from the north are equally prone to them.

It is my firm view that when an Italian has to consider someone, regardless of sex, who is said to be above him or more important or famous or worthy of respect etc., he automatically tends to visualise that person not in the social or political or professional position or location where he is to be found at work or displaying those virtues or those powers for which he is renowned, but in the privacy of his/her home performing more menial duties or obeying the laws of nature. Against that background, we are all more or less exactly the same.

It is interesting that many years ago there were on sale in Italy little terra-cotta ashtrays which had on them a rather charming picture of a toilet seat. The legend beneath it, as I recall, ran more or less like this (my free translation): 'Kings may be powerful and Popes may be wise, I don't know why, but when they sit here they are all exactly the same as I.'

There are other factors as well. The Italian nobleman lived in his city or town in almost medieval style, until quite recently. Certainly, in respect of the more primitive parts of Italy (I have Sicily particularly in mind) one can say that these conditions prevailed until less than a century ago. The houses of the rest of the inhabitants, the successors of the vassals of the Middle Ages, were all around. And so they remained. It was not unusual for the children of the humbler folk or the servants in these places to play with the children of the owners or the heirs to the title. Indeed, this used to happen until quite recently even in the more progressive parts of Italy like Tuscany where the farm cottages are not too far removed from the castle or principal farm house.

Ultimately, things changed because the nobility of tradition and of custom has disappeared and it has been replaced by a 'nobility' of money. The so-called self-made man, who usually should have made himself better, has a tendency to move away from the place where he was born. He does so because he is thinking of his bank account and therefore of the value of property, because he no longer wishes to be reminded of his original meagre surroundings and because he prefers to mix with people who have money. It is a fact that one tends to associate with those whose economic level is more or less the same as one's own. Hence the move away from one's roots.

None of these reasons have any significance for the true nobleman who, until recent times, looked upon his ancestral home or castle not in terms of its real property value but in historical and emotional terms as the seat of his family and the custodian of his traditions. But by the time things changed, the social levelling mentality had become established. The Catholic Church has endorsed the Italian lack of class consciousness, whilst paying lip service to the maintenance of the nobility. To this extent, at any rate, the Church has made a positive contribution to Italian society. It has ensured that Italians are realists.

My final point about the Catholic Church is that it has always taught us to accept with good spirit the evils that befall us. On the personal level, this philosophy of life has much to commend it; on the social plane, however, it has resulted in the Italians, particularly those from the south, very often adopting what I can only call a negative or resigned outlook on their social conditions. This mentality has been exploited both by those in authority and by those with what I might call greater entrepreneurial spirit; the former for the purposes of maintaining the status quo, the latter for their own private purposes or for purposes of crime. It can hardly be a coincidence that the Mafia and the Camorra have prospered in the south of Italy but not in the remainder of the peninsula. True, there were ancient traditions of honour, resistance to tyranny, reaction to injustice, need to safeguard certain basic individual requirements where the State could not assert its authority and the overlords tyrannized with their own private armies. But to some extent, the Church must bear responsibility because such organised criminal associations can only prevail where the individual, either because of his make-up or because of his attitude of resignation, is both unwilling and incapable of fighting back.

I suppose it could be said that resignation is a small price to pay for peace of mind. Certainly, one cannot blame it solely upon the Catholic Church. I seem to recall from the little philosophy I studied at school that both the Sceptics and the Stoics preached resignation of some sort, intellectual if not emotional, or in the form of a suspension of speech and thought. Again, it will come as no surprise to learn that both these schools of philosophy had some success in the south of Italy and very little elsewhere. The impact of the climate as I have already discussed does have considerable bearing in this context. But by preaching resignation over the centuries the Catholic Church has made the social evolution and improvement of the Italians much more difficult to attain.

*   *   *

In conclusion, allow me to summarize how the various distinctive features of the Italian people developed over the centuries. I have for many years had the opportunity of analysing Italian merits and the corresponding faults.

Indeed, it is interesting to record that in the case of Italy every single character trait coin has a very clear-cut reverse side; every virtue of which we can be proud results in a vice of which we ought to be ashamed. Let us look at them one by one.

1. From the barbarians who invaded us throughout our history we have derived our sense of adventure and our desire for travel. Also from them, however, we inherited those traits that led us to the extremes of barbarity and cruelty in which we have indulged on occasions throughout our history.

2. Through our dealings with them, and our having successfully mixed our race with theirs, we have developed an instinct for diplomacy and for what is positive, as well as a certain ability to deal with people. The reverse of this is our innate ability to lie and to cheat when we consider it necessary to achieve our ends. To this extent, we can be quite machiavellian and, where necessary, humiliatingly servile.

3. From our resistance to the invaders we have developed our resilience; the reverse of that is our utter inability to see our faults and to pull together as a nation.

4. From our constant internecine fights and struggles we have developed our political ingenuity and our machiavellism. The reverse of that is the corruption in our political, social and administrative structures.

5. From our siege mentality has come our principal asset, our resourcefulness; the reverse of that is our inability to look at ourselves as a nation and our concern with our own 'particulare', our town and our family, which are destructive of our national unity.

6. From the totality of our development and history during the Renaissance we have inherited our extraordinary, unique imagination, sense of art and beauty. The reverse of this is our fondness for form rather than for substance, which leads us to superficiality and into numerous errors of judgement; and our waste of energies in allowing our imagination a free rein.

7. From the combination of the Mediterranean weather and the blue skies we have derived our joyfulness, sensuality and love of life; the reverse of that is our occasional irresponsibility and inability to be serious.

8. From the fact that our cities developed individually and independently one of the other, and indeed constantly fought against one another, we have derived our great sense of individuality and our worldliness. That has also given us our lack of discipline, of civic sense and of punctuality.

9. From the fact that we traded with everybody throughout our history, we have ultimately got our genial tolerance and total lack of class consciousness. The reverse of that, however, is our cynicism.

10. From our Roman heritage and from the fact that we were as a people both old and knowledgeable, we have inherited a firm conviction that there is nothing new under the sun, coupled with pride in our achievements in the sense that there are very few fields about which it can be said that we did not get there first. The reverse, however, is our pessimism and disillusionment with life, and our almost permanent dissatisfaction with ourselves.

Why we should be pessimistic I do not know. It is true to say that northern Italians are on the whole less pessimistic then southerners. Indeed, some northerners are positively optimistic about life. Why people who live in Milan, which has a climate in winter which is not too dissimilar from that of Germany or England, should view life more optimistically than those who live, say, in Naples and are favoured by the sun's rays on most days of the year, is something I have never been able to explain. Perhaps their optimism is a form of despair; perhaps you must believe in your ability to mould your destiny before you can be an optimist. A fatalist, as most southerners are, can develop neither optimism nor pessimism, but only irony. Still, it is odd.

All these features go to make up a people who do not as a rule look to the future with any enthusiasm; who are ever mindful of Horace's saying 'Carpe diem', that is to say 'Grab what's available today'. The Italian on the whole adopts the stance that since he has no idea what is going to happen tomorrow he might as well be cheerful today. It is not for nothing that a very old Italian proverb says that it is much more sensible to take the egg today rather than hope to be able to eat the hen tomorrow.

A people which is ultimately tormented by its imagination because the instinctive psychological intuition with which it has been gifted makes it see the difficulties of events and the futility of long-term planning rather more than any positive side. This is, for example, one of the reasons why Italians, generally speaking, try not to enter into long-term contracts.

A people with no great sentiment for nature on its own, unless it be connected with humanity. If one looks at the history of Italian painting, there is little landscape painting for its own sake and whenever attention is dedicated to the landscape it is usually as an adjunct to the human body. And yet, we are sensitive to the style of natural beauty.

Indeed, more than one foreigner has termed the Italians children of nature. In many respects, they manifest quite primitive traits and hold equally primitive beliefs. This is not a bad thing after all: it allows them to reduce problems to their fundamentals.

For this reason the Italians have not (at least until the deification of the profit motive came into existence with the advent of American films and Coca Cola) attached as much importance to money as they have to enjoying life and being as carefree as their more obvious responsibilities allow.

*   *   *

A people quick to criticise, yet tolerant, quick to seize on the ridiculous and to expose shams, immensely susceptible to beauty and style, refined in taste, sensuous in feeling, suspicious of mysticism, realistic, demanding, practical yet superstitious, pleasure-loving.

The generally accepted view of the Italians as subservient to the senses and to the pleasures of the flesh has a long, established history. The thought has occurred more than once to a number of writers that this slavery to the senses has consumed and destroyed the Latin race. For example, D. H. Lawrence maintained that the phallic worship of the Italians - surely, not only of the Italians, but also of the Greeks and probably of Mediterranean races generally - was a step lower than the worship of physical forces and of science. Lawrence assumed that the move from paganism and sensuality to modernism and scientific development was a necessary one in the emancipation of the Italian people, when it occurred. The creativity of the Italians would accordingly be transferred from the phallus to machinery.

It is an odd notion, which I believe to be flatly contradicted by the numerous contributions made by the Italians to science which I have already analysed. Whether phallic worship has diminished since he wrote I cannot determine.

Pleasure-loving, the Italians definitely are, but does that mean that other avenues of fulfilment must be closed to them? Herein I believe lies a misconception on the part of northern races generally. Dedication to the senses and to science are by no means mutually exclusive; dedication to science and not to the senses need not of itself produce better results. It is obviously a fact of life that the greater effort one puts into any activity, the more successful one is: hence the proverbial success in teaching by people in holy orders of one form or the other, who in theory would not be distracted by commitments to family, to the senses or to society.

But that goes to the world outside the individual: what about the world inside? Are people who dedicate the whole of their life to scientific research, to the total or almost total exclusion of the pleasure of the senses, any happier, more interesting, more fulfilled or more complete persons? I wonder.

Pleasure-loving certainly, but not romantic. I have already tried to make the point that it is a total misconception to assume that Italians are romantic. The whisperings of sweet nothings into a young girl's ear are not the fruit of romantic temperament; they are merely a natural, instinctive reaction to basic needs and to a violent demand for satisfaction of one's desires. They are means to an end and are not motivated by any particular spiritual feeling or dissatisfaction or by an over-excited sensitivity or tension of the soul. Anything but that: the hot Mediterranean sun burns the mists of romanticism and mysticism away and, in any event, the Italians are far too old and cynical even in their youth to be able ever to be truly romantic.

The reality is completely different. An Italian is incapable of considering as novel and extraordinary something as basic as the relationship with a person of the opposite sex. That somewhat exciting but essentially naive approach is left to the northerners who enjoy suffering, who tend to be physically and emotionally impotent, and ultimately ashamed of themselves and of their emotions.

The average Italian is not ashamed of being himself. Indeed, he tries on occasions so hard to be himself that he becomes a bore. And because he it is, on the whole, of brief duration. This concept holds good for everything an Italian indulges in, simple or complicated, routine or exceptional; but it is especially true of his relationship with woman.

An Italian cannot look at a woman for too long still thinking that she is unique. She may be unique when he first singles her out as the object of his attentions; but not after she has responded. The only Italian I can recall who could do that was Petrarca; and it is interesting to note that he was particularly successful in England; he was liked by Chaucer, admired and followed almost to distraction by Sir Philip Sydney and literally copied by Milton, Shelley and Wordsworth. But he was a very exceptional Italian. Exceptional in his style, his appreciation of woman and his patriotic fervour. Over 600 years ago he was already moaning about the 'moral wounds that one saw so frequent in the fair body of our mother country, Italy'. His predecessor, Dante, who died in 1321 when Petrarca was seventeen, also had a similar outlook: but then, he really stared straight through Beatrice and he, too, in that respect at least, was not typically Italian, since when an Italian looks at a woman he mentally undresses her.

But let no-one with knowledge of psychiatry assume for a moment that this characteristic is a manifestation of psychical onanism. Far from it. It is merely a consequence of having a practical mind, and a concrete approach to matters sexual. There is both a spiritual and a practical value to nakedness. The spiritual one is related to beauty, the practical one to hygiene. Insofar as an Italian looks upon woman as a chattel, he wishes to inspect her in the same way as he would examine the teeth of a horse he is about to buy.

Feminists will no doubt resent this observation. But I have little doubt that if more men when choosing a wife, or women picking a husband, exercised the same care as a stockman in selecting a calf, the chances of disagreement or dissatisfaction at a later date would be greatly reduced - even more so, I would add, if prospective spouses both have a medical.

Against such background, one must reach the conclusion that the reason for all this is basic egoism, for Italians cannot as a rule ascribe outstanding attributes to any person, as that would be tantamount to admitting that there exists apart from themselves another extraordinary human being; and that, for an Italian, is impossible. That is also the reason why we consider ourselves better than the next man: as I have said, why we are not prepared to have a disc-jockey tell us what records we should listen to; why, despite our Catholic faith, we do not really love our neighbour. We all think like the boxer: 'I'm the greatest'.

Romanticism goes with misty skies and damp climates; the former force one to hope constantly for a brighter outlook and the latter provoke a certain amount of physical impotence. Neither feature is Italian.

We are transparently Roman in culture and Mediterranean in outlook. is cynical, he is inevitably difficult to please; for the very same reasons he sees things too clearly to be excited by them for too long a period. This is not to say that there may not be a sudden conflagration of emotion; but

4.

Conclusion

It is my belief that we are witnessing a new renaissance in Italy. It is partly a technological revival and partly a spiritual and psychological one.

In the first place, the country has begun to recognise that, after nearly forty years of democratic republicanism, it has got closer together than it ever was. It used to be said that the Calabrians (from the south) resembled the Greeks, the Romans resembled nobody, the Tuscans were like the Etrurians and northern Italians on the whole were very much like the Austrians and the Germans. I do not think that any of these facile explanations are acceptable today and there is certainly no scientific evidence to support them.

It is a fact that until recently no real attempt has been made to unify the people of Italy. The Roman Empire ignored any kind of fusion: all it did was to provide the people with a common language and a common culture.

Some traits have remained, others have been added, but it is on the whole not too easy to look at the question in historical terms. The only historical statement that can safely be made is to say that the movement of labour from the south of Italy to the north that has taken place since the early 1950s - and the intermarriages between southerners and northerners that have been the result of this migration - are beginning to break down the centuries-old economic, cultural and psychological differences between the two halves of Italy and are becoming a major factor in a greater unification, in political and social terms, of the peninsula as a whole.

A common trait of this greater unification is the new technological advance that can be seen in the ever increasing successes of Italian fashion, furniture, machinery and equipment which are being marketed throughout the world. That Italy should be at the forefront in these fields is no news; I have already remarked on the novelty of some of the ideas which have tempted people

CASANOVA

GIACOMO CASANOVA

È l'ultimo avanzo di un'Italia destinata
a scomparire: va a letto solo con donne.

"He is the last remnant of an Italy which is destined
to disappear: he only ever goes to bed with
women."

to steal from it. But what must be remembered above all is that Italian designers are today's artists. Without theorizing, without purporting to belong to any particular school or to be bound by any aesthetic code, the Italian designer proceeds with the strength of the beautiful things which he has seen all his life, by which he has been surrounded in his home town, which he has appreciated in the houses, the museums and the streets that he has frequented; he proceeds to build functional objects in a natural and spontaneous manner.

The Italian designs with the same ease as Giotto did when tending his sheep; his Cimabue, however, is not his master in the art but the manufacturer/entrepreneur who looks upon art as a means to an end rather than an end in itself. This is regrettable, but inevitable; even so, there is art in what the Italian designers create and that is why they are unique. They are to industrial design generally what the artists of the Renaissance were to architecture, painting and sculpture.

It will be clear from what I have already said that I do not accept the somewhat facile argument that is often put forward to the effect that whatever contribution the Italians may have made and whatever impact or influence they may be said to have had on the rest of the world in centuries past, there is very little left that they can give.

In the first place, it seems to me that the survival ability of the Italians is worthwhile considering and, maybe, even adapting to the new economical and social requirements in which Britain, amongst other advanced industrialised countries, finds itself. Inasmuch as Britain can no longer rest on its laurels and is forced to compete with the remainder of Europe and the world in the market place, it is developing certain traits and a certain approach to life which I for one would call typically Italian. The need for greater inventiveness, more personal initiative, a certain amount of aggressiveness and, in the business world if not in the personal one, some sailing rather close to the wind, are becoming fairly accepted manifestations of a new way of tackling the problems of modern British society. Necessity is, as usual, the mother of invention; Italians have been living under its yoke for centuries.

In the second place, one has only to walk through any of the streets in the centre of London to see how many images or echoes of Italy and things Italian are to be found everywhere and not merely in the Palladian architecture of its principal buildings.

Without mentioning names, it is only too easy to see the numerous shops that sell Italian goods, from clothes to handbags, from shoes to furniture. Some of them are already household names. And it simply will not do to argue that London is a cosmopolitan city and therefore everybody is represented here. I can think of at least one household name whose shop facias adorn buildings as far north as Edinburgh and Inverness.

But one does not even have to go as far as Scotland. Macclesfield, an English town if ever there was one, can boast of Arighi Bianchi, a furniture store which has been established there since the middle of the nineteenth

century in a building of exceptional architectural interest. Antonio Arighi
had come to what was then (1850) a thriving silk town from his native
Lombardy, went into partnership with Antonio Bianchi and was the founder
of a family dynasty in the furniture business which continues to this day.

One of the major modern suppliers of optical instruments is a firm founded
by two Italians and still carrying their names. The head of the cardio-thoracic
unit at Hammersmith Hospital at the time I am writing is an Italian. A
Professor of the University of Turin is at the forefront in the study of cancer
(experimenting with protein-thiols molecules.) And another Professor at
the University of Siena is an authority in the field of oncology on the
biochemical damage caused to cells by another type of molecules known
as free radicals. An Italian teacher at University College London is also
internationally known for her studies on protein-thiols.

In the field of entertainment, the Italian influence is exceptionally
prominent. Leaving aside the sphere of more serious and classical music
where the names - one thinks of Toscanini, Caruso, Gigli and Gobbi - are
too numerous to record and going on to the field of more popular
entertainment generally where the names are perhaps better known - at
random, and in no particular order of merit because some of the following
are more worthwhile than others, one can think of Semprini, Mantovani,
John Bennett, Greta Scacchi, Paola Dionisotti, Katie Boyle, Tom Conti, Bobby
Darren, Connie Francis, Madonna, Frankie Vaughan, Henry Mancini, Dean
Martin, Vic Damone, Frank Sinatra, Perry Como, Don Ameche - all of them
Italian. One can see how the Italian ability to provide the kind of
entertainment the public wants has found a fairly natural outlet in the Anglo-
Saxon world. Furthermore, Margaret Thatcher's champion female
entrepreneur, Anita Roddick, is also Italian.

And there are many others whose claims in the scientific field are of
greater importance, albeit less well known, than those of the multifarious
establishments that dispense spaghetti, pizza and other pasta dishes; these
latter are by no means to be underrated since their influence has in many
respects been much more profound than the superficial consumption of
food may show. It has run somewhat deeper and has altered habits. Indeed,
one could make a very good case for saying that the eating habits of the
entire population of Britain have changed as a result of Italian influence.
Habits not only in terms of the quality and type of food but of the times at
which that food is taken. Eating times are no longer the same in Britain,
particularly for the last meal of the day: very few people nowadays have
the traditional high tea and very many have dinner at hours later than 7 pm.

And how family menus have changed as well. Dishes with Italian names
that were unknown before World War II are now established in the kitchen
vocabulary and folklore of the proverbial man on the Clapham omnibus
who would be just as pleased as the next man (or woman) to enjoy a quick
snack of lasagne and a glass of red wine for lunch. This would have been
unthinkable say 30 years ago: beans on toast, eggs and bacon, pork pie,
you name it; and lasagne? and a glass of red wine? certainly not.

I have so far been concerned primarily with England and the English as well as Britain as a whole. But the Italians are coming to the fore in other countries as well. However, before leaving England, let us not forget that an Italian now sits in the House of Lords - Lord Forte.

But elsewhere in the world the construction of chemical, petrochemical and multifarious engineering works and dams, from North Africa to Brazil, from the Middle East to India, and especially in Third World countries has, over the past 20 years, seen an increasing contribution by Italians. In America, for example, where since the beginning of the century Italian talents have been channelled all too often into criminal activities, one has witnessed in recent years a redirection of effort, almost a rehabilitation of the name of Italy by those Americans of Italian origin who are beginning to stake a claim in spheres of society and in activities somewhat higher than the humble, but necessary and pleasure-giving dispensing of food. Greater social mobility has led to increased flexibility of outlook, so that we have at the time of writing a successful and fearless public prosecutor of the Mafia (Giuliani), the head of a major conglomerate (Iacocca), and a Judge of the Supreme Court (Scalia), all Italians.

At home, terrorism and organised crime are by no means defeated yet but the authority of the State has emerged strengthened from the war which is still being waged against the Red Brigades, the Mafia and the Camorra. But I believe that there is a more important and totally different way in which Italy is experiencing a new renaissance; it is a renaissance of culture of an entirely different kind. Despite the shift away from it in economic and political terms, there is no reason whatsoever why the Mediterranean should not become once more the centre of human activitiy. I believe it was E. M. Forster who wrote that 'the Mediterranean is the norm'. He meant it no doubt in the sense that the Mediterranean represented a cultural and artistic medium which served to balance out, as far as he was concerned, England and India, the east and the west, the two poles of his being.

There is today a wider meaning to Forster's words. The cradle of civilization may yet be able to show that it can also be its custodian, that it can act as a mediator between northern Europe and America on one side and the remainder of the world on the other. At least, in the political sense, if in no other, the Mediterranean may well prove capable of reconciling the differences between the ex-colonial powers and African countries. And if you look at the picture of the Mediterranean, which country better than Italy can represent the focus of that activity?

What is the reality in which northern people live? They live in conditions which are hardly enjoyable, have had to adapt to totally false and artificial standards, and have to struggle with an atrocious climate.

In this climate, they have little choice but to pursue material gain and the true test of their success must be the acquisition of money. Material wealth is their primary aim. It is their bank balance and not their spiritual or physical happiness which takes priority.

But can this really be the lot of humanity? Can it be right that we should expend our energy and our vital efforts adequately to house ourselves and our families in order to keep up with the Joneses? What we do ultimately is to sacrifice our life on what is obviously the wrong altar. We may have performed our duties to our families and to our society by today's standards, but what about our duties to ourselves? Should we not be searching for happiness rather than material gain, for spiritual self-satisfaction rather than smugness? This is probably a dream, but it is a dream where the Italians still have something to say. After all, have we not reminded the world of what sweet life is all about? Taking yesterday, one has only to think of the fascination of the Grand Tour. It is easy to see why it was so necessary, and so successful. It was a combination of a release from one's background and an assault on one's senses that occurred crossing the Italian border.

The release was endorsed by the change in climate, in language and in the facial expressions of the locals. The assault was both visual and aural. It started with the beauty of the Alps, it continued with the charm of the valleys and was heightened by the abundance of villas, churches and paintings. It started as a manifestation of the beauty of nature and it ended in a glorification of the aesthetic sense of man. Wherever the visitor turned, he saw what he had come to see, and was not disappointed. The musicality of the language, ranging from the 'cantilena' type of speech along the Po valley to the more refined and yet aggressive jargon of Tuscany, to the vulgarity and solidity of the Roman dialect, and the suavity of the Neapolitan idiom, ended in the subdued, softly uttered and yet threatening Sicilian speech. This assault has continued in the twentieth century and in the Italy of today. The dialects have either mellowed or disappeared, at any rate in the major centres, but the visual impact is still far from negligible. True, the countryside has been spoilt by the erection in a haphazard and wholly inappropriate manner of advertising hoardings that litter the landscape to a degree which is a national disgrace. True, motor vehicle traffic is threatening and sometimes killing the heart of the principal cities, although that is a curse common to the whole of the modern world. But some of the displays are even more dazzling, artificial though they are, than they were one or two centuries ago, and not to be found elsewhere in Europe.

The visitor is pleasantly shocked by the elegant window displays. In any food shop that he may pass or enter, the abundance of products is truly amazing. Sometimes the arrangements are gargantuan; legs of pork, hams, on and off the bone, cheeses of all lengths, shapes, sizes, colours, stacked one on top of the other, sometimes in pyramidal form, other times at random, but always with a visual impact, an orgy of food if not of bodies. The presentation techniques in Italian food shops are unrivalled. Even if you walk in on a full stomach, you suddenly feel temptation and perhaps even pangs of hunger.

This is continued at the greengrocers'. The choice is again probably the widest in Europe but it is the way in which what is for sale is displayed that catches the eye. A box of fennel will be placed next to dark red lettuce, a bright yellow endive next to radishes, multi-coloured peppers all mixed together. The eye is tempted even where the purse is inadequate. And the displays actually walk out of the shop, almost as though they felt that they had to find more room on the pavement, almost as if the boxes of fruit wished to embrace the passer-by in a pleasurable clasp.

Even if you are in a hurry and you pop into one of the many bars (too many: are there any other countries in the world where there are as many cafes and snack bars as in Italy?); even if you walk into one of these establishments, the choice of rolls, sandwiches, the movement and vivacity of people, the gesticulating and the noise, above all the noise: they all conspire to create a picture of life that is unique in colour, sound and smells.

If you are in search of a little respite and enter one of the many churches (and how many: is there any other country in the world that has as many churches as Italy?), the peace you will find is again a voluptuous one. Gone is the coldness of the northern Gothick. Apart from the few examples of dignified Romanic style, it is the Baroque which prevails. The church is full; full of statues, pictures, votive items, candles. The representations of the saints in statues or paintings seem more human than elsewhere; they almost seem less saintly.

Clearly these are monuments to a God who is not to be found in the skies but on earth, a robust God, almost as Michelangelo painted him, a God tolerant of human foibles as no other God could be. A human God, a God, if the statement is not blasphemous, who loves a good table. A God of style and beauty.

Just as in the Renaissance we set the cultural tone and we taught the world the fashion by which they should learn to live, so I believe that we can still teach the world how to preserve its sanity amidst the chaos that so-called progress and mass-communications has brought about.

Where else can we look for guidance? Can you with any degree of conviction mention any nation in the world who can claim to have made a greater contribution to happiness than that of Italy? I am not considering either political or economic leadership, but merely feeling for life.

I do not wish to be carried away on any great wave of enthusiasm for Italy which I am only too well aware also has problems. But if I am a nationalist at all, which I doubt, I am a cultural and not a political one.

I quite see the many obstacles that Italy has to overcome: our total lack of civic sense, antiquated civil and criminal procedures, poverty, slums and backwardness, let alone illiteracy in the south, our constitutional inability to pull together, our chaotic institutions, a primitive bureaucracy, a medieval outlook on political life, servilism and obsequiousness to those in authority or those who can be of use or from whom favours are expected (the modern equivalent of the kissing of hands of yesteryear), our exasperated individualism, lack of discipline, inconstancy, moodiness and envy for those with ability that forces many of our better men (musicians, artists, film directors, or whatever) to go abroad for recognition, our disrespect for those in uncorrupted authority. All these are enormous problems and we have to face them. But the Italians are not alone with problems.

I repeat, I'm only concerned with happiness. Few Italians can teach anyone civic sense, political efficiency, militarism, organization, or respect for authority. These qualities, even where they exist, may make for a comfortable life in society, but of themselves they do not contribute to happiness. They have not prevented our social order from being distinguished by violence, drug-taking, contempt for life, disregard of old age, disinterest in those worse off than ourselves, lust for money and power, sexual abuse.

I have to say, too, that generally speaking, an Italian is not easy to please; and, I know, generally speaking, he is not too happy about his lot either. He is most unhappy with his country, about which he is always complaining. He is dissatisfied with the way it is run and says it is ruined. He moans about his politicians, his bureaucrats, his diplomatic representatives, the police and everything else around him for, with some justification, he believes that he deserves better than he is being given.

He looks around himself caught in, say the Rome rush-hour traffic, considers the increased number of violent robberies, thinks of how sycophantic he has to be to preserve his employment and how subservient to those in authority if he wants to achieve anything, how long he has to wait in a queue in a government office to obtain a certificate which is said to be necessary before even the slightest administrative step can be taken. He hears with disgust the news of the poor and the weak who are being tried for petty or non-existent offences when the big and powerful get away with siphoning funds abroad in breach of exchange-control regulations and, literally, with murder. He wonders what is happening to the world when the rate of incest and child abuse is on the increase even in Italy (let alone England): and he feels totally helpless.

He then has to comfort himself and he does so in a field where nobody can interfere and where his artistic and aesthetic perceptions are allowed their full rein: he cooks and he eats. This is not to say that he himself does the cooking; he may or he may not. His mother may, or his mother-in-law or his wife, assuming that there are still any Italian wives left who are willing to cook, or his sister or his friends. It does not matter. The point is there is spontaneous comfort found in the notion that we shall all go out and have a nice meal at some restaurant, if we can, or we shall all meet at someone's home where we 'shall have ourselves a banquet'. It is in food that the Italian gets his own back over the misfortunes that he thinks are hitting him and where his true nature comes to the fore.

And quite right too. Tell me what you eat and I shall tell you what you are has become an English idiom; it is so true. And need we be reminded that Italians eat the best food in the world.

*   *   *

But enough of philosophy. I have been serious for long enough. That will not do for an Italian.

Let me conclude on a lighter note. First, I would take you through a whole day, from when you woke up until you went to bed and demonstrate that there was not a single moment when you could afford to ignore what the Italians had done. Finally, there will be some readers wondering why I have not considered the 'Casanova' factor in more depth. Well, I cannot say I am in any way a Casanova expert, but I am more than pleased to offer my views on the Italian 'male of the species'. Of course, this could prove to be the most controversial issue in the entire book. Ah, well.

I shall start with the beginning of a new day.

If your alarm clock wakes you up, it is a fruit of the Italian development of horology. If your radio is on, then you owe it to Volta who discovered electricity and to Marconi who developed radio wavelengths.

I have already recorded the invention of the handkerchief and 'eau de Cologne', two pleasant adjuncts to good appearance and manners.

Equally, I have said enough about the contribution of the Italians to the motor car, if you are using it to get to work.

Stuck on a motorway or expressway somewhere? Think of the first 'Autostrada'.

Similarly, if you buy a morning paper or read a paperback, Italians were there first.

When it comes to food, whether or not you accept my view that, if you eat anything worth eating, it must be Italian, and leaving on one side the ever increasing popularity of the espresso or cappuccino coffee, it is a fact that, unless you use your hands, you owe it to the Italians that a fork enables you to rise above the level of the monkeys.

If in your spare time you tend to your garden, or go to the theatre, ballet, bowling or to the circus, Italians were there first.

If you are interested in the weather, consider that the barometer, the thermometer and the hygrometer are Italian inventions.

Apart from cricket and soccer, many of the hobbies you might indulge in, like gaming, horse-riding, mountain-climbing, or anything artistic, have been influenced by what the Italians have done. Our contribution to music and art is enormous; and matchless. Our sense of beauty and style is unique.

If you are a student, then, whatever your subject, we have made a major contribution to it, be it art, economics, law, metallurgy, medicine, music, physics, or whatever.

Dropping in at the club on your way home? Do not forget Francesco Bianco, who founded White's; and our invention of playing cards.

But perhaps, having reached this far, you are getting tired and bored by my reminders, and you think you ought to go to bed with, depending on your tendencies, a good book (which you may have borrowed from a Public Library - Italians established the first) or a good partner.

Quite right too. But even there you will not escape the Italians.

First of all, if you are heeding present day prophylactic advice, you will not have forgotten about the condom that was a seventeenth-century Italian invention. Secondly, it is now time to propound Barone's law: in bed, the Italians are supreme. Ha! There he goes again, you will be saying to yourself, adding that whatever I may have stated before which I could prove, this time I am certainly in the wrong and cannot make my point. Italian men or women cannot be better than any other. Perhaps. But *I* am not so sure. Let us take the men first.

I realise that the myth of the Latin Lover is said to be now exploded: hardened feminists have seen to that. The Latin Lover is a Gigolo who is not exciting and who expects too much. Budding Casanovas please note: all men are the same.

Untrue. Generally speaking (in this particular context I am referring to men of my generation - early 50s...) the Italian male, especially the southern Italian, knows better than most how to make a woman feel grand. Proof, however, is a different matter.

It has always fascinated me to consider that although Italians are very well aware of their ability in this field and when talking to one another and comparing it to that of other nationalities, they need little convincing that they are justified in believing it to be great, they seem exceedingly shy of making a public point of it. Is this because of the difficulties of proof? I quite accept that any such superiority is not something that is capable of easy verification. Leaving aside mind-boggling competitions, one cannot very conveniently test ability in the bedroom with the same ease as one has, for example, a wine-tasting or a football match. But the matter goes a little further, I believe, since it is not an ability that can be determined by all and sundry: like the appreciation of a fine claret or burgundy, or a good artistic performance, it can only be left to the initiated and the experienced. Any comment passed on it by those who do not have the age and knowledge of the world to make an actual comparison, is worthless.

It seems to me that the only people who can actually decide the point I am making, apart from the Italians themselves who have already reached a conclusion about it, are experienced women in their early 40s or older. The judgement of no other person has any value in this context.

Have you ever noticed how Italian men look at women? Their look is not hesitant or sly or out of the corner of an eye as though something forbidden were about to happen. It is open, direct, almost indecent in a sense, as though the man had spent the night before with the woman who is being stared at. It is, on the one hand, confident, eager, full of anticipation and expectation; or on the other, critical, disappointed, disinterested without in any way being neglectful. It says, depending on the circumstances: 'I am interested, what next?' or 'I am not interested, but it is not your fault.' Indeed, it is my firm belief that one can always recognise an Italian, in a restaurant or at a party or in any public place, by the way he looks at a woman. The process of exciting her starts early. I go further and say that Italians themselves recognize one another quite often in this particular way.

Equally significant is the manner in which an Italian will talk to a woman.

For example, entertaining her across a two-seater dining table in an intimate restaurant, an Italian will normally lean slightly forward, displaying a gentle, constant, confident smile, his voice vibrating with real, or feigned interest.

Am I being too imaginative or perhaps too naive? I don't think so. This kind of Italian look makes certain women cringe; and those who react in this way probably do not deserve to be looked at in the first place. For the real woman, however, that look has a totally different effect: it makes her feel wanted and feminine; it justifies all the troubles she has taken about her appearance and her attire; it provides the inner satisfaction that is transferred to her face and to her limbs. It causes a glow to develop on her cheeks, a more jaunty step, a shrug of the head and the mane to come about. It makes her day, even if nothing else should happen; it creates well-being in her body and happiness in her soul. That male look is part of the same ability, if not destiny, of the Italians to give pleasure; it is to the heart what good food is to the stomach and beauty to the eye: it is part of the Italian tradition and of the mystique of the Mediterranean.

I admit that it is sometimes impertinent and, if used by ill-mannered or insensitive persons, rude and intrusive. But there are two sides to every coin. The patent admiration of and desire for women in turn makes woman herself more conscious of her attractions and consequently more desirable. This desirability in turn provokes desire so that a circle is established which makes both man and woman happy, at least for the time being. And on the basis that one should grasp happiness where one finds it, this is not a bad idea after all.

Such an approach to woman starts in the Italian family where the mother is queen and is developed within a society where women are neither segregated nor neglected. It is a concomitant of the fact that the stag party as an institution does not exist in Italy, any more than all male clubs do, any more than that, after dinner, Italian women are expected to leave the room whilst the port is passed round. In a similar context, an Italian youth is just as likely to go to a football match with one or more girl friends as he is to have an outing there with the boys.

Against this background the presence and importance of a woman, the feeling that she radiates, is taken for granted by Italians from a very early age. They do not grow up either ignorant or terrified of her as sometimes happens in more emotionally restrained and scientifically progressive countries; and this is the reason why they are not at all concerned when, more frequently nowadays, they come across a confident woman eager to assert her newly recognised rights and independence in social and sexual matters.

One final consideration which is of some significance. Until recently, Italian men have not had any tendency to over indulge as far as alcohol is concerned. Northerners, on the contrary, seem to enjoy drunkeness; and that spells doom for their sexual life. To that extent, if to no other, Italians enjoy the inbuilt physical advantage of not having their sexual performance weakened by drink.

And what shall I say about Italian women? Decency, discretion and, above all, my Italian wife, prevent me from expanding on this aspect of the subject matter.

Let me conclude. I believe that food and women represent the Italians' national leanings, just as art and beauty are their centuries-old style. It is a unique combination that has made them what they are regardless of who they are.

But enough said. I shall leave you with one last thought about the Italians: we are also modest.

Ciao.

List of Authorities

References to the *Encyclopaedia Britannica* are as follows:
a) **Micropaedia.** References are expressed as follows: the letter followed by Block Roman numerals, followed by the page number. Thus, for example, R - IV - p. 278, followed by either the name of the inventor or the subject matter of the invention;
b) **Macropaedia.** References are expressed by two numerals, namely the volume and the page.

Other authors or texts are quoted in full.

Reference to 'Treccani' are references to the *Encyclopaedia Treccani* 1931-4 edition.

References to 'Harwin' are references to the *Harwin Chronology of Inventions Innovations and Discoveries* 1987 edition, where there are no pages but only references to years.

References to 'Carter' are to the *Dictionary of Inventions and Discoveries* edited by E. F. Carter published by F. Muller - 1966.

References to 'Bibliographical Dictionary of Scientists' are to the *Bibliographical Dictionary of Scientists* published by Pitman, 1969 edition.

SECTION 1: Architecture and Buildings

Harwin 1432 (Brunelleschi)
10 - p. 811 (Alberti)
13 - p. 933 (Palladio)
F. E. Halliday - *Cultural History of England* (Thames and Hudson) - p. 148 (Palladio)
R - VIII - p. 859 (San Gimignano)

SECTION 2: The Arts

Ballet

5 - p. 452 (dancing - da Piacenza)

2 - p. 647/8 (dancing - Belgioioso)
2 - p. 649 - R - X - p. 431 (dancing)
R - I - p. 373 (dancing Vigano Angiolini)
R - I - p. 765 (dancing Gastoldi)
R - X - p. 412 (dancing Vestris)
2 - p. 650 (Blasis)
R - II - p. 664 (Cecchetti)
R - VI - p. 124 (Legnani)

Caricatures

R - IV - p. 523 (Ghezzi)

Literary Criticism

10 - p. 1038 (Valla)
R - II - p. 621 (Castelvetro)

Music and Musical Instruments

R - IV - p. 785 (D'Arezzo)
R - VI - p. 22 (Landini)
4 - p. 448 (Frottola)
14 - p. 60 (Griffori)
10 - p. 440 (harpsichord)
Treccani - Vol. I - p. 729 (bassoon)
R - X - p. 449 (first violin)
10 - p. 442 (spinets)
17 - p. 7 (Gabrieli) and Treccani Vol. XXXII p. 134
R - VI - p. 201 (Rinuccini)
R - I - p. 134 (Agazzari)
R - VII - p. 563 (oratorio)
R - IV - p. 316 (Frescobaldi)
13 - p. 645 (Monteverdi)
Harwin 1617 (Sonata)
4 - p. 23 (Rossi)
10 - p. 442 (Cristofori)
R - IX - p. 597 (Stradivari)
R - II - p. 150 (Bonporti)
R - VI - p. 289 (Locatelli)
R - IV - p. 54 (Farinelli)
R - IV - p. 455 (Geminiani)
R - IX - p. 832 (Tartini)
R - X - p. 84 (Traetta)
Carter 128 (mechanical piano)
12 - p. 692 (Leoncavallo)
6 - p. 673 (Russolo)
Harwin 1981 (Di Giugno)

Opera Houses

The *Concise Oxford Dictionary of Opera* (Rosenthal-Warrack OUP 1964) (San Cassiano Opera House).

Painting and History of Art

R - II - p. 486
R - II - p. 486 (P. Uccello) Campagnola
R - X - p. 363 (Vasari)
12 - p. 98 (Michelangelo)
R - I - p. 753 (Baldinucci)
R - IV - p. 523 (Ghezzi)
R - VII - p. 18 (Morelli)
R - VI - p. 626 (Marinetti)

Pornography (Erotic Literature)

Boccaccio - the Decameron
John Addington Symonds - Renaissance in Italy, Vol. 5 - p. 103 (Cinzio)

Pottery

T. Wilson - Ceramic Art of the Italian Renaissance - British Museum Publications 1987 (Piccolpasso and ornamentation)

Theatre and Acting

1 - p. 60 and 12 - p. 212 (acting)
4 - pp. 984 and 987 (Commedia dell'Arte)
17 - p. 537 (Urbino stage)
18 - p. 223 (Ruzzante)
4 - p. 983 (theatrical contract)
17 - pp. 537 and 553 (Serlio)
17 - p. 537 and 18 - p. 243 (Palladio)
17 - p. 537 (Salviati)
17 - p. 537 (Sabbatini)
17 - p. 541 (Vigarani)
3 - p. 909 (Bernini)
R - X - p. 337 (Valentino)

SECTION 3: Clothes and Dressing up

Fashions

F. Boucher - A History of Costume in the West (Thames and Hudson)

Lace

R - V - p. 467 (lace)

Make-Up (Cosmetics)

R. Corson - Fashions in make-up, - Peter Owen, London 1974 - p. 103 - (cosmetics)

Spectacles (Eye Glasses)

R - IV - p. 16 (Spina)

Textiles and Velvet

18 - p. 171 (textiles)
Harwin 1854 (Bonelli-loom)

SECTION 4: **Communications**

Canals

3 - p. 753 (Naviglio Canal)

Flying

Treccani - XVIII - p. 257 (flying Guidotti)
Carter 16 (balloon night flight)
Carter 7 (jet plane)

Hydrofoil/Ships and Biplanes

R - V - p. 240 (hydrofoils)
Harwin 1905 (hydrofoil biplane)

Libraries

10 - p. 857 (Montecassino - library)
10 - p. 858 (Florence library)

Motor Car

2 - p. 764 (battery)
11 - p. 311 (Romagnosi)
Colonnetti - *Grandi Primati Italiani* - p. 57 (Pacinotti)
R - VIII - p. 1 (Pirelli)
R - VIII - p. 1 (Pirelli)
R - X - p. 391 and 11 - p. 780 (Venturi)
R - I - p. 674 (autostrada)

Newspapers

R - IV - p. 444 and 15 - p. 236 (newspapers)

Paperbacks

R - VI - p. 585 and 15 - p. 225 (Manuzio - paperbacks and imprint)

Photography

14 - p. 328 and Treccani VI - p. 132 (photography) Treccani XXVII - p. 951 (Porro)

Postal Systems

14 - p. 884 (post)

Printing

Harwin 1477 (maps)
R - V - p. 468 and R - VI - p. 585 (Griffo)
R - VII - p. 918 (Petrucci)
R - II - p. 113 (Bodoni)
Rizzatti (Ed. Vallardi) Gl' Italiani e il Bel Paese (*La Cultura Scientifica*) - p. 201 and
208 (Milan 1915) - (paper factories) *Biographical Dictionary of Scientists (Pitman
1969) (Aselli's book)*

Scientific Societies

2 - p. 1020 (scientific societies)

Signalling

18 - p. 67 (Cardano)
18 - p. 68 (Volta)

Steam Engines

R - VIII - p. 130 (Dellaporta)
Carter 104 (magic lantern)
Carter 85 (incubators)
Carter 89 (kite)
Carter 169 (electric telegraph)
Carter 133 (telescope)

Telephones

Colonnetti - Grandi Primati Italiani (Meucci) *Colonnetti - Grandi Primati Italiani* (Marzi)

SECTION 5: Economics, Law and Social Sciences

Anthropology

R - X - p. 418 (Vico)

Banking and Book-keeping

3 - p. 37 (Pacioli)
John Addington Symonds - *Renaissance in Italy* - 1875 edition, Vol. 1, p. 193 (Bardi-Peruzzi)
Montanelli - Gervaso - *L'Italia dei Comuni* - p. 169 (Letter of Credit)
Treccani - XXX - pp. 655/6 (Banco di San Giorgio)

Chronicles

R - II - p. 436 (Caffaro di Caschifellone)

Criminal Associations

R -VI - p. 478 (Mafia)

Criminology

R - I - p. 916 (Beccaria)
Salvatorelli - *Sommario di Storia D'Italia* p. 385 (Leopold II)

Economics

R - IV - p. 470 (Genovesi)
R - IV - p. 386 (Galiani)

Insurance

Edler de Roover (as quoted in text) - (marine insurance)
Edler de Roover (as quoted in text) - (insurance policy)
Treccani - XXXIII - p. 1035 (Tonti)

Law

R - VI - p. 26 (Lanfranc)

R - X - p. 321 (Vacario)
R - I - p. 702 (Azzone)
4 - p. 988 (law merchant)
4 - p. 988 and R - II - p. 2O (Bill of Exchange)
Calasso - Medio Evo del Diritto - Vol. 1 (Eleonora)
4 - p. 988 (company law)
4 - p. 988 (bankruptcy)
13 - p. 1071 (patents)
13 - p. 1071 (patents)
1 - p. 955 (military law)
R - IV - p. 472 (Gentili)
Montanelli - Gervaso - L'Italia dei Comuni - p. 293 (law of the sea)
Treccani - XXX - pp. 655/6 (cheques)

Statistics

R - X - p. 438 (Villani)

Time and Motion Studies

R - II - p. 320 (time and motion studies)

SECTION 6: Folklore and Hobbies

Botanical Gardens and Botany

7 - p. 902, 3 - p. 64 and 4 - p. 685 (botanical gardens)
Biographical Dictionary of Scientists (Cesalpino)
2 - p. 1020 and 3 - p. 66 (Malpighi)
Biographical Dictionary of Scientists (P. Alpini)

Festivals

Thomas Ashby - *Some Italian Scenes and Festivals* - Methuen 1929 p. 8

Funerals

R - II - p. 1 (funerals)
Treccani - XXX - p. 378 - (Sabbioneta)

Gaming

7 - p. 868 and II - p. 557 (Probability Theory) 3 - p. 901 (playing cards)

Gardens and Horticulture

7 - pp. 893/4 (parterres)
Treccani - X - p. 853 (gardening book)
Treccani - XXXI - p. 452 and Harwin 1545 (conservatory)
Treccani - XI - p. 840 (De Crescenzi)
Harwin 1877 (viticulture)

Heraldry

8 - p. 796 (Bartolo da Sessoferrato)

Lotteries

11 - p. 114 (the Florence 'lotto')

Magic

R - VII - p. 1016 (Pinetti)

Traditional Tales

R - IX - p. 600 (Straparola)
John Addington Symonds - *Renaissance in Italy* - Vol. 5, p. 103 (Machiavelli)

SECTION 7: Food and Drink

Gastronomy

7 - p. 940 (cooking)
R - IV - p. 230 (fork)
Biographical Dictionary of Scientists (P. Alpini)
Harwin 1946 (espresso machine)
Harwin 1800 (pasta)
Carter 8 (alcohol distillation)

Ice Cream

R - V - p. 276 (Ice-cream)
Harwin 1896 (Ice-cream cones)

SECTION 8: Living Style

Aesthetics

1 - p. 154 (Croce)
Carter 131 (plastic noses)

Animals

4 - p. 635 (Franconi - circus diameter)
R - IV - p. 278 (lion taming)

Calligraphy

R - IV - p. 232 (Poggio)
R - I - p. 415 (Niccoli)

The Church in England

R -VI - p. 27 (Lanfranc)
R - I - p. 401 (Anselmo)

Civic Amenities

John Addington Symonds - *Renaissance in Italy* -Vol. 3 - p. 42 (jetty)
John Addington Symonds - *Renaissance in Italy* - Vol. 3 - p. 42 (aqueduct)
John Addington Symonds - *Renaissance in Italy* - Vol. 3 - p. 42 (Venice)
John Addington Symonds - *Renaissance in Italy* - Vol. 3 - p. 42 (flags)
4 - p. 744 (horology)
Montanelli - Gervaso - *L'Italia dei Comuni* - p. 174 (chimney breast)
Treccani - XIII - p. 141 (clock)
Carter 186 (water chlorination)

Pedestrianisation

Go there and see for yourself!

Clocks and Watches

Treccani XIII - p. 141 (clock)
Allix - 'Carriage Clocks' - p. 5 (horology)
Harwin 1335 (automatic striking clock)
Harwin 1704 (jewelled watch)

Clubs

Algernon Bourke - *History of White's* - pp. 11-13 (White's Club)

Contraception

2 - p. 1067 (condoms)

Cryptology Cryptography and Cryptanalysis

5 - p. 332 (de Lavinde)
Harwin 1411 ('Pasini' cipher) 5 - p. 332 (Simonetta)

Dictionaries

5 - p. 714 (Calepino's dictionary)

Diplomacy

R - IV -p. 472 (Gentili)
R - IV - p. 473 (Gentili) R - I - p. 984 (Bentivoglio)

Education

6 - p. 337 and R - II - p. 131 (Bologna)
R - VII - p. 757 (Paris)
R - VII - p. 898 (Perugia)
John Addington Symonds - *Renaissance in Italy* - Vol. 2 - p. 84 (Vicenza)
John Addington Symonds - *Renaissance in Italy* - Vol. 2 - p. 84 (Arezzo)
R - VII - p. 670 (Padova)
R - VII - p. 190 (Naples and Salerno)
John Addington Symonds - *Renaissance in Italy* - Vol. 2 - p. 84 (Vercelli)
John Addington Symonds - *Renaissance in Italy* - Vol. 2 - p. 85 (Ferrara)
John Addington Symonds - *Renaissance in Italy* - Vol. 2 - p. 86 (Florence)
John Addington Symonds - *Renaissance in Italy* - Vol. 2 - p. 86 (Pavia)
6 - p. 344 (Vergerio)
R - I - p. 848 and 6 - p. 344 (Barzizza)
John Addington Symonds - *Renaissance in Italy* - Vol. 4 - p. 172 (Alberti)
R - VI - p. 1020 (Montessori)
6 - p. 780 (Bandini)
6 - p. 785 (Zara)

Gemstones

7 - p. 978 (Peruzzi)
Carter 46 (crystals)

Glass

8 - p. 184 (colourless glass)

Lighthouses and Lighting

10 - p. 952 ('Lanterna' at Genoa)
11 - p. 179 (Cascariolo)

Manners

R - II - p. 622 (B. Castiglione)
R - II - p. 604 (Della Casa)
Montanelli - Gervaso - *L'Italia dei Comuni* - p. 192 (handkerchief)
H. V. Morton - *A Traveller in Southern Italy* - p. 362 (eau de cologne)
R - IV - p. 151 (Firenzuola on women's beauty)
Carter 179 (umbrella)

SECTION 9: Politics and War

Atom Bombs

11 - p. 800 (Fermi)
R - IV - p. 102 (Fermi) R - VII - p. 280 (Fermi)

Bureaucracy

John Addington Symonds - *Renaissance in Italy* - Vol. 1, p. 74 (bureaucracy)

Politics and Power

17 - p. 609/610 (Machiavelli)
8 - p. 465 (Guicciardini)
R - VII - p. 41 (Mosca)
Garzanti - *Enciclopedia Europea* 1978 Ed. Vol. VII, p. 333 (Mattei)

Trade Unions

Salvatorelli - *Sommario di Storia d'Italia* p. 125 (trade unions)

Treaties

Index to British Treaties - HMSO - Vol. 2 - p. 4 (treaties)

War

Harwin 1326 (cannons)
8 - p. 489 (Colleoni - gun-train)
R - VIII - p. 6 (pistols)
R - III - p. 7 (Colleoni)
R - IX p. 831 (Tartaglia)
Treccani - Vol. XXXIV - p. 1031 (D'Avalos)
Biographical Dictionary of Scientists (Ramelli)
Carter 8 - (air gun)
Treccani - Vol. II - p. 409 (Alfonso D'Este)
Treccani - Vol. IX - p. 545 (Cavalli)
R - VII - p. 361 (Sobrero)
William Percy Jolly - *Marconi* - Constable - London 1972

SECTION 10: Sport and Travel

America

Common knowledge (Colombo's discovery of America and Vespucci's naming of it)

Archaeology

R - I - p.963 and 1 - p. 1078 (Belzoni) R - III - p. 329 (Pizzicolli)

Bowling

3 - p. 86 ('bocce')

Canada

R - II - p. 423 (Caboto)

Fencing

7 - p. 224 (fencing)
7 - p. 225 (fencing)

Horse-Riding

15 - p. 836 (Grisone)
15 - p. 836 (Pignatelli)
15 - p. 836 (Caprilli)

Map-Making

Treccani - XXIV - p. 329 (maps)

Mountain-Climbing

Garzanti - Enciclopedia Europea 1978 Ed. Vol. 1, p. 314 (Rotario D'Asti)
Rheinhold Messner's exploits are modern and well known

River Nile

R - IV - p. 511 (Gessi)

Boating and) Sailing

2 - p. 1157 (boat race)
John Addington Symonds - Renaissance in Italy - Vol. 1, p. 31 (compass)
16 - p. 158 (sails)
P. Riccardi - Biblioteca Matematica Italiana - Modena 1873 (eight- point compass)
Treccani - XI - p. 840 (Crescenzio's compass)
Treccani - XI - p. 840 (detailed 'portolan' chart)

Travel and Exploration

R - VIII - p. 91 (Polo)
11 - p. 472 and R - VIII - p. 141 (portolans)
R - X - p. 474 (Vivaldi)
R - VII - p. 833 (Pegolotti)
Christopher Columbus
R - X - p. 410 (Vespucci)
R - II - p. 423 (Caboto)
R - VI - p. 623 (Marignolli)
R - X - p. 404 (Verrazzano)

R - X - p. 338 (Valignano)
R - VIII - p. 563 (Ricci)

SECTION 11: The Sciences

Astronomy

Harwin 1364 (astronomical clock)
11 - p. 520 (Fontana)
11 - p. 520 (F. Cassini)
11 - p. 917 (Schiaparelli)
R - II - p. 615 (G. D. Cassini)
R - I - p. 1048 (Bianchini)
R - VII - p. 985 (Piazzi)
R - III - p. 618 (Donati)
R - IX - p. 15 (Secchi)
R - VIII - p. 957 (Schiaparelli)

Autopsies

11 - p. 813 (post-mortems)
2 - p. 356 (autopsies)

Barometer

11 - p. 780 and R - X - p. 56 (Torricelli)

Biology

11 - p. 210 (Aselli)
2 - p. 1026 and R - II - p. 164 (Borelli)
11 - p. 831 and 12 - p. 109 (Redi)
R - VIII - p. 461 (Redi)
11 - p. 831 (Bassi)
R - VI - p. 19 (Lancisi)
2 - p. 1024 and R - I - p. 313 (Amici)
R - IV - p. 615 (Golgi)
R - VII - p. 244 (Negri)
R - VIII - p. 112 (Pontecorvo)

Chemistry

Carter 119 (nitric acid)
Carter 76 (gold wire)
Carter 56 (silver coins gilding by Brugnatelli)
2 - p. 333 and 13 - p. 334 (Avogadro)
R - VIII - p. 809 (Piria)
R - IX - p. 45 (Selmi)
2 - p. 333 (Cannizzaro)
Carter 82 (helium gas)
R - VII - p. 220 (polypropylene)

Contagious Diseases

12 - p. 109 (syphilis and theory of contagious diseases)

Geology

R - I - p. 497 (stratigraphy)

Geometry

7 - p. 1113 (Saccheri)
7 - p. 1091 (Torricelli) 7 - p. 1090 (Grandi)

Hydraulics

11 - p. 780 and R - X - p. 56 (hydraulics)
R - IV - p. 783 (Guglielmini)
R - IV - p. 328 (Frisi)

Longevity

Treccani - Vol. XI - p. 416 (longevity)

Mathematics

13 - p. 349 and 10 - p. 818 (Fibonacci)
10 - p. 811 (Pacioli)
11 - p. 677 (Brunelleschi)
11 - p. 642 (Del Ferro)
R - IX - p. 831 (Tartaglia)
R - IV - p. 106 (Ferrari)
11 - p. 662 and 7 - p. 858 (Tartaglia, Ferrari, Cardano)
R - II - p. 655 and 11 - p. 643 and 1 - p. 740 (Cavalieri)
11 - p. 643 (Torricelli)
R - II - p. 701 (Ceva)
Biographical Dictionary of Scientists (Mengoli)
7 - p. 1113 (Saccheri)
5 - p. 738 (Riccati)
R - V - p. 991 (La Grange)
R - VIII - p. 711 (Ruffini)
R - I - p. 1034 (Betti)
R - III - p. 233 (Cremona)
11 - p. 630 (Beltramini)
R - VIII - p. 563 (Ricci)
R - VII - p. 819 (Peano)
1 - p. 740 (Cesaro)
1 - p. 758 (Volterra)
11 - p. 637 (Zermelo)
1 - p. 796 (Levi-Civita)
1 - p. 764 (Tonelli, Cesari, Digiorgi)

Medicine

11 - p. 828 and R - VIII - p. 808 (Salerno)
11 - p. 813 (post-mortems)
R - VIII - p. 809 (Saliceto)
2 - p. 536 (Liucci) *Biographical Dictionary of Scientists* (Eustachio)
R - III - p. 15 (Colombo)
Treccani - XXI - p. 707 (VD)
Treccani - XXXIV - p. 1013 (Varolio)

R - IV - p. 40 (Falloppio) and 2 - p. 1067
R - I - p. 573 (Aselli)
2 - p. 1022 and Treccani Vol. XXVIII - p. 972 (Redi)
1 - p. 956 (Bellini)
R - VIII - p. 886 (Santorio)
Readers' Digest Universal Dictionary p. 932 (Malpighi and microscope use)
2 - p. 1020 and 3 - p. 55 (Malpighi)
11 - p. 829 (Malpighi and blood)
Treccani XXIX - p. 488 (transfusions)
15 - p. 748 and 5 - p. 1121 (Valsalva)
11 - p. 831 (Ramazzini)
11 - p. 830 and 2 - p. 536 (Morgagni)
10 - p. 900 and 12 - p. 112 (Spallanzani)
Carter 21 - (blood pressure)
Treccani XXV - p. 880 (Pacinian corpuscles)
R - VIII - p. 711 (Ruffini)
Treccani - XV - p. 609 (ear)
5 - p. 1133 (Corti)
Treccani - XV - p. 681 (pneumothorax)
Harwin 1896 (sphygmomanometer)
Harwin 1937 (electro-convulsive therapy)

Metallurgy

11 - p. 1063 and Treccani IV p. 706 (Biringuccio)

Nobel Prizes

Nobel Foundation

Philosophy

Carter 27 (Bruno)
R - IX - p. 870 (Telesio)

Physics

Carter 29 (cam)
Carter 137 (jet propulsion)
Carter 137 (Di Giorgio)
Carter 77 (centrifugal governor)
Carter 143 (rainbow theory)
Treccani XXVII - p. 951 (Fabrizzi)
10 - p. 924 (Leonardo) - diving
10 - p. 929 (Leonardo) - light propagation
11 - p. 232 (Leonardo) - screw machine
11 - p. 236 (Leonardo) - gears
11 - p. 249 (Leonardo) - bearings
11 - p. 780 (Leonardo) - fluid flow engineering
12 - p. 55 (Leonardo) - Hygrometer
12 - p. 511 (Leonardo) - 'camera oscura'
17 - p. 746 (Leonardo) - underwater exploration
18 - p. 766 (Leonardo) - water turbine
Codex Atlanticus Folio 276 (Leonardo) flying machine
French Institute - Manuscript B, Folio 83 (Leonardo) – photometry

French Institute - Manuscript C, Folio 22 (Leonardo)
Harwin 1488 (crossbow gun)
Montanelli-Gervaso - *L'Italia della Controriforma* - p. 388 (repeater gun)
Montanelli-Gervaso - *L'Italia della Controriforma* - p. 388 (parachute)
James McDonald - Wordly Wise (Constable 1984) - p. 215 (bicycles)
Carter 149 - (rope making machine)
Carter 3 - (retractable undercarriage)
Carter 27 - (explosive bullets)
Carter 165 - (submarine)
Carter 171 - (tensile testing machine)
Carter 152 - (handsaw for marble)
Carter 78 - (grinders)
7 - p. 851 (Galileo)
18 - pp. 97 and 415 (Galileo)
7 - p. 851 (Galileo)
7 - p. 852 (Galileo)
10 - p. 350 (Galileo)
11 - p. 520 (Galileo)
11 - p. 762 (Galileo)
11 - p. 830 (Galileo)
R - IV - p. 388 and 14 - p. 387 (Galileo)
16 - p. 273 (Galileo)
7 - p. 852 (Galileo)
6 - p. 849 (Galileo)
7 - p. 868 (Galileo)
17 - p. 799 (Galileo)
13 - p. 302 (Galileo)
12 - p. 55 (Galileo)
18 - p. 321 (Galileo)
Carter 51 - (dredger)
Carter 31 - (cardan joint)
Carter 74 - (gimbal suspension)
Carter 107 - (light refraction theory)
Harwin 1616 (thermometer)
8 - p. 702 (Ferdinand II)
R - X - p. 56 (Torricelli)
R - X - p. 476 (Borelli and Viviani)
6 - p. 646 (Grimaldi)
R - II - p. 164 (Borelli)
R - II - p. 487 (Campani)
7 - p. 382 (Delana)
7 - p. 859 (Galvani)
R - VII - p. 985 (Piazzi)
2 - p. 1034 (Beccaria)
R - IX - p. 15 (Secchi)
Treccani - XXII - p. 819 (Melloni)
Treccani - XXXV - p. 392 (and)
Harwin 1824 (wine press)
Colonnetti - *Grandi Primati Italiani* (Barsanti and Matteucci) and Carter 16
Colonnetti - *Grandi Primati Italiani* (Pacinotti) and Treccani 1934 Ed. Vol. XVII
Treccani Vol. XXIX - p. 328 (Righi)

Colonnetti - *Grandi Primati Italiani* (Ferraris)
Carter 133 (electricity generation)
Carter 105 (lamp bulbs vacuum)
Carter 68 (arc electric steel furnace)
Carter 28 (oil-filled electric cable)
Colonnetti - *Grandi Primati Italiani* (Marconi)
Carter 2 (aerial)
Harwin 1937 (Segre)

Short Bibliography

ASCHAM, Roger, *The Schoolmaster*. London: John Daye, 1570. *The Schoolmaster*. Edited by Lawrence V. Ryan 1967
ASHBY, Thomas, *Some Italian Scenes and Festivals*. London: Methuen, 1929
BARZINI, Luigi, *The Italians*. London: H. Hamilton, 1987
BOCCACCIO, Giovanni, *The Decameron*. London: W.W. Norton, 1984
BOURKE, Algernon, *History of Whites*. London: Waterlow & Sons, 1892
BRAND, Charles Peter, *Italy and the English Romantics*. Haarlem: Cambridge University Press, 1957
BRITTON, Frank, *London Delftware*. London: J. Horne, 1987
BURFORD, E.J., *Royal St. James's*. London: Hale, 1988
BUXTON, John, Sir Philip Sydney & The English Renaissance. London: Macmillan, 1987
BYRON, *Don Juan*. London: John Murray, 1st two Cantos, 1819, 3-5, 1821, 6-14, 1823, 15 & 16, 1824 (modern edition) Penguin English Poets, 1977
COLSON, Percy, 'White's' 1693 to 1950. London: Heinemann, 1951
DIXON-HUNT, John, *Gardens and Groves*. London: Dent, 1986
DIXON-HUNT, John, 'The Wider Sea' (A Life of Ruskin). London: Dent, 1982
DOUGLAS, Norman, *Old Calabria*. London: Century, 1983
GOETHE, Johan Wolfgang, *Italian Journey*. London: Penguin, 1970
GUTTERIDGE, Harold Cooke, *Nelson and The Neapolitan Jacobins*. London: See Navy Records Soc. Vol.25, 1894. Edited by H.C. Gutteridge, 1903
HALLIDAY, Frank Ernest, *Illustrated Cultural History of England*. London: Thames & Hudson, 1981
HAWTHORNE, Nathaniel, *The Marble Faun 1860* (also in The Works Vol.4). Ohio State University Press 1986
HITCHENS, Christopher, *The Elgin Marbles*. London: Chatto & W.: The Hogarth Press, 1987
HUTTON, Edward, *Italy and The Italians*. London: William Blackwood & Sons, 1902. *In Unknown Tuscany*. London: Methuen, 1909. *Why Italian?* Firenze: Tip, Rinaldi, 1934
HUTTON, William, *History of Derby*. London: J&J Robinson, 1971
JOLLY, William, Percy, *Marconi*. London: Constable, 1972
JUCKER, Ninetta, *Italy*. London: Thames & Hudson, 1970
LEWIS, W.S. (Editor), *Selected Letters of Horace Walpole*. London: Folio Society, 1951
MACHIAVELLI, Niccoló, *Il Principe*. Numerous editions since 1513. Latest, London: Penguin, 1961

MAYES, Stanley, *The Great Belzoni.* London: Putnam, 1959

MONTANELLI-GERVASO, *Storia d'Italia.* Milan: Rizzoli, 1959-1987

NICHOLLS, Peter, *Italia, Italia.* London: Macmillan, 1973

POCOCK, Tom, *Horatio Nelson.* London: Bodley Head, 1987

RIPA, Cesare, *Iconologia.* London: 'By the care of P. Tempest', 1707

RUSKIN, John, *The Works: Library Ed. (1902-'12).* Edited by E.T. Cook & A.D.O. Wedderburn. *Mornings in Florence.* Orpington: George Allen, 1899. *Letters To His Parents.* Clarendon Press, Harold Shapiro, 1972

SALVATORELLI, Luigi, *Sommario di Storia d'Italia.* London: G. Allen & Unwin, 1940

SCOTT-FOX, David, *Mediterranean Heritage.* London: Routledge & Kegan Paul, 1978

SELLS, Lytton, *The Italian Influence in English Poetry.* London: G. Allen & Unwin, 1955

SHAPIRO, Harold (Ed.), *Ruskin in Italy.* Oxford: Clarendon Press, 1972

STENDHAL, *Rome, Naples & Florence en 1817.* London: Henry Colburn, 1818 or London: John Calder, 1959

STOCKER, Giglioli C., *Naples in 1799.* London: John Murray, 1903

SYMONDS, John Addington, *Renaissance in Italy.* 7 Vols. London: Smith Elder & Co, 1875-1886

TREVELYAN, George Macauley, *English Songs of Italian Freedom.* London: Longmans, 1911. *Englishman and Italians: Some Aspects of Their Relations Past and Present.* London: Humphrey Milford, 1919

TROLLOPE, Anthony, *Travelling Sketches.* London: Reprinted from 'Pall Mall Gazette', 1866

UKERS, William Harrison, *All About Coffee.* New York: Tea & Coffee Trade Journal, 1922

WICKS, Margaret, *The Italian Exiles in London 1816-1848.* Manchester: Manchester University Press, 1937

WILLEY, David, *The Italians.* London: BBC Books, 1984

WILSON, Timothy, *Ceramic Art of Italian Renaissance.* London: British Museum Publications, 1987

Index

Note: the names of the 'discoverers' are shown in capitals